Poverty Discourses in Teacher Education

As economies across the world continue to struggle, there is growing evidence that the vulnerable in society, especially children, are paying the greatest cost in terms of reduced opportunities for access to equitable life chances, the most vital of these being education. Juxtaposing the ongoing failure of education systems to address disadvantage with the widespread belief in the vital importance of the training of teachers raises another issue, namely that remarkably little is known about the effective preparation of pre-service teachers to ameliorate educational disadvantage and, additionally, that little attention appears to be given to this in most teacher preparation programmes.

This book attempts to redress this balance and is structured by three themes that focus on national policy, pre-service teacher preparation programmes and individual pre-service teachers. The book reveals a disheartening picture of complex patterns of inequality across and within individual countries, together with an incomplete understanding of the intersectional mechanisms – political, ideological, social and cultural – that link poverty and educational disadvantage. Contributions from five different countries, however, provide evidence of positive signs that interesting, innovative and intellectually sound developments are happening at a local level and offer a valuable contribution to the debate about how teacher education can create levers for change.

The chapters in this book were originally published as a special issue of *Journal of Education for Teaching*.

Olwen McNamara is Professor of Education at the University of Manchester, UK. Her research interests are in teacher professional learning, particularly mathematics education, practitioner research and social justice. Nationally, she has served on the Executive Council of the British Education Research Association and as Chair of the Research Committee of the Universities' Council for the Education of Teachers.

Jane McNicholl is an Associate Professor of Science Education at the University of Oxford, UK. Her main research interests have included the development of professional knowledge for teaching secondary science in the school context, policy and practice in initial teacher education and issues of social justice in teacher education.

Poverty Discourses in Teacher Education

Edited by
Olwen McNamara and Jane McNicholl

LONDON AND NEW YORK

First published 2018
by Routledge
2 Park Square, Milton Park, Abingdon, Oxon, OX14 4RN, UK

and by Routledge
711 Third Avenue, New York, NY 10017, USA

Routledge is an imprint of the Taylor & Francis Group, an informa business

© 2018 Taylor & Francis

All rights reserved. No part of this book may be reprinted or reproduced or utilised in any form or by any electronic, mechanical, or other means, now known or hereafter invented, including photocopying and recording, or in any information storage or retrieval system, without permission in writing from the publishers.

Trademark notice: Product or corporate names may be trademarks or registered trademarks, and are used only for identification and explanation without intent to infringe.

British Library Cataloguing in Publication Data
A catalogue record for this book is available from the British Library

ISBN13: 978-0-8153-8524-0

Typeset in Myriad Pro
by codeMantra

Publisher's Note
The publisher accepts responsibility for any inconsistencies that may have arisen during the conversion of this book from journal articles to book chapters, namely the possible inclusion of journal terminology.

Disclaimer
Every effort has been made to contact copyright holders for their permission to reprint material in this book. The publishers would be grateful to hear from any copyright holder who is not here acknowledged and will undertake to rectify any errors or omissions in future editions of this book.

Contents

Citation Information — vii
Notes on Contributors — ix
Preface — xi
Peter Gilroy

Introduction: Poverty discourses in teacher education: understanding policies, effects and attitudes — 1
Olwen McNamara and Jane McNicholl

1. Poverty and the ideological imperative: a call to unhook from deficit and grit ideology and to strive for structural ideology in teacher education — 5
Paul C. Gorski

2. Responding to poverty through education and teacher education initiatives: a critical evaluation of key trends in government policy in England 1997-2015 — 14
Katharine Burn and Ann Childs

3. Education and child poverty in times of austerity in Portugal: implications for teachers and teacher education — 31
Maria Assunção Flores and Fernando Ilídio Ferreira

4. Teacher prep 3.0: a vision for teacher education to impact social transformation — 44
Kerry Kretchmar and Ken Zeichner

5. The impact of adopting a research orientation towards use of the Pupil Premium Grant in preparing beginning teachers in England to understand and work effectively with young people living in poverty — 61
Katharine Burn, Trevor Mutton, Ian Thompson, Jenni Ingram, Jane McNicholl and Roger Firth

CONTENTS

6 Rethinking initial teacher education: preparing teachers for schools in low socio-economic communities in New Zealand   78
Lexie Grudnoff, Mavis Haigh, Mary Hill, Marilyn Cochran-Smith, Fiona Ell and Larry Ludlow

7 Discussing poverty with student teachers: the realities of dialogue   95
Hanneke Jones

8 Student teachers' perceptions of the effects of poverty on learners' educational attainment and well-being: perspectives from England and Scotland   110
Sue Ellis, Ian Thompson, Jane McNicholl and Jane Thomson

9 Seeing disadvantage in schools: exploring student teachers' perceptions of poverty and disadvantage using visual pedagogy   127
M. L. White and Jean Murray

Index   143

Citation Information

The chapters in this book were originally published in the *Journal of Education for Teaching*, volume 42, issue 4 (October 2016). When citing this material, please use the original page numbering for each article, as follows:

Preface
Preface
Peter Gilroy
Journal of Education for Teaching, volume 42, issue 4 (October 2016) p. 373

Introduction
Poverty discourses in teacher education: understanding policies, effects and attitudes
Olwen McNamara and Jane McNicholl
Journal of Education for Teaching, volume 42, issue 4 (October 2016) pp. 374–377

Chapter 1
Poverty and the ideological imperative: a call to unhook from deficit and grit ideology and to strive for structural ideology in teacher education
Paul C. Gorski
Journal of Education for Teaching, volume 42, issue 4 (October 2016) pp. 378–386

Chapter 2
Responding to poverty through education and teacher education initiatives: a critical evaluation of key trends in government policy in England 1997–2015
Katharine Burn and Ann Childs
Journal of Education for Teaching, volume 42, issue 4 (October 2016) pp. 387–403

Chapter 3
Education and child poverty in times of austerity in Portugal: implications for teachers and teacher education
Maria Assunção Flores and Fernando Ilídio Ferreira
Journal of Education for Teaching, volume 42, issue 4 (October 2016) pp. 404–416

Chapter 4
Teacher prep 3.0: a vision for teacher education to impact social transformation
Kerry Kretchmar and Ken Zeichner
Journal of Education for Teaching, volume 42, issue 4 (October 2016) pp. 417–433

CITATION INFORMATION

Chapter 5
The impact of adopting a research orientation towards use of the Pupil Premium Grant in preparing beginning teachers in England to understand and work effectively with young people living in poverty
Katharine Burn, Trevor Mutton, Ian Thompson, Jenni Ingram, Jane McNicholl and Roger Firth
Journal of Education for Teaching, volume 42, issue 4 (October 2016) pp. 434–450

Chapter 6
Rethinking initial teacher education: preparing teachers for schools in low socio-economic communities in New Zealand
Lexie Grudnoff, Mavis Haigh, Mary Hill, Marilyn Cochran-Smith, Fiona Ell and Larry Ludlow
Journal of Education for Teaching, volume 42, issue 4 (October 2016) pp. 451–467

Chapter 7
Discussing poverty with student teachers: the realities of dialogue
Hanneke Jones
Journal of Education for Teaching, volume 42, issue 4 (October 2016) pp. 468–482

Chapter 8
Student teachers' perceptions of the effects of poverty on learners' educational attainment and well-being: perspectives from England and Scotland
Sue Ellis, Ian Thompson, Jane McNicholl and Jane Thomson
Journal of Education for Teaching, volume 42, issue 4 (October 2016) pp. 483–499

Chapter 9
Seeing disadvantage in schools: exploring student teachers' perceptions of poverty and disadvantage using visual pedagogy
M. L. White and Jean Murray
Journal of Education for Teaching, volume 42, issue 4 (October 2016) pp. 500–515

For any permission-related enquiries please visit:
http://www.tandfonline.com/page/help/permissions

Notes on Contributors

Katharine Burn is a Fellow at the Department of Education, University of Oxford, UK.

Ann Childs is Associate Professor of Science Education at the Department of Education, University of Oxford, UK.

Marilyn Cochran-Smith is Professor of Teacher Education for Urban Schools and Director of the doctoral program in curriculum and instruction at Lynch School of Education, Boston College, USA.

Fiona Ell is Associate Dean and Head of ITE at the Faculty of Education and Social Work, University of Auckland, New Zealand.

Sue Ellis is a Professor at the School of Education, University of Strathclyde, UK.

Fernando Ilídio Ferreira is based at the Institute of Education, University of Minho, Portugal.

Roger Firth is Associate Professor of Geography Education at the Department of Education, University of Oxford, UK.

Maria Assunção Flores is an Associate Professor based at the Institute of Education, University of Minho, Portugal.

Peter Gilroy is the Editor of the *Journal of Education for Teaching*.

Paul C. Gorski is Associate Professor at the School of Integrative Studies, George Mason University, USA.

Lexie Grudnoff is a Principal Lecturer in the School of Learning, Development and Professional Practice and is currently the Deputy Dean (Teacher Education) for the Faculty of Education, University of Auckland, New Zealand.

Mavis Haigh is Associate Professor at the Faculty of Education and Social Work, University of Auckland, New Zealand.

Mary Hill is Associate Professor at the Faculty of Education and Social Work, University of Auckland, New Zealand.

Jenni Ingram is Associate Professor of Mathematics Education at the Department of Education, University of Oxford, UK.

Hanneke Jones is Lecturer in Primary Education at the School of Education, Communication and Language Sciences, Newcastle University, UK.

NOTES ON CONTRIBUTORS

Kerry Kretchmar is Associate Professor of Education in the Education Department, Carroll University, USA.

Larry Ludlow is a Professor at the Lynch School of Education, Boston College, USA.

Olwen McNamara is Professor of Education at the University of Manchester, UK.

Jane McNicholl is an Associate Professor of Science Education at the University of Oxford, UK.

Jean Murray is the Research and Knowledge Exchange Leader at The Cass School of Education and Communities, University of East London, UK.

Trevor Mutton is Associate Professor at the Department of Education and is Director of Professional Programmes, University of Oxford, UK.

Ian Thompson is an Associate Professor of English Education, and a Fellow of St. Hugh's College, Oxford, UK.

Jane Thomson is a Lecturer at the School of Education, University of Strathclyde, UK.

M. L. White is Senior Lecturer in Education at The Cass School of Education and Communities, University of East London, UK.

Ken Zeichner is Boeing Professor of Teacher Education at the College of Education, University of Washington, USA.

Preface

Poverty and educational disadvantage are, as Olwen McNamara and Jane McNicholl argue in their Introduction to this special issue, inextricably linked. Student teachers, almost by definition, are not educationally disadvantaged and so are likely to find it difficult to identify, let alone address, such disadvantage, especially when it is coupled to the pernicious effects of grinding poverty. This special issue points to the fact that student teachers bring with them mindsets concerning children and poverty which need to be both identified and challenged if, as teachers, they are to help children break free from their disadvantaged backgrounds.

Moreover, as the contributors demonstrate, the problem is worldwide. Indeed, JET has recently published research which indicates that student teachers bring with them assumptions about their pupils which are extraordinarily hard to address (see, for example, Ye 2015 with reference to China, and Ebersöhn et al. 2015 with reference to South Africa).

Another element of this situation identified in the issue is the way in which teacher education has had to accommodate political policies which are supposed to address poverty and disadvantage, policies which are often based on a political ideology rather than on hard empirical evidence. Despite the tension involved in negotiating a path between ideology and evidence, there are effective ways in which teacher educators can address the link between poverty and disadvantage, and examples are provided in the special issue.

Just over a decade ago, Nelson Mandela urged world leaders to recognise that 'Like slavery and apartheid, poverty is not natural. It is man-made and it can be overcome and eradicated by the actions of human beings' (Mandela 2005, 1). As this special issue reveals, the actions of teacher educators and their students are a vital part of the process of addressing social and educational injustice.

References

Ebersöhn, L., T. Loots, I. Eloff, and R. Ferreira. 2015. "In-service Teacher Training to Provide Psychosocial Support and Care in High Risk and High Need Schools: School-based Intervention Partnerships." *Journal of Education for Teaching* 41 (3): 267–284.

Mandela, N. 2005. Nelson Mandela's Speech to Trafalgar Square Crowd, via. Accessed July 1, 2016. www.makepovertyhistory.org/docs/mandelaspeech.doc

Ye, W. 2015. "When Rural Meets Urban: The Transfer Problem Chinese Pre-service Teachers Face in Teaching Practice." *Journal of Education for Teaching* 42 (1): 28–49.

Peter Gilroy

INTRODUCTION

Poverty discourses in teacher education: understanding policies, effects and attitudes

Olwen McNamara and Jane McNicholl

There is overwhelming evidence in this special issue that even the developed world is a long way from delivering the educational improvements that will 'temper the deleterious effects resulting from cross-generational cycles of disadvantage' and, in the process, 'generate wider benefits in terms of better health, crime and social capital outcomes' (Machin 2006, 19). Analysis in this special edition reveals a disheartening picture of complex patterns of inequality across and within individual countries, together with an incomplete understanding of the intersectional mechanisms – political, ideological, social and cultural – which link poverty and educational disadvantage.

Juxtaposing the continuing failure of education systems to address disadvantage, with the widespread belief that in the best performing school systems the key factor for success is the selection and training of teachers (Barber and Mourshed 2007), raises another concern. The issue is that remarkably little is known about the effective preparation of pre-service teachers to ameliorate educational disadvantage and, additionally, that little attention appears to be given to this in most teacher preparation programmes. Concern about this matter led to the formation of the Poverty and Teacher Education (PaTE) group at Oxford University Department of Education, subsequent to a conference day for initial teacher education (ITE), students and partners on the educational effects of poverty within Oxfordshire. Following this event, PaTE group meetings were initiated with invited colleagues from several universities and, in the two years since then, membership of the informal group has grown organically with the intention of developing and deepening research knowledge and publications in the area. Towards this end, PaTE members have presented their research in symposia at the British Education Research Association (BERA) conferences in 2013 and 2014 and at the European Conference on Educational Research (ECER) in 2015. The impetus to compile this special edition came again from the PaTE group and includes some of the work presented at the three conferences, together with other invited contributions.

The volume overall evidences some positive signs that interesting, innovative and intellectually sound developments are happening at a local level in a number of countries. But, as many of the targeted policy initiatives described also demonstrate, turning around an education system is a complex business given that neither the reasons for the disadvantage nor the solutions are primarily internal to the system. In England, for example, constructions of characteristics such as ethnicity, gender, diversity and inclusion have, over the last two decades, been subject to increasing scrutiny in education policy development, and more specifically teacher education policy. However, understanding of the impact of poverty per se has not been signalled as a priority for the (albeit increasingly full) agendas of mainstream ITE providers. Instead, policy metaphors for poverty include 'widening participation' and 'closing the gap' and prescriptions for change centre on teacher expectations and pupil aspirations. Simplistic therapies that offer schools the possibility of reducing the outward manifestations of 'the gap' incline teachers to a deficit pathology, rather than generating understanding of the structural factors within society that cause poverty and the insidious mechanisms through which it operates. Existing research on teachers' and head teachers' perceptions and attitudes to social class and poverty in the classroom suggest that many often lack a critical perspective on context (Gorski 2012; Lupton and Thrupp 2013) and evidence presented in this journal indicates that pre-service teachers' attitudes to poverty are also often deeply ingrained and resistant to change.

An insightful analysis elucidating how and why such attitudes develop towards disparities in educational outcomes is given by Paul Gorski in his excellent framing article for this special edition. He identifies dominant societal ideologies about poverty as the problem and argues that how we interpret the educational disparity determines our understanding of the problem, which in turn determines the solutions we are capable of imagining. Issues that are taken up in contributions from across three continents, drawing on perspectives from five countries: US, New Zealand, Portugal, England and Scotland. The special issue is structured by three embedded organising themes that focus variously at national policy level (Theme 1), ITE programme level (Theme 2) and individual pre-service teacher level (Theme 3).

Theme 1 explores how education polices, and specifically teacher education policies, conceptualise and address poverty, its influence on learning and teaching in schools and its impact on educational outcomes. Reflecting on this theme, Ann Childs and Katharine Burn from Oxford University, UK, focus on the key education and teacher education policies designed by two successive UK governments (during the period 1997–2015) with the aim of mitigating the effects of poverty on children and young people in England. They consider the implications of the government initiatives for those tasked with preparing pre-service teachers to address the effects of multiple and complex educational disadvantage. This is followed by a contribution from the University of Minho, Portugal, in which Maria Flores and Fernando Ferreria outline government policy and practice in response to the severe and continuing economic crisis in Portugal, and reflect upon the complex and multiple deprivations experienced across society as a result of the austerity measures, and especially their impact on education and child poverty. They explore the profound and possibly long-term implications for teachers and teacher education.

Theme 2 has contributions from three countries– the USA, New Zealand and England, and offers analyses and case studies of how ITE programmes are framing, and seeking to address, the link between poverty and educational disadvantage. The first article from Kerry Kretchmar, Carroll University, Wisconsin, USA, and Ken Zeichner, University of Washington, USA, describes the features of college and university-based teacher education programmes and non-university-based (self-proclaimed) 'reform' programmes in the USA. They present the case for a new generation of third-way programmes that, through place-based learning, offer teachers a more nuanced understanding of the effects of poverty and prepare them to work for and with communities to address it. The second contribution is from Katharine Burn and colleagues at Oxford University, UK, and reports on an initiative of their ITE programme in which pre-service teachers undertake an enquiry into schools' use of the Pupil Premium Grant (a government initiative which targets funds specifically to children in England deemed to be at an educational disadvantage). The third contribution in this theme is offered by Lexie Grudnoff, Mavis Haigh and colleagues at the University of Aukland, New Zealand, and Marilyn Cochran-Smith and Larry Ludlow at Boston College, USA. It presents a brief but stark contextual analysis of the differential achievement of socio-economic and ethnic groups in New Zealand and then describes the programme that the authors designed around six 'facets of practice for equity', in order to prepare pre-service teachers for teaching in low socio-economic communities. The final article by Hanneke Jones at Newcastle University, UK, reports on her use of dialogic enquiry with pre-service teachers as a tool for understanding socio-economic disadvantage and promoting the social justice agenda.

Theme 3 explores pre-service teachers' understandings of, and attitudes towards, poverty and to what extent these can be changed or developed during their programme of study. It encompasses two articles. The first, a UK cross national study from Scotland and England in which Sue Ellis and Jane Thomson from the primary ITE course at the University of Strathclyde, Scotland, and Ian Thompson and Jane McNicholl from the secondary ITE course at Oxford University, England, report on pre-service teachers' perceptions of poverty, how they understand its effects on pupils' educational achievement and what they believe they can do to effect change. The final article by ML White and Jean Murray at the University of East London, UK, describes exploratory research into the development of innovative visual pedagogies with a view to offering a forum to discuss the social justice agenda and support and nurture pre-service student teachers' capacity to articulate their views about the effects of poverty on educational attainment.

As even advanced economies across the world continue to struggle and falter, there is growing evidence that the weak and vulnerable in society, especially children, pay the greatest cost in terms of reduced opportunities for access to equitable life chances. The most vital of these is of course education. This volume, we hope, offers an insight and valuable contribution to a debate about how ITE can, at macro, meso and micro levels, create levers for change. We hope that it illustrates how ITE programmes can illuminate the complex intersectionality of poverty with ethnicity, gender, culture, language and class, by creating safe spaces in which pre-service teachers can discuss discourses of disadvantage and oppression and understand them in relation to their own narrative histories and value systems. And, in doing so, that they become sensitised to the use of deficit labels and the stigmatising of learners and, importantly, that they retain an awareness of how their pedagogies and practices situate the learners' self-perceptions and self-efficacy, and impact on the learners' multi-layered identities and experiences of the world.

Disclosure statement

No potential conflict of interest was reported by the authors.

References

Barber, M., and M., Mourshed. 2007. "How the World's Best Performing School Systems Come out on Top." McKinsey & Company. Accessed March 16, 2016. http://www.smhc-cpre.org/wp-content/uploads/2008/07/how-the-worlds-best-performing-school-systems-come-out-on-top-sept-072.pdf

Gorski, P. C. 2012. "Perceiving the Problem of Poverty and Schooling: Deconstructing the Class Stereotypes That Mis-Shape Education Practice and Policy." *Equity & Excellence in Education* 45 (2): 302–319.

Lupton, R., and M. Thrupp. 2013. "Headteachers' Readings of and Responses to Disadvantaged Contexts: Evidence from English Primary Schools." *British Educational Research Journal* 39 (4): 769–788.

Machin, S. 2006. OECD Social, Employment and Migration Working Papers No. 32. *Social Disadvantage and Education Experiences*. Accessed March 16, 2016. http://www.oecd.org/social/soc/36165298.pdf

Poverty and the ideological imperative: a call to unhook from deficit and grit ideology and to strive for structural ideology in teacher education

Paul C. Gorski

ABSTRACT
In this article I explore the educational equity implications of three popular ideological positions that drive teachers' and teacher educators' understandings of, and responses to, poverty and economic injustice in schools: deficit ideology, grit ideology, and structural ideology. The educator's ideological position, I illustrate, determines their understandings of conditions such as socio-economic-based outcome disparities. Those understandings, in turn, determine the extent to which the strategies they can imagine have the potential to eliminate or mitigate those disparities. I then argue that teacher education for equity and economic justice must equip pre- and in-service educators with a *structural ideology* of poverty and economic injustice, based on a sophisticated understanding of relationships between structural inequalities and educational outcome disparities, rather than a *deficit* or *grit* ideology, both of which obscure structural inequalities and, as a result, render educators ill-equipped to enact equitable and just teaching, leadership and advocacy.

'Raise your hand,' I instructed the students, 'if you believe you have worked hard in your life'. We were in the third meeting of Poverty, Wealth, and Inequality, a class taken predominantly by elementary education students at a public university in the United States. I had just graded their first assignment, an essay in which they described how their socio-economic identities influence their attitudes about their future students whose families are experiencing poverty. I had noticed that virtually all of the students told the same story: *My grandparents worked hard. My parents worked hard. My parents taught me I can become whatever I want to become through hard work. Everything I have accomplished has come through hard work.* Many, including students whose parents or grandparents had experienced poverty, wrote as though their families were exceptional in this regard. *Thank goodness my family was responsible and worked hard. Who knows where I might have ended up.* Every student raised her or his hand.

I was not surprised by this outcome. The students, all well-intentioned enough that they opted to take an elective class about poverty and inequality, merely parroted the dominant US view about 'success' (Gans 1996). The world is a meritocracy, they were saying. What one achieves is directly proportional to how hard one works. My students – people who had chosen a career path that would require extremely hard work and that, save for the few who were born into wealth or who one day would become upper level administrators, all but assured them a future without class privilege – like most everybody else in the US had been socialised into this view from birth (McNamee and Miller 2009). *Everybody has an opportunity. Work hard like me and my parents and their parents and you can be Bill Gates.*

I invited the students to look around the room at all of the raised hands. 'What do you see?' Some appeared startled, their narrative of exceptionality shaken.

'Everybody works hard?' one student asked timidly. 'There must be more to the story than hard work?' another proposed.

With this we began our exploration on socioeconomically based educational outcome disparities and how to eliminate them.

In this essay, I draw on the principles of equity literacy (Gorski 2016a; Gorski and Swalwell 2015; Swalwell 2011) in order to demonstrate what my students and I began to uncover in class that day. The students were not lacking desire to develop the knowledge and skills necessary to create equitable learning environments for their future students. Nor, thanks to their more methods-oriented coursework, were they short on practical strategies or ideas for solving the 'achievement gap'. The trouble, instead, was that a majority of the students had been socialised to fundamentally misunderstand poverty and its impact on educational outcome disparities. As a result, despite good intentions, the strategies they were capable of imagining – trendy instructional interventions, the cultivation of grit in students experiencing poverty, programmes designed to encourage higher levels of parent involvement by economically marginalised families – sidestepped completely the causes of the disparities they felt desperate to redress. The trouble was not dispositional or practical. Instead it was ideological, borne of faulty belief systems that, if not reshaped, would undermine their potentials to be the equitable teachers they hoped to be.

With this in mind, my purpose is to argue that when it comes to issues surrounding poverty and economic justice the preparation of teachers must be first and foremost an ideological endeavour, focused on adjusting fundamental understandings not only about educational outcome disparities but also about poverty itself. I will argue that it is only through the cultivation of what I call a *structural ideology* of poverty and economic justice that teachers become *equity literate* (Gorski 2013), capable of imagining the sorts of solutions that pose a genuine threat to the existence of class inequity in their classrooms and schools. After a brief clarification of my case for the importance of ideology, I begin by describing deficit ideology, the dominant ideological position about poverty that is informed in the US and elsewhere by the myth of meritocracy (McNamee and Miller 2009), and its increasingly popular ideological offshoot, grit ideology (Gorski 2016b). After explicating these ideological positions and how they misdirect interpretations of poverty and its implications, I describe structural ideology, an ideological position through which educators understand educational outcome disparities in the context of structural injustice and the unequal distribution of access and opportunity that underlies poverty (Gorski 2016a). I end by sharing three self-reflective questions designed to help me assess the extent to which my teacher education practice reflect the structural view.

Ideology matters

In the US, as in many parts of the world, discourses about the 'achievement gap' are thick with references to parent involvement. Those discourses tend to revolve around establishing and bemoaning this fact: parents and other caregivers from economically disadvantaged families are less likely than their wealthier peers to participate in family involvement opportunities that require them to visit their children's schools (Desimone 1999; Hickman, Greenwood, and Miller 1995; Noel, Stark, and Redford 2013). Although research has shown that the same parents and caregivers may be just as likely as their wealthier peers to be engaged in their children's learning at home (Williams and Sanchez 2012), their lower rate of at-school involvement often, particularly in the popular press, is presumed to be one of the core causes of the socio-economic 'achievement gap' (see, e.g. Barton 2004; Bridges 2013).

There is no debate; this is a fact: parents and caregivers from families experiencing poverty do not visit their children's schools for family involvement opportunities at the same rate as wealthier parents and caregivers. The question from a policy and practice intervention perspective – from an equity literacy perspective – is, how do we interpret this fact? How does our ideological position influence what we define as the problem to be resolved? After all, how we interpret the disparity drives our understanding of the problem. Our understanding of the problem drives the solutions we are capable of imagining. Our choices of solutions determine the extent to which the strategies and initiatives we adopt threaten the existence of inequity or threaten the possibility of equity (Gorski 2013, 2016a). It all tracks back to ideology.

When asked why these sorts of disparities exist – why, indeed, poverty itself exists – people tend to attribute them in ways that reflect one of two big ideological positions. On one end of the continuum are people, including educators and policy-makers, who see people experiencing poverty as the agents of their own economic conditions. They adhere to deficit ideology (Gorski 2008a; Sleeter 2004), believing that poverty itself is a symptom of ethical, dispositional, and even spiritual deficiencies in the individuals and communities experiencing poverty. This is the dominant view in the US (Gans 1996) and, in my experience working with educators in more than 20 countries spanning five continents, a common view among people most everywhere who have not experienced poverty. Its adherents are likely to believe that in-school involvement disparities, like other disparities, are a reflection of these deficiencies. They might assume, despite decades of research demonstrating otherwise (e.g. Compton-Lilly 2003, Grenfell and James 1998), that low-income people do not value education, for example, and point their initiatives at attempting to fix this supposed deficiency.

On the other end of the continuum are people who tend to understand poverty and issues such as the family involvement disparity as logical, if unjust, outcomes of economic injustice, exploitation, and inequity. Adherents to a structural ideology (Gorski 2016b), they are likely to define gaps in in-school family involvement as interrelated with the inequities with which people experiencing poverty contend. So, recognising people experiencing poverty as targets, rather than causes, of these unjust conditions, they might understand lower rates of in-school involvement as a symptom of in-school and out-of-school conditions that limit their abilities to participate at the same rates as their wealthier peers. These conditions, such as families' lack of access to transportation or schools' practices of scheduling opportunities for in-school involvement in ways that make them less accessible to people who work evenings (as economically marginalised people are more likely than their wealthier peers to do) are rendered invisible by the deficit view.

To be clear, deficit and structural ideology are at the far ends of a long continuum of ideological positions. They do not constitute a binary. Still, as I have described elsewhere (Gorski 2016b), I generally can predict the extent to which a school's policies and initiatives related to poverty and educational disparities reflect a more or less deficit or structural view by asking the person in the institution with the most power a single question: *Why, on average, do parents from families experiencing poverty not attend opportunities for family involvement at their children's schools with the same frequency as their wealthier peers?* Based on the response I generally can predict the effectiveness of the school's policies and initiatives meant, at least ostensibly, to eradicate educational disparities across socio-economic status. This is why, in my view, any evaluation of a school's or school system's commitment to equity begins, not with an accounting of this or that policy or practice intervention, but rather with an accounting of the ideological positions of the institutional leaders – the views that determine the policies and practices those leaders are likely to adopt.

It also is why as a teacher educator I attend to ideology. No set of curricular or pedagogical strategies can turn a classroom led by a teacher with a deficit view of families experiencing poverty into an equitable learning space for those families (Gorski 2013; Robinson 2007).

The dangers of deficit ideology and its cousin, grit ideology

As described earlier, deficit ideology is rooted in the belief that poverty is the natural result of ethical, intellectual, spiritual, and other shortcomings in people who are experiencing it. Adherents to deficit ideology point to educational outcome disparities – differences in test scores or graduation rates, for example – as evidence of these shortcomings (Sleeter 2004; Valencia 1997). Low rates of in-school family involvement among parents experiencing poverty or higher relative rates of school absences among students experiencing poverty is interpreted, in their view, as evidence that people experiencing poverty do not value their children's education. People experiencing poverty are the problem; their attitudes, behaviours, cultures and mindsets block their potential for success.

Sometimes these deficit ascriptions are explicit. For example, Payne (2005), the most active purveyor of deficit ideology in North America, explicitly ascribes a wide variety of negative attributes to people experiencing poverty as part of her argument that we alleviate educational outcome disparities by adjusting the mindsets of economically marginalised people. She describes people experiencing poverty as ineffective communicators, promiscuous, violent, criminally oriented, addiction-prone and spiritually under-developed, and explains in her description of a generalised and universal 'mindset of poverty' that they do not value education the way middle class and wealthy people do (Payne 2005).

A majority of her claims about the mindsets of people experiencing poverty have been debunked (Gorski 2008a), her core book, *A Framework for Understanding Poverty* (2005), exposed for containing innumerable factual errors meant to paint the cultures of people experiencing poverty as the determining factor in educational outcome disparities (Bomer et al. 2008). People experiencing poverty, as it turns out, are just as diverse as any other group defined around a single identity. Unfortunately, reality is of little mitigating consequence against ideology. Payne, like other deficit ideologues, speaks to the existing misperceptions and biases of her primarily classroom-teacher audience. *People in poverty are broken. Here's how to fix them.*

This is the power of deficit ideology and why it poses the most danger in sociopolitical contexts in which people are socialised to believe equal opportunity exists. Despite the debunking, despite the inaccuracy and oppressiveness (Bomer et al. 2008; Gorski 2008a, 2008b) of her approach, Payne remains the most far-reaching voice about poverty and education in North America.

This also is why it is important to build teacher education processes related to equity concerns around the goal of ideological shifts. If a teacher believes people experiencing poverty are inherently deficient, no amount of instructional strategies will adequately prepare that teacher to see and respond to the conditions that *actually* underlie educational outcome disparities (Berliner 2006, 2013), from structural issues like housing instability to building-level issues like policies – for example, harsh punishments for school absences – that can punish students experiencing poverty for their poverty. As a teacher, can I believe a student's mindset is deficient, that she is lazy, unmotivated, and disinterested in school *and also* build a positive, high-expectations relationship with her?

Just as importantly, what realities does deficit ideology obscure and to what are we *not* responding when we respond through deficit ideology? Can we expect to eradicate outcome disparities most closely related to the barriers and challenges experienced by people experiencing poverty by ignoring those barriers and challenges – the symptoms of economic injustice?

Returning to the example of family involvement, the natural inclination of the educator who ascribes to deficit ideology is to believe that parents experiencing poverty do not show up because they do not care. The logical response to that interpretation is to try to convince people experiencing poverty to care. Across the US schools invest time and resources into initiatives designed to solve a problem that does not exist, not only wasting time and resources, but also risking the further alienation of the most marginalised families. What they too often fail to see are the barriers that make opportunities for family involvement less accessible to families experiencing poverty, so those barriers go unaddressed. This is deficit ideology, the inverse of equity.

As advocates for a more sophisticated examination of educational outcome disparities have grown louder about the trouble with the deficit view (Dudley-Marling 2007; Ullucci and Howard 2015), an enticing but equally troublesome alternative has emerged. Growing out of the notoriety of grit theory (Duckworth et al. 2009), the idea that there are particular personal attributes that enable some people to overcome adversity that might overwhelm others, grit ideology differs from deficit ideology in one important way. Unlike people who adhere to deficit ideology, who must wholly ignore structural barriers in order to attribute outcome inequalities to the mindsets of the targets of those barriers, adherents to grit ideology recognise the structural barriers. However, rather than cultivating policy and practice to eradicate those barriers, they enact strategies to bolster the grit of economically marginalised students (Gorski 2016b).

The most obvious trouble with grit ideology is that, of all the combinations of barriers that most impact the educational outcomes of students experiencing poverty, which might include housing instability, food insecurity, inequitable access to high-quality schools, unjust school policies, and others, not a single one is related in any way to students' grittiness. As Kohn (2014) has noted, adherents to a grit ideology are grasping for amoral solutions to inequity and injustice, which are moral problems. Kundu (2014), who warned of the 'relentless focus on grit' as a remedy to educational outcome disparities, explained how the grit view is a cousin to deficit ideology. 'By overemphasizing grit', Kundu wrote, 'we tend to attribute a student's underachievement to personality deficits like laziness. This reinforces the idea that individual effort determines outcomes' (80). It also ignores the fact that the most economically disadvantaged students, who show up for school *despite* the structural barriers and the inequities they often experience in school, already are, by most standards, the most gritty, most resilient students (Gorski 2013).

Like deficit ideology, grit ideology is no threat to the existence of educational outcome disparities. In the end, it only can lead to strategies that sidestep the core causes of those disparities, requiring students to overcome inequities they should not be experiencing.

The hope of structural ideology

Educators with a structural ideology understand that educational outcome disparities are dominantly the result of structural barriers, the logical if not purposeful outcome of inequitable distributions of opportunity and access in and out of school (Gorski 2016b). As mentioned earlier, this inequitable access tracks most closely to the symptoms of income and wealth inequality (Berliner 2006, 2013) – to economic injustice and its implications. Outside of schools, lack of access to adequate financial resources might mean that students experiencing poverty are coping with some combination of unstable housing, food insecurity, time poverty, and inadequate or inconsistent health care (Gorski 2013; Pampel, Krueger, and Denney 2010). They likely have less access than wealthier peers to Internet technology, books, tutoring, formal opportunities to engage with the arts, and other resources and experiences that bolster school achievement (Bracey 2006; Buchmann, Condron, and Roscigno 2010). Often students experiencing poverty are even cheated within their schools out of similar levels of access to experienced teachers, higher order pedagogies, affirming school cultures, arts education, co-curricular programmes, and other resources and opportunities their wealthier peers may take for granted (Almy and Theokas 2010; Barr and Parrett 2007). The barriers and challenges are diverse, but they do have this in common: they are wholly unrelated to the mindsets of families experiencing poverty. They have this in common, too: as long as they exist, educational outcome disparities will exist; there simply is no way to eradicate educational outcome disparities while sidestepping structural injustice (Berliner 2013).

What makes this reality difficult to manage in a teacher education context is that all of these outside-of-school inequities appear to most current and future educators far outside their spheres of influence (Gorski 2012). In fact, neither teachers nor schools are equipped with the knowledge, resources, or time to resolve these conditions – especially not in the immediate term. This is, in part, what makes deficit and grit ideology so alluring: they allow educators to define problems in ways that call for straightforward and practical solutions. *Teach families the value of education. Cultivate resilience in students.* With a structural ideology educators see big structural conditions they cannot rectify so easily or practically.

The hope of structural ideology is that, even if schools and educators cannot fully rectify those conditions, equity policy and practice should be responsive to those conditions and not punish economically marginalised students for their implications. Returning to the example of family involvement, rather than blaming parents experiencing poverty for lower at-school involvement rates, the educator with structural ideology steps back and reflects with greater equity literacy. Do we organise opportunities for family involvement in ways that are responsive to the challenges economically marginalised families face, perhaps a lack of paid leave, difficulty securing transportation, the inability to afford childcare, and the necessity of working multiple jobs? Even if we cannot eliminate these barriers entirely, can we create policy and practice that do not exacerbate them? Are we able to identify all the way in which structural inequalities are being reproduced in our classrooms and schools, in our spheres of influence, and eradicate those? Do we have the will, upon doing so, to expand our spheres of influence and find ways to address the structural conditions that underlie school outcome disparities?

This is equity literacy: having the knowledge that a commitment to equity requires us to ask these questions and then having the will to ask them. There is no path to equity literacy that does not include the adoption of a structural ideology because there is no way to cultivate equity through an ideological standpoint, like deficit or grit ideology, that is formulated to discourage direct responses to inequity.

Conclusion: holding myself accountable to structural ideology in my teacher education practice

In teacher education, if we only prepare future educators to be aware of outcome disparities or to think of achievement gaps solely in terms of test score disparities, 'dropout' rates, or other symptoms of economic injustice, and not as the *opportunity gaps* that they actually are, we may be inviting them, even if unintentionally, to slide into a deficit or grit view. If we equip them with practical instructional strategies but fail to facilitate the difficult ideological work necessary to become responsive to structural barriers within their spheres of influence (even if they cannot eliminate those inequities altogether) we become facilitators of deficit ideology. It is not easy. I have written about the challenges I have faced attempting to cultivate these shifts in my teacher education students (see Gorski 2012), as I try to navigate the ideologies they bring with them and their experiences in many of their other classes, where they are treated as mindless technicians concerned only with easily implementable strategies (DiAngelo and Sensoy 2010).

In order to ensure that I sustain a structural approach I have crafted a series of reflective questions that I occasionally revisit. I offer these, not in judgement of others' practice, but in hopes that they might inspire a similar ideological commitment in colleagues who, like me, struggle to cultivate in their students equity literacy – the ideological shifts necessary to become a threat to the existence of inequity in their spheres of influence.

Question 1: Am I helping students develop a language that problematises deficit framings?

When students refer to school 'dropouts' I encourage them to restate their concerns using 'pushout' instead. It helps them learn how a simple shift in perspective provides a more sophisticated equity understanding. Similarly, the term 'generational poverty' is popular in the US, suggesting poverty persists because it is passed generation to generation. I encourage my students to think, instead, of 'generational *injustice*', wherein families experience generations of economic injustice, making its impact more and more insidious.

Question 2: Am I in any way suggesting that educational outcome disparities can be eradicated by fixing economically marginalised people's mindsets rather than by fixing the conditions that economically marginalise people?

I must ensure that I am not, in any explicit or implicit way, supporting the former, thereby validating the deficit view many teacher education students learn in other contexts.

Question 3: Am I providing students with adequate structural context so that they will understand and learn how to respond to the core causes of educational outcome disparities?

I must ensure that I have high expectations of my teacher education students as thinkers and theorists, as people who desire to make and are capable of making big theoretical connections. Any discussion of practical 'diversity' or 'equity' strategies is inadequate without this structural context.

Disclosure statement

No potential conflict of interest was reported by the author.

References

Almy, S., and C. Theokas. 2010. *Not Prepared for Class: High-Poverty Schools Continue to Have Fewer in-Field Teachers*. Washington, DC: The Education Trust.
Barr, R. D., and W. H. Parrett. 2007. *The Kids Left behind: Catching up the Underachieving Children of Poverty*. Bloomington, IN: Solution Tree Press.
Barton, P. E. 2004. "Why Does the Gap Persist?" *Educational Leadership* 62: 8–13.
Berliner, D. 2006. "Our Impoverished View of Educational Reform." *Teachers College Record* 108 (6): 949–995.
Berliner, D. 2013. "Effects of Inequality and Poverty vs. Teachers and Schooling on America's Youth". *Teachers College Record* 115. Accessed December 14, 2015. http://www.tcrecord.org
Bomer, R., J. Dworin, L. May, and P. Semingson, 2008. "Miseducating Teachers about the Poor: A Critical Analysis of Ruby Payne's Claims about Poverty". *Teachers College Record,* 10 (11). [On-line]. Accessed January 24, 2015. http://www.tcrecord.org/content.asp?ContentsId=14591
Bracey, G. W. 2006. "Poverty's Infernal Mechanism." *Principal Leadership* 6 (6): 60.
Bridges, L. 2013. *Make Every Student Count: How Collaboration among Families, Schools, and Communities Ensures Student Success*. New York: Scholastic.
Buchmann, C., D. J. Condron, and V. J. Roscigno. 2010. "Shadow Education, American Style: Test Preparation, the SAT, and College Enrollment." *Social Forces* 89 (2): 435–462.
Compton-Lilly, C. 2003. *Reading Families: The Literate Lives of Urban Children*. New York: Teachers College Press.
Desimone, L. 1999. "Linking Parent Involvement with Student Achievement: Do Race and Income Matter?" *The Journal of Educational Research* 93: 11–30.
DiAngelo, R., and O. Sensoy. 2010. "'OK, I Get It! Now Tell Me How to Do It!': Why We Can't Just Tell You How to Do Critical Multicultural Education." *Multicultural Perspectives* 12 (2): 97–102.
Duckworth, A. L., C. Peterson, M. D. Matthews, and D. R. Kelly. 2009. "Grit: Perseverance and Passion for Long-Term Goals." *Journal of Personality and Social Psychology* 92 (6): 1087–1101.
Dudley-Marling, Curt. 2007. "Return of the Deficit." *Journal of Educational Controversy* 2 (1): 1–13.
Gans, H. 1996. *The War against the Poor: The Underclass and Antipoverty Policy*. New York: Basic Books.
Gorski, P. C. 2008a. "Peddling Poverty for Profit: Elements of Oppression in Ruby Payne's Framework." *Equity & Excellence in Education* 41 (1): 130–148.
Gorski, P. C. 2008b. "The Myth of the 'Culture of Poverty.'" *Educational Leadership*, 65 (7): 32–36.
Gorski, P. C. 2012. "Teaching against Essentialism and the Culture of Poverty." In *Cultivating Social Justice Teachers: How Teacher Educators Have Helped Students Overcome Cognitive Bottlenecks and Learn Critical Social Justice Concepts*, edited by P. Gorski, K. Zenkov, N. Osei-Kofi, and J. Sapp. 84–107. Sterling, VA: Stylus.
Gorski, P. C. 2013. *Reaching and Teaching Students in Poverty: Strategies for Erasing the Opportunity Gap*. New York: Teachers College Press.
Gorski, P. C. 2016a. "Equity Literacy: More than Celebrating Diversity." *Diversity in Education* 11 (1): 12–14.
Gorski, P. C. 2016b. "Re-Examining Beliefs about Students in Poverty." *School Administrator* 73 (5): 16–20.
Gorski, P., and K. Swalwell. 2015. "Equity Literacy for All." *Educational Leadership* 72 (6): 34–40.

Grenfell, M., and D. James. 1998. *Bourdieu and Education: Acts of Practical Theory*. Bristol, PA: Falmer.

Hickman, C. W., G. Greenwood, and M. D. Miller. 1995. "High School Parent Involvement: Relationships with Achievement, Grade Level, SES, and Gender." *Journal of Research & Development in Education* 28: 125–134.

Kohn, A. 2014. "Grit? A Skeptical Look at the Latest Educational Fad." *Educational Leadership* 74: 104–108.

Kundu, A. 2014. "Grit, Overemphasized; Agency, Overlooked." *Phi Delta Kappan* 96: 80.

McNamee, S. J., and R. K. Miller. 2009. *The Meritocracy Myth*. Lanham, MD: Rowman & Littlefield.

Noel, A., P. Stark, and J. Redford. 2013. *Parent and Family Involvement in Education, from the National Household Education Surveys Program of 2012*. Washington, DC: US Department of Education.

Pampel, F. C., P. M. Krueger, and J. T. Denney. 2010. "Socioeconomic Disparities in Health Behaviors." *Annual Review of Sociology* 36: 349–370.

Payne, R. K. 2005. *A Framework for Understanding Poverty*. Highlands, TX: aha! Process.

Robinson, J. G. 2007. "Presence and Persistence: Poverty Ideology and Inner-city Teaching." *Urban Review* 39: 541–565.

Sleeter, C. E. 2004. "Context-Conscious Portraits and Context-Blind Policy." *Anthropology & Education Quarterly* 35 (1): 132–136.

Swalwell, K. 2011. "Why Our Students Need Equity Literacy." *Teaching Tolerance Online*, December 21. http://www.tolerance.org/blog/why-our-students-need-equity-literacy

Ullucci, K., and T. Howard. 2015. "Pathologizing the Poor: Implications for Preparing Teachers to Work in High-Poverty Schools." *Urban Education* 2: 170–193.

Valencia, R. R. 1997. "Introduction." In *The Evolution of Deficit Thinking*, edited by R. R. Valencia, ix–xvii. London: Falmer Press.

Williams, T. T., and B. Sanchez. 2012. "Parental Involvement (and Uninvolvement) at an Inner-City High School." *Urban Education* 47: 625–652.

Responding to poverty through education and teacher education initiatives: a critical evaluation of key trends in government policy in England 1997-2015

Katharine Burn and Ann Childs

ABSTRACT

This paper presents a comparative critique of key education and teacher education policies in England adopted by New Labour (1997–2010) and the Coalition government (2010–2015). It focuses on direct measures intended to alleviate the effects of poverty on young people's educational outcomes, and on teacher education policies with implications for preparing teachers to tackle such problems. It questions the consistency, coherence and effectiveness of the policies pursued by each administration and analyses the similarities and differences between them. Particular attention is paid to the conceptions of professional knowledge and educational research that underpin their assumptions about the role of teachers' professional learning in seeking to break the link between young people's socio-economic status and their educational outcomes. While policies implemented by both administrations are deeply imbued with neoliberal perspectives, our analysis highlights important differences, the effects of which may become more apparent as the Conservatives exercise their independent authority over education.

Introduction

This paper presents a critical examination of government policies in education and teacher education in England that address, explicitly or implicitly, issues of poverty and disadvantage. It covers the period 1997–2015, dealing first with the policies of successive Labour administrations and then with those of the Coalition government. While all political parties within those administrations and each successive Secretary of State for Education expressed their commitment to addressing the educational inequalities associated with socio-economic disadvantage and while each intervened in significant ways in initial teacher education (ITE), only some of the initiatives undertaken to address educational inequalities also had specific implications for teacher preparation or professional development. The paper therefore tackles each issue in turn: first, questioning the coherence and consistency of Labour policies (1997–2010) concerned with addressing the impact of poverty on education, and then applying the same critique to interventions in teacher education with implications for preparing teachers to respond effectively to the barriers to learning associated with economic disadvantage.

A similar two-pronged approach is taken to the Coalition government (2010–2015). The paper concludes by examining similarities and differences between the two types of administrations, demonstrating that while they were both committed to pursuing neoliberal policies that combined increasingly tight regulation in some domains with principles of diversity and 'consumer' choice in others, thereby exemplifying classic features of a quasi-market system (Levacic 1995), there were also highly significant differences between them. These differences can be seen not only in the extent to which schools alone were regarded as responsible for, or capable of, overcoming the educational inequalities that arise from socio-economic disadvantage, but also in their diverse conceptions of the kinds of professional knowledge with which teachers need to be equipped in order to contribute effectively to that endeavour. In turn, those different conceptions also gave rise to profoundly different views of research based or theoretical knowledge and of the roles that universities should play, both in its creation and effective dissemination.

The Labour government 1997–2010

> Incoherence and inconsistency in the plethora of 'Third way' education policies addressing issues of poverty and disadvantage.

The Labour Party that triumphed in the landslide victory of May 1997 had promised a dramatic break with the neoliberal policies of the preceding Conservative administrations, which they characterised and condemned as a 'ruthless free-for-all' (Power and Whitty 1999, 599), essentially premised on the laissez-faire principles of free-market capitalism. While this characterisation failed to acknowledge the role of state intervention and tightening regulation that the Conservatives had also introduced (most obviously in the form of a national curriculum), it allowed New Labour to promise an alternative 'third way': balancing market principles of choice and competition with appropriate, well-informed direction. Education policy would be formulated, it was claimed, 'on the basis of "what works" rather than being driven by any one ideological approach' (Power and Whitty 1999, 599). In fact, as Power and Whitty went on to argue, the extent to which Labour embarked on a new course is debatable: despite some 'Old Labour "first way" thinking' New Labour's strategies [were] largely an extension of the second way "neo-liberalism" of the previous Conservative governments' (535).

Powell (2000, 46) has shown that New Labour policies concerned with combating the effects of poverty and disadvantage tended to be couched in 'the terms of inclusion and exclusion'. Equal opportunities discourse was 'constructed around the problem of how to enable "them" ("the different") to overcome barriers that prevent them from becoming like "us" ("the normal")' (48). The language of 'inclusion' as a response to economic disadvantage was also prevalent within educational policy, as Furlong (2005), has noted:

> Raising educational standards has been one of the government's key priorities because at one and the same time education is seen as being able to create economic growth in the flexible, knowledge-based economies of the twenty-first century, and to promote social inclusion by creating pathways out of poverty. (123)

The Labour government's declared commitment to tackle the educational inequalities associated with socio-economic disadvantage was quickly matched by a plethora of new initiatives. *Education Action Zones* (EAZ) were introduced in June 1998 in 25 different areas, as a 'fresh approach' to the 'deep-seated problems' of improving the performance of schools in challenging circumstances through 'partnerships of schools, the business sector, local authorities and community organisations' (DFEE 1998, para 1.2). The *Sure Start* initiative, announced the same year and initially operating as a series of local programmes, was designed to 'give additional professional help to families with young children in areas of poverty' (Power and Whitty 1999, 537), focusing on the improvement of health services and family support, including increased provision of childcare, alongside early education. Parents were seen as important partners in determining the nature of the local programmes. A third initiative, the *Excellence in Cities (EiC)* programme, established in March 1999, was built on the principle of schools in inner city and deprived urban areas working together to raise standards. Additional funding was spent on learning mentors and learning support units, alongside provision for those pupils designated as 'gifted and talented' and access to high-quality information and communications technology resources in new City Learning Centres.

This series of specific programmes was followed in Labour's second administration by a much more wide-ranging and ambitious programme, *Every Child Matters* (*ECM*), which called for extensive inter-professional collaboration. Launched in 2003 (across England and Wales), it encompassed children and young adults and, as Williams (2004, 407) explains, it argued for 'a more universal approach to children: propos[ing] universal prevention and early intervention, rather than just targeted protection, and draw[ing] these into the goal of ending child poverty and enabling every child to reach their potential'. At its heart was a commitment to inter-professional collaboration: a network of support, including health and social services working closely with schools, to combat the effects of disadvantage. Within *ECM*, the *Sure Start* local programmes were replaced by Sure Start Children's Centres, operated by local authorities, providing easy access to a full range of services.

While this range of programmes indicates a strong commitment to tackling educational disadvantage, it has been argued that 'the sheer number of separate initiatives' led to 'a lack of overall coherence' in policy direction (Walford 2006, 5). This can be seen in the different assumptions reflected in each initiative about the impact of poverty and how it could be redressed. While *EiC*, for example, seemed to be based on the premise that compensatory educational interventions alone could overcome the barriers to learning created by economic deprivation, *Sure Start* and *ECM* were underpinned by an awareness that the transformation of young people's educational outcomes also depended on action in other arenas, including health services and access to high-quality childcare. They also reflected different views about the most effective agents in addressing educational inequalities associated with poverty. While some programmes, such as the *EAZs*, were based on the principles of public–private partnership, encouraging business investment in local communities, *Sure Start* initially sought to engage and empower parents as active partners, only to find that the Sure Start Children's Centres developed under *ECM* effectively vested power in local authorities. According to Glass (2005), the emphasis of ECM also shifted from concern with child development to the provision of childcare, reflecting an assumption that parental inclusion within the labour market would contribute most effectively to improving children's educational outcomes.

More damning, perhaps, than lack of coherence is Walford's (2006) claim that other educational policies pursued by New Labour actually tended 'in the opposite direction', effectively increasing inequality. On these grounds, he particularly indicted the extension of diversity within secondary education through the introduction of more specialist schools. Pioneered by the previous Conservative administration in its creation of sponsored City Technology Colleges, this was a policy with strong neoliberal resonances, both in its involvement of the private sector and in its emphasis on parental choice and the promotion of competition between different kinds of providers. Labour extended the policy, first by creating further specialist designations, such as Beacon Schools (high-performing schools given additional funding to share their good practice with others identified as 'failing') and in 2000 by establishing the first in a series of 'academies', privately sponsored schools (independent of the then local education authorities) in areas of socio-economic disadvantage. While these sponsored academies were explicitly intended to address long-standing problems of under-achievement, it is important to examine Walford's claim that they may well have increased, rather than decreased, educational inequalities. This followed Ball, Bowe, and Gewirtz's (1996) earlier demonstration that increases in diversity of provision, combined with the operation of parental choice, could operate to reinforce inequality and hierarchies of social class. Where such detailed analysis has been undertaken, for example, by Gorard (2005, 2014), the conclusion seems to be that the earliest academies did *not* in fact lead to an increase in segregation, but this was *only* because:

> The schools selected at the outset were among the most disadvantaged and so where they changed their intake as a result of Academisation, this was no threat to local levels of socio-economic segregation between schools. For example, where new Academies ended up taking a smaller share of local free school meal (FSM) eligible pupils, this meant neighbouring schools had to take more and so the local clustering of poorer children in specific schools would reduce. (Gorard 2014, 269)

Unfortunately, however, in terms of addressing educational disadvantage, Gorard also concluded that there was 'no evidence' that the earliest academies were, in general, 'performing any better for equivalent pupils than the schools they replaced' (Gorard 2005, 369).

New Labour teacher education policies: mandated standards with the capacity to enrich teachers' knowledge undermined by the diversification of training routes.

New Labour's teacher education policies reflected the same combination of state regulation and free-market mechanisms that had been employed by the preceding Conservative administrations. Where the Conservatives had intervened in the early 1990s to specify the precise number of days that postgraduate student-teachers should spend in school-based training (DFE 1992), the Labour government imposed tighter forms of control by intervening in the content of ITE (Furlong et al. 2000), establishing national standards for the award of Qualified Teacher Status and setting out a national curriculum for ITE programmes. The neoliberal, market-based elements of Labour's policy can be discerned, as Childs (2013) has discussed elsewhere, in its diversification of the routes into teaching, through the creation of new school-based routes: the employment-based Graduate Teacher Programme and Teach First.

Unsurprisingly, the contrast between the regulatory tendencies (towards formalising the content of ITE programmes) and the more liberal promotion of choice and competition (embedded in the diversification of ITE training routes) created profound tensions in terms of preparing new teachers to work effectively with young people living in poverty. While the former provided considerable scope to examine the ways in which social class, poverty and disadvantage combine to affect the educational outcomes of pupils and to investigate research claims about the kinds of interventions that have most potential to make an impact, the latter tended to inhibit any sustained focus on such theoretical or research-based perspectives.

The potential inherent in the new Standards for Qualified Teacher Status (TTA 2003) derived from requirements related to understanding the diverse needs of young people as a precursor to effective personalised provision. Standard Q18, for example, required teachers to 'understand how children and young people develop' and 'to recognise specific sorts of developmental, social, religious, ethnic, cultural and linguistic influences that impact on the progress and well-being of the young people whom they teach'. Standards Q19 and Q25 both acknowledged clearly that the 'promotion of equality and inclusion' depended on the capacity to 'take practical account of diversity'.

In theory, the force of these standards was backed by the Office for Standards in Education (Ofsted) inspections and other accountability systems, such as the annual survey of newly qualified teachers. Yet, it must be acknowledged that presentation of the issue in terms of 'inclusion' and the enumeration (in Standard Q18) of the very wide range of influences affecting child development about which student-teachers were expected to learn make it difficult to judge the extent to which ITE providers' efforts were focused *specifically* on equipping student-teachers to understand the nature of the interaction between poverty and education or to translate those understandings into particular pedagogical responses. The best that can be claimed, perhaps, is that the Universities Council for the Education of Teachers at least acknowledged and mapped out the profound implications of the *ECM* agenda in terms of teachers' professional knowledge. Kirk and Broadfoot (2007), for example, outlined six implications for ITE:

(i) A need for an analysis of the policy context of ECM.
(ii) A need to reassess the place of knowledge in teacher education.
(iii) A need for student-teachers to undergo 'sustained study of the theoretical perspectives of child development, on human learning, on the environmental and other obstacles to human flourishing, on conditions which maximise learning, and on the manifold ways in which learning is facilitated and managed'.
(iv) A need to develop an understanding of the inter-professional context.
(v) An emphasis on developing skills in students-teachers which 'give greater prominence to the subtleties of the interpersonal interaction skills required in discussions in inter- professional contexts'.
(vi) The need for ITE to rework their partnership arrangements, making it possible for them to draw on the necessary knowledge and expertise in different contexts (12–13).

Although none of these are the exclusive domain of either university or school partners, arguably implications (i), (ii) and (iii) required significant input from different kinds of research traditions (sociological as well as psychological) which universities were well-placed to provide. Yet, it was precisely this kind of sustained theoretical analysis and research-informed perspective that was rendered problematic by the diversification of ITE since the new routes all reduced the role of universities. The reduced scope for this kind of analysis was evident even within the Teach First programme, despite the scheme's declared commitment to breaking the link between parental wealth and children's educational outcomes.

Inspired by Teach for America, but adapted to local circumstances (Ellis et al. 2016), Teach First sought to overcome the 'scourge' (Wigdortz 2012) of educational underachievement among the poor by recruiting well-qualified graduates, prepared to commit to teaching for at least two years in a London secondary school in 'challenging circumstances', as defined with reference either to the school's public examination results at 16+ or to the proportion of pupils eligible for Free School Meals. While recruitment was successful (allowing the gradual expansion permitted by the government, from 186 participants in 2003 to 485 in 2009), the location of most professional learning 'on-the-job' meant that there was relatively little time and few sustained opportunities for psychological or sociological examination of the ways in which poverty and structural inequalities tends to affect young people's engagement with, and capacity to exploit, different kinds of educational provision. With limited opportunity for university-based study (approximately 20 days within the introductory six-week 'Summer Institute', with other days devoted to school induction and school-centred learning, and just six further study days over the course of the year), the strongest influences on new recruits' understanding and practice were likely to be the perspectives that they encountered within school, although this may have been mediated by the programme's explicit ethos.

Occupational socialisation has been shown to be the strongest factor counteracting attempts at educating innovative teachers, even in tightly integrated partnership ITE programmes (Wideen, Mayer-Smith, and Moon 1998; Brouwer and Korthagen 2005) designed to facilitate the use of research to interrogate existing practices. Where the scope for alternative perspectives is significantly reduced, so too is the potential to challenge prevailing assumptions. The programme thus lacked precisely the opportunity for 'sustained study of the theoretical perspectives of child development, on human learning, on the environmental and other obstacles to human flourishing, on conditions which maximise learning' that Kirk and Broadfoot (2007, 12) had regarded as necessary within the *ECM* agenda.

It could be argued that the explicit commitment of Teach First to breaking the connection between educational attainment and parental income may have helped challenge the essentially conservative dynamic of an apprenticeship training model. Yet, the fact that a strong component of the Teach First 'vision' was the presumed need to 'raise pupils' aspirations' (see Teachfirst.org/leadership development programme 2015) meant that the programme tended to operate with an essentially unhelpful deficit model, of the kind condemned by Gorski (2012). The assumption that educational outcomes could be transformed by an emphasis on raising young people's aspirations and changing their attitudes has also been shown, in a series of research reviews commissioned by the Joseph Rowntree Foundation, to lack any secure evidence (Carter-Wall and Whitfield 2012; Cummings et al. 2012).

The Coalition government 2010–2015

Coalition contradictions between freedom and regulation in responding to educational inequalities: a new compensatory initiative backed by new accountability mechanisms.

Key figures in the Coalition government, established in May 2010, declared their commitment to ensuring social mobility and emphasised the essential role of education in overcoming disadvantage. The first Education Secretary, the Conservative Michael Gove, proclaimed 'the gap in attainment between rich and poor' to be 'a scandal' (Gove 2010b), while the Liberal Democrat Schools Minister, David Laws, professed similar determination to break down 'this stubborn attainment gap between richer and poorer pupils' (Laws 2014). The policy solutions that they advanced remained distinctly neoliberal in their emphasis on diversification, but this was combined with a neo-conservative drive towards a more traditional curriculum and more rigorous testing. They were also accompanied by a new compensatory initiative, which promised increased educational funding for *all* pupils identified as economically disadvantaged, while reinforcing the drive to narrow the gap with new accountability mechanisms.

In terms of the diversification of schooling, a fundamental change was made to the academy policy, allowing any school rated 'good' or 'outstanding' by Ofsted to apply for conversion to academy status. While early converters received some additional resources, the policy was essentially promoted in terms of the freedoms it offered: 'less bureaucracy and an opportunity to thrive, free from interference from government' (Gove 2011b). The new 'converter Academies' were still bound by admissions criteria set for all state schools, but could develop their own curriculum, rather than being constrained by the National Curriculum which, ironically, was simultaneously being made more rigorous.

In a more radical move, the Coalition also permitted the establishment of entirely new 'free' schools. Officially enjoying the same 'freedoms' as academies, and required to be run on a not-for profit basis, they could be established by a wide range of organisations, including businesses, but also encompassing charities, universities, existing academies or independent schools, community and faith groups, parents and teachers. The policy emphasis on wresting control of education from local government was underlined, however, by the fact that no new schools (of any kind) could henceforward be established by local authorities.

While these policies, as we have noted, could be presented in neoliberal terms as driving improvement by increasing diversification and parental choice, Gorard (2014) has observed that under the Coalition, the process of 'academisation' was essentially 'driven by the purported school improvement agenda'. The declared commitment to addressing the relationship between educational outcomes and socio-economic inequalities that had officially underpinned previous sponsored conversions of 'failing' schools in areas of economic disadvantage was 'now largely ignored' (2014, 269).

In marked contrast to this neglect, a much more explicit commitment to 'closing the gap' in educational outcomes between the poor and their more affluent peers was embodied in the Pupil Premium Grant. Although this was merely the latest in a long line of 'compensatory' initiatives (Mortimore and Whitty 1997), it was much more wide-ranging than many because of its application to every eligible student, wherever they lived. Originally championed by the Liberal Democrats, the policy provided specific funds, 'an additional £2.5 billion a year' (Laws 2010), that schools were expected to use to improve the educational outcomes of pupils in receipt of Free School Meals. The policy was accepted as part of the Coalition Agreement, and instituted in the first year of government.

In examining this range of policies, some of which represented the continuation and expansion of policies driven forward by New Labour, the over-riding picture is again one of inconsistency, with the impact of certain policies effectively undermining the stated aims of others. As Gorard has demonstrated, the expansion of the academies programme emphatically failed to decrease segregation. Data drawn from the Annual Schools Census (1989–2012), the Department of Education School performance tables (2004–2012) and the National Pupil Database revealed that 51% of Converter Academies took less than half of their 'fair share' of free school meals pupils, in contrast to only 3% of Sponsor-led academies (Gorard 2014, 273). Although Gorard did not conclude that the presence of particular kinds of academies actually exacerbated problems of segregation (noting, in fact, that any causal link might well operate in the opposite direction), his work demonstrated that local authorities with both types of academy were linked to higher levels of segregation than local authorities with a higher proportion of maintained schools.

The introduction of the Pupil Premium Grant did, however, appear to represent a more determined and focused policy initiative, reinforced in a variety of ways (with implications for teacher education), but perhaps most obviously by accountability mechanisms. The formal inspection framework was revised to ensure that judgements about schools' effectiveness took particular account of the achievement of pupils registered as eligible for Free School Meals at any point in the previous six years. In July 2014, Ofsted declared that 'headteachers know that their schools will not receive a positive judgement unless they demonstrate that they are focused on improving outcomes for pupils eligible for the pupil premium' (Ofsted 2014, 4). Although the same report claimed that the funding was 'making a difference in many schools', it conceded that it would take more time to establish whether it would actually lead to a narrowing in the attainment gap.

> One consistent emphasis in Coalition policies: increasing the role of schools and reducing that of universities in both the production of research and the process of teacher education.

The Coalition's teacher education policies also reflected a continued commitment to diversification, both in the range of applicants they sought and in the development of new routes that ran counter to their regulatory tendencies in other respects. More significantly, they represented the continuation and intensification of a sustained attack on the role of universities. As Furlong (2005) has previously argued, Conservative policies in this respect had long been driven by ideological objectives, but their ferocity escalated after the Coalition came to power, with Gove explicitly condemning certain 'academics who have helped run the university departments of education' as members of 'the Blob', 'Marxist sympathisers' and 'enemies of promise' (Gove 2013).

In opposition, the Conservatives' teacher education policy had primarily been expressed in terms of improving the quality of teachers because of the essential role they were expected to play in raising the achievement and social mobility of the most disadvantaged (Gove 2010a). Improvement was proposed through diversification of the profession: the recruitment of ex-service personnel and high-achieving business people, through 'Troops to Teachers' and a 'Teach Now' initiative (an expansion of Teach First). As Childs and Menter reflect, while the emphasis on diversifying the range of applicants had a 'more neo-liberal slant', policies designed to bring troops into teaching to improve discipline and a simultaneous focus, in new teacher standards, on developing teachers' subject knowledge 'resonate more with neo-conservative perspectives of tradition and control' (2013, 106).

The 'Troops to Teachers' programmes were formally launched in June 2013 (DFE 2013) while the Teach First programme nearly trebled in size over the five years of the parliament, to reach 1400 participants (including primary and early years' teachers), placed in 10 different regions (see Teachfirst.org/about our history 2015). Although the Department for Education (DFE) did not in fact establish a 'Teach Now' programme, Teach First also began targeting career changers, with such success that they accounted for 22% of the participants enrolling in 2014 (Teach First 2014).

While these policies were primarily concerned with the nature of the teaching workforce, the principle of diversification was also applied in a much more radical way to the organisational structures and recruitment processes of ITE, through the establishment of School Direct. The thrust of this policy towards 'school-led' ITE was consistent with moves made by the Conservatives in the early 1990s, establishing that that all postgraduate trainees (on secondary programmes) should spend at least two-thirds of their time in school (DFE 1992), but the emphasis in Gove's reforms on school *leadership* of ITE implied a fundamental shift in power relations, and organisational arrangements.

Gove sought to justify an increased role for schools by drawing on Mourshed, Chijioke and Barber (2010) report for McKinsey:

> What they found was that the best systems embed professional and talent development in schools ... In Finland trainees receive extensive classroom teaching practice under the guidance and supervision of experienced teachers. In Singapore I saw trainees learning how to improve their craft and strengthen their classroom management skills by observing the very best teachers at work in the classroom. All of these nations currently outperform us educationally and the emphasis they place on both intensive school-based classroom training and continual school-based professional development is at the heart of their success. (Gove 2011a)

The policy was signalled in the Government White paper, *The Importance of Teaching* (DFE 2010b), and fleshed out in a subsequent implementation plan (DFE 2011). It was to be facilitated by creating a network of Teaching Schools, expected to 'lead the school system in training and developing outstanding teachers' (DFE 2011), an expectation that extended beyond initial training, to further professional development of 'teachers, support staff and head teachers' and 'the raising of standards through school-to-school support' (DFE 2014). School Direct training placements would be allocated directly to Teaching School partnerships, which might choose whether *or not* to collaborate with a particular HEI. The School Direct routes expanded with extraordinary speed, accounting for 351 of secondary trainees in 2012–2013 (little more than 1% of the total cohort) and for 17,609 places allocated for 2015–2016 (just over 40%) (DFE 2013). This far exceeded Gove's original suggestion of 10,000 by the end of the parliament (Gove 2012).

As Furlong has noted, this further diversification of routes into teaching was matched by the introduction of a 'new and slimmed-down list of teachers' standards' (2013, 44). While reference was still made to essential knowledge and understanding that should underpin teachers' practice, including understanding of 'how a range of factors can inhibit pupils' ability to learn', the main thrust of the reform was to emphasise teachers' demonstrable competences. Extensive guidance (some 150 pages) that had accompanied the previous standards was simply removed, offering maximum flexibility to ITE providers in the design of their programme.

A more extreme form of flexibility had, however, already been offered to schools, some two months earlier, with the announcement in July 2012 that academies and free schools could choose to bypass ITE altogether and simply recruit untrained teachers. This additional freedom amply illustrates the tensions inherent in the Coalition's blend of neoliberal and neo-conservative policies, which sought to regulate the nature and content of ITE programmes even as they liberated schools from the obligation to engage with them at all. The essential contradictions are further highlighted by Gove's decision in 2015 to commission a review of Initial Teacher Training, which recommended the establishment of a new core curriculum to be included in any ITE programme (Carter 2015). The inconsistencies evident in these two decisions precisely mirrored those playing out in relation to the school curriculum: a review process largely premised on Hirsch's notion of 'core knowledge', intended to equip all young people with the knowledge that would give them access to power (Gibb 2015), conducted at the same time as academies and free schools were exempted from its mandate.

As argued earlier, any move to make the role of universities more marginal within ITE has the potential to reduce the theoretical understandings of beginning teachers about the ways in which issues of poverty, social class and disadvantage affect young people's capacity and commitment to engage with particular kinds of educational opportunities. This is particularly problematic if the alternative perspectives that are offered serve to perpetuate unhelpful assumptions about those living in poverty. Moreover, there is little evidence in the international comparisons on which the Coalition government originally drew, that reducing the university-based components of ITE would improve their effectiveness. Indeed, Gove's (2011a) appeal to practices in Finland and Singapore dramatically overstated the role of school-based provision in those countries and obscured their fundamental commitment to developing research-informed knowledge and understanding and the capacity to subject routine practices to systematic critical evaluation.

In Finland, for example, the successive periods of classroom experience accounted for only about a third of the ITE programme (Sahlberg 2012), *half* as much as in existing postgraduate programmes in England. In summarising the Finnish's programme's key features, Sahlberg argued that it was supported by 'scientific knowledge' and focused on 'thinking processes and cognitive skills employed in conducting research' (Jakku-Sihvonen and Niemi 2006). He particularly alluded to the 'systemic integration of scientific educational knowledge, didactics and practice in a manner that enables teacher to enhance their pedagogical thinking, evidence-based decision-making and engagement in the scientific community of educators' (Sahlberg 2012, 6). All prospective teachers were required to achieve a full Master's degree, demonstrating knowledge and understanding of the 'advanced fields of educational science' and the 'interdisciplinary nature of educational practice' as well as their own capacity to 'design, conduct and present original research on practical or theoretical aspects of education' (2012, 11). This, it was argued, would equip them not only to adopt a research orientation towards their own practice, but also to evaluate the findings of others' research, discerning its value in interpreting and responding to the particular classroom situations that they faced.

It is true that the notion of teachers as researchers as well as users of research was endorsed by the Coalition's policies, but even as it apparently embraced this idea, the government consistently sought to reduce the role of universities, not only excluding them from ITE, but marginalising them in the production of research since that too could be entrusted to schools. Indeed, designation as a Teaching School carried with it a formal commitment to:

- build on existing research and contribute to alliance and wider priorities;
- base new initiatives within your alliance on existing evidence and ensure you can measure them;
- work with other teaching schools in your area, or nationally, where appropriate;
- ensure that your staff use existing evidence;
- allow your staff the time and support they need take part in research and development activities;
- share learning from research and development work with the wider school system (DFE 2014).

While the use of 'existing evidence' might well imply reliance on academic research, the Coalition's consistent policy drive to reduce the influence of universities and to prioritise certain kinds of research over others was reflected in two other policy initiatives. Both were related to the generation of knowledge intended to equip teachers to overcome the inequalities in educational outcomes associated with socio-economic disadvantage and they took the form of significant financial contributions to the Educational Endowment Foundation (EEF) and to the 'Closing the Gap Test and Learn' project.

Although officially an independent grant-making charity, the establishment of the EEF was supported by a Department for Education grant of £110 million (DFE 2010a). Its declared objective was to 'break the link between family income and educational achievement, ensuring that children from all backgrounds can fulfil their potential' which it sought to achieve by:

- Identifying and funding promising educational innovations that address the needs of disadvantaged children.
- Evaluating these innovations to extend and secure the evidence on what works and can be made to work at scale.
- Encouraging schools, government, charities and others to apply evidence and adopt innovations found to be effective (EEF 2011).

Closing the Gap (CTG), a sustained research initiative involving Teaching Schools and their local alliances, was similarly intended 'to help improve the evidence-base for what works in closing the attainment gap for disadvantaged pupils' while also stimulating 'robust research and development in schools' (see Curee.co 2015).

At first, in contrast to the thrust of ITE policies which seemed to be encouraging schools to assert their independence of universities (or at least their authority within school/HEI partnerships), the rhetoric with which CTG was launched appeared to reflect a commitment to 'strengthening relationships' between schools and HEIs, building tighter links 'between the teaching profession and universities', thereby 'helping to develop the academic standing of the teaching profession' (CfBt.com 2015). The initial phase was undertaken by the University of Durham, working in conjunction with the Centre for the Use of Research and Evidence in Education (CUREE), to identify a series of potentially powerful interventions that schools could trial in a two-year programme (CUREE 2015). The capability phase was entrusted to the CfBT Education Trust (now the Education Development Trust) and to the University of Oxford, with the latter specifically expected to support small-scale professional enquiry into pupils' and teachers' experience of the interventions, including analysis of the reasons for their success (or failure) (Childs, Firth, and Thompson 2015).

Although this approach might seem to represent a well-coordinated commitment both to tackling the educational outcomes of socio-economic disadvantage and to developing a more research-literate teaching profession, capable of sustaining the continued professional learning of its members, in effect, its key focus on finding interventions which 'work' to close the gap reflected the discredited assumption (Mortimore and Whitty 1997) 'that social inequality and "gaps" in outcomes can be eliminated through educational interventions alone' (Ellis et al. 2016, 60). This is the same assumption that underpinned the publication of the EEF/Sutton Trust Toolkit (Higgins et al. 2014), designed to provide an easily accessed and straightforward guide to research evidence about the effectiveness of particular interventions (presented in relation to their cost).

While publication of the toolkit obviously reflected an endorsement of research, much of it conducted by university-based researchers, its very nature meant that it could only encompass particular kinds of research: studies able to generate quantitative measures of impact. A similar premise underpinned CTG, which was based on the use of randomised control trials to determine which of the seven selected interventions 'worked' to close the gap. The role of the university was limited, in Durham's case, to working with CUREE to select the interventions and, in Oxford's case, to provide regional training (each typically lasting one day, at three separate points within the two-year project) to strengthen and enhance the Teaching Schools' capacity to engage in research. However, such limited contact, three points over two years, with participants representing 673 Teaching Schools made it difficult to ensure the kind of significant and sustained interactions necessary to build the 'stronger links between universities and schools' (CfBt.com 2015) that had originally been promised. In addition, even though existing university partners of Teaching Schools were formally invited to training events, attendance was sparse and the direct involvement of universities other than Oxford was not mentioned in the final project report (Churches 2016). Any potential that there might have been to bring in more critical examination of the ways in which poverty affects young people's engagement in education, or (more radically) to question the assumption that educational innovations *alone*, without attention to structural inequalities, can reverse established patterns of relative achievement between advantaged and disadvantaged pupils seems not to have been realised.

By reducing the role of educational research to a narrow technicist notion of 'what works', the Coalition government restricted the scope to equip teachers with the full range of knowledge and understanding necessary to tackle the barriers to learning that derive from socio-economic disadvantage and structural inequalities. Their actions reflected an essential distrust of theoretical perspectives informed by sociological or sociocultural research. While the Coalition retained an explicit commitment to the use of 'research' within ITE, reflected within the suggested ITE curriculum proposed by Carter (2015), there was no requirement for teachers in free schools or academies ever to engage with that curriculum since they were not obliged to gain a teaching qualification. While universities still appeared to have some role as the suppliers of research, they were essentially marginalised and excluded from any role in developing teachers' abilities to evaluate research critically or to implement it in contextually sensitive ways. Teachers were expected to draw on research as expert technicians, having been told 'what works'. While they might play a part in generating the evidence that informed pronouncements, they were effectively barred from contributing to those judgements and received little encouragement to engage with the questions of why or how particular strategies work and thus of how they might be adapted or developed to make them more effective, or effective in different contexts.

Similarities and differences between labour and coalition policies

Having examined the policies espoused and enacted by both the New Labour and Coalition governments across the period 1997–2015, we conclude by clarifying the extent of the similarities and differences between them. While both are undoubtedly deeply imbued with a neoliberal perspective, there are in fact profound differences between them, the effects of which are likely to become more apparent over the next few years as the Conservatives exercise their independent authority over education.

> A shared commitment to compensatory policies and the establishment of a quasi-market through diversification and choice.

Both New Labour and the Coalition governments sought to address the gap between the outcomes of wealthier and poorer pupils by directing resources into specific educational provision for the most disadvantaged. The essential difference, however, was that while successive Labour administrations channelled funding into particular regional initiatives such as the *EAZ* and *Excellence in Cities* programme, the Pupil Premium Grant linked funding to *individual* pupils and thus effectively made *all* schools clearly accountable for the achievement of children identified as economically disadvantaged. The funding and the accountability measures associated with it undoubtedly succeeded in focusing attention on the educational outcomes of young people living in poverty, even in more affluent areas, although it is accepted that little impact can yet be seen on their attainment (Ofsted 2014).

A second broad similarity is that both New Labour and the Coalition governments argued that diversification of educational provision and increased parental choice would serve to drive up standards (through competition between schools) and thus to improve the educational outcomes of disadvantaged pupils. As we have noted, this neoliberal idea was originally borrowed from the Conservatives by New Labour. The first Conservative, privately sponsored City Technology College, was followed under New Labour by a range of specialist schools, and specifically by a series of privately sponsored academies that replaced 'failed' schools in areas of socio-economic disadvantage. Although the achievements of these particular academies continue to be debated, the best that can be said of them is that they did not exacerbate the problems of disadvantage by increasing social segregation (Gorard 2005). Little more can be claimed of the extraordinary wave of diversification unleashed by the Coalition's academy programme. As Gorard (2014) has demonstrated, there is still no evidence either that they have reduced social segregation or that they have achieved any kind of differential impact in terms of value-added scores.

The principle of diversification was also applied by both New Labour and the Coalition governments to the issue of teacher quality, which was regarded as another important means of improving the educational outcomes of those living in poverty. Teach First was enthusiastically embraced by policy-makers in all parties because of its avowed commitment and demonstrable success in attracting 'high-flying' graduates into teaching, expanding by 2014 to become the largest recruiter of graduates in the UK, (Birchall 2014). The scheme's most dramatic expansion took place, however, under the Coalition government, which was also responsible for the 'revolutionary' changes (Gove 2012) heralded by the introduction of School Direct and the establishment of the Teaching School alliances that underpinned this fundamental shift of responsibilities within ITE.

Profoundly different conceptions of universities' role impacting on teachers' theoretical understandings of the educational impact of poverty and disadvantage.

While previous Labour governments had promoted a number of employment-based routes into teaching, these were always seen as 'alternative' routes intended to make the profession more accessible to particular kinds of career changers or mature applicants; they were never intended to replace established partnership programmes, nor were they driven by the ideological opposition to the role of universities in ITE that characterised some of the more intemperate pronouncements of Coalition ministers (see, for example, Gove 2013). While the extraordinary expansion of School Direct in fact concealed considerable diversity of provision (allowing some well-established partnerships to maintain their essential character), the contribution of universities within teacher preparation was effectively marginalised in many contexts, and the stability of its continuing provision called into question. Despite the early protestations of the Schools Minister, Nick Gibb, that the DFE was not 'abandoning universities' (Gibb 2012) and the affirmation by the Carter Review (2015) of the importance of teachers learning to use research, the role assigned to universities in teacher education was essentially reduced in the Coalition's policies to the provision of research findings. These, it was presumed, should be presented not as theoretical models of children's learning to be drawn on in interpreting and responding to learners' needs in any particular context, but as clearly delineated and empirically validated teaching strategies, ideally validated through the use of randomised control trials. Unfortunately, although the use of such research methods does not by definition preclude consideration of the specific contexts in which certain strategies do and do not work, the emphasis on simplification of the research to make it accessible tends to promote the expectation that certain strategies should be universally applicable. Moreover, the fact that randomised control trials cannot in themselves explain why or how particular strategies work also leaves teachers (who have been told merely that they do) poorly equipped to adapt and or modify them appropriately if the need arises.

The same differences between Labour and the Coalition (in terms of their conception of the kinds of knowledge and understanding that teachers need) are also reflected in changes that each made to the standards for award of Qualified Teacher Status (DFE 2012). While revisions under Labour included consideration of the knowledge and understanding that teachers would need to respond effectively to the *ECM* agenda (Teacher Training Agency 2003), the new standards issued by the Coalition (DFE 2012) paid relatively little attention to teachers' underlying knowledge and understanding of the barriers to learning faced by young people in particular circumstances. Even when the DFE reflected again on the kinds of knowledge on which effective teaching would depend and accepted the recommendations of the Carter Review (2015) that greater attention should be paid within the ITE curriculum to knowledge of child and adolescent development, no specific reference was made to any kind of sociological understanding of social class or of the psychological implications of deprivation. As Diane Reay has argued:

> With no access to sociological and historical understanding of social class and in particular the positioning of the working classes within education, initial teacher trainees are left ill informed … and ill equipped to broach, let alone tackle, the greatest problem the education system faces: that of working class educational underachievement, alienation and disaffection. (Reay 2006, 303)

It is unsurprising, therefore, that despite the range of policy initiatives detailed here, there were few signs of *sustained* progress in the endeavour that came to be increasingly narrowly framed in terms of closing the 'achievement gap'. While the overall failure might be attributed to the limited time for which some interventions were sustained, the most consistent policies across the whole period were essentially based on establishing a quasi-market: promising increased freedom and diversity in order to maximise 'choice', while effectively seeking to mandate achievement through punitive accountability mechanisms. Not only is the claim that diversification tends to reduce the effects of disadvantage widely disputed (Feinberg and Lubienski 2009), but these policies are also premised on the discredited assumption that the efforts of schools alone can redress the effects of wider structural inequalities. While schools undoubtedly *do* make a significant difference to the outcomes of pupils living in poverty (Mortimore and Whitty 1997), and have an essential role to play in equipping new entrants to the profession to contribute effectively to that work, there is little evidence to suggest that they will become any more effective by assuming sole responsibility for it.

Indeed, the consistent message to be drawn from a recent collection of studies examining international teacher education programmes that have achieved notable success in preparing teachers to work in high-poverty schools (Lampert and Burnett 2016) is that their effectiveness in challenging unhelpful deficit models depends on providing beginning teachers with sustained opportunities to examine the nature of poverty in specific contexts (including its intersection with other factors such as race and social class). As Lampert and Burnett's (2016) collection richly demonstrates, this is a process facilitated by serious engagement with appropriate theoretical frameworks and with the kind of reflexive practice promoted by practitioner research training. These are precisely the components of teacher preparation that are lost in the policy drive towards on-the-job training, a drive with enthusiastic promoters elsewhere (Zeichner 2014) but so far most passionately embraced by the Coalition government in England and its Conservative successor.

Disclosure statement

No potential conflict of interest was reported by the authors.

References

Ball, S. J., R. Bowe, and S. Gewirtz. 1996. "Circuits of Schooling: A Sociological Exploration of Parental Choice of School in Social Class Contexts." *Sociological Review* 43: 53–78.
Birchall, M. 2014. *The times Top 100 Graduate Employers 2014–15*. London: High Fliers Publications.
Brouwer, N., and F. Korthagen. 2005. "Can Teacher Education Make a Difference?" *American Educational Research Journal* 42 (1): 153–224.
Carter, A. 2015. *Carter Review of Initial Teacher Training (ITT)*. London: DFE.
Carter-Wall, C., and G. Whitfield. 2012. *The Role of Aspirations, Attitudes and Behaviours in Closing the Educational Attainment Gap*. Joseph Rowntree Foundation. Accessed November 5, 2014. http://www.jrf.org.uk/publications/aspirations-attitudes-educational-attainment-roundup
CfBt.com. 2015. Accessed November 5. http://www.cfbt.com/en-GB/What-we-do/School-improvement/Teacher-development
Childs, A. 2013. "The Work of Teacher Educators: An English Policy Perspective." *Journal of Education for Teaching* 39 (3): 314–328.
Childs, A., R. Firth, and I. Thompson. 2015. "Who and Why? Motives and Agendas for Key Stakeholders." Paper presented at the British Educational Research Association Conference, Belfast, September.
Childs, A., and I. Menter. 2013. "Teacher Education in 21st Century England – A Case Study in Neoliberal Public Policy." *Revista Española de Educación Comparada* 22, 93–116.
Churches, R. 2016. *Closing the Gap: Test and Learn*. London: DFE. https://www.gov.uk/government/uploads/system/uploads/attachment_data/file/495580/closing_the_gap_test_and_learn_full_report.pdf.
Cummings, C., K. Laing, J. McLaughlin, I. Papps, L. Todd, and Woolner, P. 2012. *Can Changing Aspirations and Attitudes Impact on Educational Attainment*. Joseph Rowntree Foundation. Accessed November 5, 2014. http://www.jrf.org.uk/sites/files/jrf/education-attainment-interventions-full.pdf
Curee.co. 2015. Accessed November 5. http://www.curee.co.uk/ctg/overview
DFE. 1992. *Initial Teacher Training (Secondary Phase) Circular 9/92*. London: DFE.
DFE. 2010a. *Press Release 3 November 2010*. Accessed November 5, 2015. https://www.gov.uk/government/news/new-endowment-fund-to-turn-around-weakest-schools-and-raise-standards-for-disadvantaged-pupils
DFE. 2010b. *The Importance of Teaching. The Schools White Paper 2010*. London: The Stationery Office.
DFE. 2011. *Training Our Next Generation of Outstanding Teachers*. London: The Stationery Office.
DFE. 2012. *Teachers' Standards*. Accessed November 5, 2015. https://www.gov.uk/government/uploads/system/uploads/attachment_data/file/208682/Teachers__Standards_2013.pdf#

DFE. 2013. *Initial Teacher Training Performance Profiles: Academic Year 2012 to 2013*. Accessed November 5, 2015. https://www.gov.uk/government/collections/statistics-teacher-training

DFE. 2014. *Teaching Schools: A Guide for Potential Applicants, National College for Teaching and Leadership*. Accessed November 5, 2015. http://www.education.gov.uk/nationalcollege/index/support-for-schools/teachingschools.htm

DFEE. 1998. *Handbook for Education Action Zones*. London: DFEE.

EEF. 2011. *Challenge for the New Education Endowment Foundation Laid Bare*. Accessed November 5, 2015. https://educationendowmentfoundation.org.uk/news/challenge-for-the-new-education-endowment-foundation-laid-bare/

Ellis, V., M. Maguire, T. A. Trippestad, Y. Liu, X. Yang, and K. Zeichner. 2016. "Teaching Other People's Children, Elsewhere, for a While: The Rhetoric of a Travelling Educational Reform." *Journal of Education Policy* 31 (1): 60–80.

Feinberg, W., and C. Lubienski. 2009. *School Choice Policies and Outcomes: Empirical and Philosophical Perspectives*. New York: State University of New York Press.

Furlong, J. 2005. "New Labour and Teacher Education: The End of an Era." *Oxford Review of Education* 31 (1): 119–134.

Furlong, J. 2013. "Globalisation, Neoliberalism, and the Reform of Teacher Education in England." *The Educational Forum* 77: 28–50.

Furlong, J., L. Barton, S. Miles, C. Whiting, and G. Whitty. 2000. *Teacher Education in Transition: Re-forming Teaching Professionalism*. Buckingham: Open University Press.

Gibb, N. 2012. *Oral Evidence at the Education Select Committee 14 March 2012*. Accessed November 5, 2015. http://www.publications.parliament.uk/pa/cm201012/cmselect/cmeduc/1515/120314.htm

Gibb, N. 2015. *Welcome Address to E.D. Hirsh, Policy Exchange Annual Lecture on Education, 17 September, 2015*. Accessed November 5, 2015. http://www.policyexchange.org.uk/modevents/item/the-annual-education-lecture-with-e-d-hirsch

Glass, N. 2005. "Surely Some Mistake?" *The Guardian*, January 5. Accessed November 5, 2015. http://www.theguardian.com/society/2005/jan/05/guardiansocietysupplement.childrensservices

Gorard, S. 2005. "Academies as the 'Future of Schooling': Is This an Evidence-Based Policy?" *Journal of Education Policy* 20 (3): 369–377.

Gorard, S. 2014. "The Link between Academies in England, Pupil Outcomes and Local Patterns of Socio-Economic Segregation between Schools." *Research Papers in Education* 29 (3): 268–284.

Gorski, P. C. 2012. "Perceiving the Problem of Poverty and Schooling: Deconstructing the Class Stereotypes That Mis-Shape Education Practice and Policy." *Equity and Excellence in Education* 45 (2): 302–319.

Gove, M. 2010a. *Michael Gove to the Local Government Association*. Accessed November 5, 2015. https://www.gov.uk/government/speeches/michael-gove-to-the-local-government-association

Gove, M. 2010b. *Speech to the Westminster Academy, 9th September 2010*. Accessed November 5, 2015. https://www.gov.uk/government/speeches/michael-gove-to-westminster-academy

Gove, M. 2011a. *Michael Gove to National College*. Accessed November 5, 2015. https://www.gov.uk/government/speeches/michael-gove-to-the-national-college

Gove, M. 2011b. *Education and Economic Success Speech to the Education World Forum*. Accessed November 5, 2015. https://community.oecd.org/docs/DOC-20737

Gove, M. 2012. *National College Annual Conference 14th June 2012*. Accessed November 5, 2015. http://www.education.gov.uk/inthenews/speeches/a00210308/michael-gove-at-the-national-college-annual-conference

Gove, M. 2013. "'I Refuse to Surrender to the Marxist Teachers Hell-Bent on Destroying Our Schools': Education Secretary Berates 'The New Enemies of Promise' for Opposing His Plans." *Mail Online*, March 22. Accessed November 5, 2015. http://www.dailymail.co.uk/debate/article-2298146/I-refuse-surrender-Marxist-teachers-hell-bent-destroying-schools-Education-Secretary-berates-new-enemies-promise-opposing-plans.html

Higgins, S., M. Katsipataki, D. Kokotsaki, R. Coleman, L. E. Major, and R. Coe. 2014. *The Sutton Trust-Education Endowment Foundation Teaching and Learning Toolkit*. London: Education Endowment Foundation. https://educationendowmentfoundation.org.uk/uploads/toolkit/EEF_Toolkit_-21st_November_2014.pdf.

Jakku-Sihvonen, R., and H. Niemi, eds. 2006. *Research-based Teacher Education in Finland: Reflections by Finnish Teacher Educators*. Turku: Finnish Educational Research Association.

Kirk, G., and P. Broadfoot. 2007. "Every Child Matters and Teacher Education: A UCET Position Paper." London: UCET. Accessed July 26, 2016. http://www.ucet.ac.uk/393.

Lampert, J., and B. Burnett, eds. 2016. *Teacher Education for High Poverty School*. New York: Springer International Publishing.

Laws, D. 2010. *Address to the Association of Teachers and Lecturers, 29 March 2010*. Accessed November 5, 2015. https://www.atl.org.uk/Images/David%20Laws%20at%20ATL%20conference%20-%20 29th%20March%202010.pdf

Laws, D. 2014. *Speech on Grammar Schools 19 June 2014*. Accessed November 5, 2015. https://www.gov.uk/government/speeches/david-laws-speech-on-grammar-schools

Levacic, R. 1995. *Local Management of Schools: Analysis and Practice*. Buckingham: Open University Press.

Mortimore, P., and G. Whitty. 1997. *Can School Improvement Overcome the Effects of Disadvantage?* London: Institute of Education, University of London.

Moursher, M., C. Chijioke, and M. Barber. 2010. *How the World's Most Improved School Systems Keep Getting Better*. New York: McKinsey & Company.

Ofsted. 2014. *The Pupil Premium: An Update (Reference No:140088), the Office for Standards in Education, Children's Services and Skills*. Accessed November 5, 2015. https://www.gov.uk/government/publications/the-pupil-premium-an-update

Powell, M. 2000. "New Labour and the Third Way in the British Welfare State: A New and Distinctive Approach." *Critical Social Policy* 20: 39–60.

Power, S., and G. Whitty. 1999. "New Labour's Education Policy: First, Second or Third Way?" *Journal of Education Policy* 14 (5): 535–546.

Reay, D. 2006. "The Zombie Stalking English Schools: Social Class and Educational Inequality." *British Journal of Educational Studies* 54 (3): 288–307.

Sahlberg, P. 2012. "The Most Wanted: Teachers and Teacher Education in Finland." In *Teacher Education around the World: Changing Policies and Practices*, edited by L. Darling-Hammond and A. Lieberman, 1–21. Abingdon: Routledge.

Teach First. 2014. *Change Career, Change Lives*. Accessed November 5, 2015. http://www.teachfirst.org.uk/leaders-life/our-career-changers

Teacher Training Agency. 2003. *Qualifying to Teach: Professional Standards for Qualified Teacher Status and Requirements for Initial Teacher Training*. London: TTA.

Teachfirst.org/about our history. 2015. Accessed November 5. http://www.teachfirst.org.uk/about/our-history

Teachfirst.org/leadership development programme. 2015. Accessed November 5. http://graduates.teachfirst.org.uk/leadership-development-programme

Walford, G. 2006. *Education and the Labour Government: An Evaluation of Two Terms*. Abingdon: Routledge.

Wideen, M., J. Mayer-Smith, and B. Moon. 1998. "A Critical Analysis of the Research on Learning to Teach: Making the Case for an Ecological Perspective on Inquiry." *Review of Educational Research* 68: 130–178.

Wigdortz, B. 2012. *Success against the Odds: Five Lessons in How to Achieve the Impossible – The Story of Teach First*. London: Short Books Ltd.

Williams, F. 2004. "What Matters is Who Works: Why Every Child Matters to New Labour. Commentary on the DfES Green Paper Every Child Matters." *Critical Social Policy* 24: 406–427.

Zeichner, K. 2014. "The Struggle for the Soul of Teaching and Teacher Education in the USA." *Journal of Education for Teaching* 40 (5): 551–568.

Education and child poverty in times of austerity in Portugal: implications for teachers and teacher education

Maria Assunção Flores and Fernando Ilídio Ferreira

ABSTRACT
In recent years Portugal has experienced a severe financial and economic crisis, with implications for all sectors of society, particularly education. Salary cuts, high rates of unemployment, high taxation and worsening career progression are just some ways in which the teaching profession has been affected. Recent policy changes have also impacted on initial teacher education. This paper gives a brief characterisation of the emerging picture within the context of crisis, drawing on data from continuing research on the effects of poverty on teaching and teacher education. It looks at student teachers' experiences during practicum in regard to issues of poverty at school, as well as the ways in which poverty is framed and discussed during their initial teacher preparation. Key findings point to student teachers' perceptions about poverty and its impact on children's well-being and equal opportunities; the strategies they employ to deal with poverty at school; and the complex role of the teacher in promoting equity and social justice through facilitating access to powerful knowledge for all children. Implications for teacher education are discussed, particularly the need to foster social and cultural dimensions of teacher education.

Introduction

Over the last few years Portugal has gone through a severe financial and economic crisis, with implications for all sectors of society. Austerity measures have been intensified since the implementation of the memorandum of understanding with the International Monetary Fund, the European Central Bank and the European Commission (known as the Troika). These measures have greatly affected people's lives, in terms of unemployment, low income, high taxation, poverty and inequalities, as well as through their impact on social protection, health and education. Thus, alongside the financial and economic downturn, a social crisis has also become apparent.

In the education sector, salary cuts, high rates of unemployment, high taxation and worsening opportunities for career progression are just a few examples of the ways in which the teaching profession has been affected. Recent research, for instance, has demonstrated the increase in bureaucracy and the low morale of the teaching workforce (Flores 2014a). The goal of this paper is twofold: first, to provide a brief characterisation of

Portugal's education sector, the emerging context of crisis and the austerity measures that have affected schools and teachers' work and education; and second, to look at preliminary findings from continuing research on the effects of poverty on teaching and teacher education. In particular, the paper focuses on student-teachers' experiences during practicum in regard to issues of poverty at school, and the ways in which poverty is framed and discussed during their initial preparation.

Economic crisis, austerity measures and child poverty in Portugal

Portugal was one of the 12 countries most affected by the world recession (UNICEF 2014). The impact has been visible in the deterioration of the situation of families, and this has been mostly related to job losses, underemployment, higher taxes and cuts in social transfers and public services which occurred between 2008 and 2012. The intervention of the Troika in 2011 led to worsening living conditions and an increase in poverty. Alongside this was the growing emigration of qualified young Portuguese people, due to the lack of employment. Data from Eurostat, issued in June 2015, indicate that Portugal had the fifth highest rate of unemployment among young people in the European Union. The rate increased from 7.6% in 2008 to 13.2% in 2015. Long-term emigration from Portugal, a country with around 10.5 million inhabitants, increased with the recession. According to a recent report (Pires et al. 2014), on an average, around 80,000 people per year left Portugal between 2007 and 2012. In 2013, the number increased to 110,000 people, including a huge number of young qualified people.

In 2012, roughly a quarter of Portugal's population were 'at risk' of poverty or social exclusion, according to Eurostat data (EU 2014). In 2011, the Portuguese government cut public sector wages, increased taxes and slashed spending on social welfare programmes that provided social security benefits. Austerity measures were adopted as part of a larger goal to reduce the national deficit below 5.9%. Although successful in reducing the deficit, the austerity measures severely harmed the status of the Portuguese workforce and those in need of public support. Between 2008 and 2012, the proportion of children aged 17 or less who were living in jobless households nearly doubled in Portugal and Spain (UNICEF 2014).

Throughout the country many social canteens were created within the context of the government's programme of 'food emergency'. In the first half of the year of 2015, around 8.6 million meals were served. In partnerships with Mayors, local authorities and parents' associations, schools have also reinforced the social support to children and their families, by keeping school canteens open during summer holidays to provide children with 'the only full hot meal' (www.jn.pt/PaginaInicial/Nacional/Interior.aspx?content_id=4731106).

Portugal has one of the most unequal income distributions in Europe, and poverty levels are high (OECD 2014). There had been a long-term gradual decline in both inequality and poverty, but the economic crisis has halted this. The number of poor households is rising, with children and young people being particularly affected. Unemployment has impacted on the risk of poverty (40.5%) and on social exclusion (25.7%). The risk of child poverty among families experiencing unemployment was higher than for the rest of the population.

The effects of the financial and economic crisis on education have been clearly visible (INE-Portugal 2015). Children have been at higher risk of poverty and social exclusion than any other population group (since 2010), and they have been the most affected by the increase in poverty and social exclusion. The risk of poverty for children is inversely proportionate to their parents' level of schooling. Child poverty is lower where parents have higher levels of schooling: 37.5% for those whose parents have not completed at least secondary education; 14.1% for those whose parents concluded secondary or post-secondary education (non-higher education) and 4.1% for those whose parents held higher qualifications.

Despite the important progress made by Portugal over the last three decades following entry to the then European Economic Community, existing performance data related to education are still below the average of the EU. For example, 40% of 25–64-year-olds have completed at least the secondary education in Portugal, compared with 75.2% in EU. The school dropout rate for 18- and 24-year olds is 19.2 and 11.9%, respectively (PORDATA 2014). In Portugal, the 'New Opportunities' programme was launched in 2005 to provide individuals who left school with a second opportunity to do their studies, and to assist those in the labour force who wanted to acquire further qualifications. As a result of this initiative, graduation rates rose by more than 40% between 2008 and 2010. In 2010, more than 40% of the students concerned were older than 25 (OECD 2014). In 2011, however, the Ministry of Education abolished the programme, citing among other reasons, concerns related to how competencies were certified.

The work of schools and teachers is now greatly influenced not only by the need to educate children, but also by social issues, especially by the alarming dimension of poverty and the greater social intervention demands.

The education sector in a context of crisis

According to a recent report, 'The State of Education in a State under an intervention programme' (Benavente et al. 2014), the budget for education in Portugal increased from 1.4% of the gross domestic product (GDP) in 1972, to 4.6% in 1995 and 5.7% in 1998. Currently, it is around 3.8%, one of the lowest in the EU. The report characterises the changes in the education sector after 2011 as follows: (i) increased number of pupils per class; (ii) return to selecting pupils through national exams at all levels of schooling, in order to guide some to vocational programmes; (iii) increased workload for teachers; (iv) reduced staffing levels, especially related to the school curriculum restructuring leading to the disappearance of cross-disciplinary areas (e.g. project work) and school support for pupils.

This situation has led to 151% increase in teacher unemployment compared to 2011; (v) creation of mega-clusters of schools (a number of schools in a given municipality that federated under the leadership of one principal); (vi) promotion of school rankings based on national exams; (vii) reinforcement of so-called key subjects, such as Portuguese and Maths; (viii) abolition of transversal (areas that are covered by any teacher such as education for citizenship, Portuguese) and cross-curricular areas such as study under guidance (support for pupils to study at school) and project area (project work done by pupils and teachers without a given list of contents to be covered); and (ix) reduced attention given to subjects such as physical education, artistic education, civic education and health education.

The teaching workforce has lost more than 30,000 jobs (www.dn.pt/inicio/portugal/interior.aspx?content_id=3417596) and is now the profession with the highest level of unemployment, with 26.4% of teachers registered as unemployed and looking for jobs (based on IEFP official data in August 2012, in the subsequent years IEFP did not disclose data). Teachers' salaries have also been reduced, alongside an increased workload and worsening working conditions (see Flores, Ferreira, and Parente 2014). Research has demonstrated the intensification of teachers' work, the increase in bureaucracy and the low morale of the teaching workforce (Flores 2014a). In a recent nationwide survey ($n = 2702$), the majority of teachers (61.6%) admitted that their motivation had decreased in the three years since 2012 (Flores, Viana, and Ferreira 2014). The majority of the teachers participating in the study (96.7%) claimed that teachers' workloads had increased over the past three years, that there was a greater control over their work (75.6%), that there was an increase in teachers' public accountability (74.6%), and an accentuation of criticism of teachers (92.2%). Respondents blamed, to a great extent, the role of the media in the deterioration of the public image of teaching and teachers.

At the same time, more pressure has been put on schools and teachers to increase student attainment, as a result of concerns with national and international assessment programmes. Issues of accountability and performativity have been identified in some recent policy initiatives, especially those related to school internal and external evaluation, teacher evaluation and pupil assessment, with particular emphasis on national exams for new entrants into the teaching profession, and for pupils in year 4, year 6 and year 9 in Portuguese and Maths.

Alongside these developments, a number of policy initiatives have been introduced in order to deal with the complex demands of school life as a result of the financial, economic and social crisis. Since 2012, emergency and compensatory policies, programmes and measures have been put in place by the Ministry of Education, such as: (i) the definition of 'learning goals' in pre-school; (ii) the development of the third generation of TEIP (the so-called Educational Territory of Priority Intervention, TEIP 3), in order to deal with policies for priority education in socially and economically deprived areas where dropout rates are above the national average (in total, 16% of Portuguese schools benefit from this government programme); (iii) the 'Alternative Curriculum Paths' aimed at pupils in elementary education who experience learning difficulties, recurrent academic failure, risk of social exclusion and/or school dropout; (iv) the 'Integrated Programme for Education and Training' which is a socio-educational policy initiative aimed at the inclusion, in a transitional way, of young people aged 15–18 who are at risk of social and/or school exclusion; (v) the school programme for 'Food Reinforcement' (PERA Portugal, Ministério da Educação e Ciência 2012) which aims to provide pupils in need with a meal in the morning (around 14,000 and 12,000 pupils benefited from this programme in 2012/2013 and 2013/2014, respectively); and (vi) The 'Education and Training Programmes' aimed at 15–25-year olds and adults (18 years or above) which seek to deal with school dropout and school failure, to support pupils at risk of leaving school, to reintegrate those who have given up school and to consolidate school training with double certificates (vocational and academic) at the level of secondary education.

It is therefore important to analyse the ways in which teacher education, particularly the practicum, is responding to the challenges posed by these policy changes and the complex social and economic context, and this can be done through considering student teachers' perspectives.

Initial teacher education (ITE) in the post-bologna context in Portugal

Like many European countries, Portugal has undergone a restructuring of ITE programmes as a result of the implementation of the Bologna process. According to the legal framework

(Decree-Law n° 43/2007), the professional qualifications for teaching (from preschool to secondary education) are to be based on a number of key elements: (i) a higher professional qualification for teachers (at a second cycle level, i.e. Master's degree); (ii) a curriculum based on leaning outcomes in the light of teacher performance; (iii) a research-based qualification; (iv) the importance of practicum (observation and collaboration in teaching situations under the supervision of a mentor/supervisor); (v) school–university partnerships; and (vi) the quality assurance of teachers' qualification and of initial teacher education (Ministério da Educação 2007). Thus, in order to become a teacher, a three-year degree (*licenciatura*) is needed, plus a Master's degree in teaching (usually a two-year programme). This implies a separation between training in the first cycle (*licenciatura*) and training at second cycle level (master's degree). In 2014, a new legal framework for ITE in Portugal was published (Decree-Law n° 79/2014) which includes the following curriculum components: (i) training in the subject matter; (ii) general educational training; (iii) specific didactics (for a given level of teaching and subject matter); (iv) cultural, social and ethical education; and (v) professional practice. However, the cultural, social and ethical education component receives no specific credits.

The new configuration, within the context of a consecutive model, has been seen as a drawback in relation to previous models of teacher education. (Previously, the so-called integrated model included four to five years of training in which student-teachers would benefit from training in educational sciences and subject matter simultaneously from the very beginning of the course, plus one year of practicum in a school.) The new model is based on a more fragmented curriculum through different courses in every semester, some of them subdivided into modules, often as a result of academic disputes over disciplinary territories. This model emphasises subject knowledge and didactics, which implies that the professional practice occurs more at universities with less time spent in schools (e.g. Flores 2011; 2014b; Flores 2016; Flores et al. 2016). This trend towards academisation is evident elsewhere in Europe as ITE shifts focus from practical skills towards academic meritocracy (Ek et al. 2013). However, in other European countries and elsewhere, ITE has followed the opposite trend (see, for instance, the UK and the USA).

By and large, recent policy changes have impacted upon ITE, in terms of curriculum and knowledge fragmentation, and an emphasis on the didactics component, making it difficult to focus on the wider social and cultural problems in which teachers work. It is also important to note that in Portugal teacher surplus and unemployment became intertwined realities, with implications for the recruitment of student-teachers in higher education institutions and for new teachers' job expectations.

Methods

This paper reports on data drawn from continuing research on the effects of child poverty on teaching and teacher education in a context of social and economic crisis. It addresses the following research questions: How do student-teachers look at poverty and its effects on pupils and schools during practicum? What kinds of poverty situations do they describe? What do they learn from their practicum experience, particularly in regard to strategies to deal with poverty? How does ITE address poverty?

Student-teachers enrolled in ITE programmes for preschool and primary schools were invited to participate in the project. Nineteen volunteered for the study, out of a total of 24 students enrolled in the Master's degree for preschool teaching and 28 enrolled in the preschool and primary school programme. All were female and their ages ranged from 21 to 24 years. Eleven were studying for a Master's degree in preschool and 7 a Master's degree in both preschool and primary school.

None of the researchers taught in these programmes. One of the researchers asked the directors of the Master's degree programmes for permission to invite the students to participate in the study and to obtain informed consent. Data were collected during a seminar at the university in May 2015.

Student-teachers were asked to complete a two-page written narrative focusing on a number of questions that sought to explore their beliefs, conceptions and experiences of poverty during their practicum at first-degree level (initiation to professional practice) and at Master's degree level (supervised teaching practice). During practicum student-teachers have the opportunity to observe and to teach a number of lessons under the supervision of a cooperating teacher and a university supervisor. Written narratives are powerful in providing participants with the opportunity to reflect on their learning experiences, as well as to raise awareness and promote reflection on beliefs and implicit theories, and to make sense of their own experience (Elliott 2005). Through these narrative accounts the participants were invited to look back on specific moments or situations, and the learning from them, through a process of meaning-making (Hollway and Jefferson 2000; Elliott 2005). This is particularly relevant within the context of teacher education, and in this case after practicum. Issues of time and space and the social context (Clandinin, Pushor, and Orr 2007) are in this regard of paramount importance.

Data analysis was undertaken according to two phases. The first phase was a vertical analysis (Miles and Huberman 1994), according to which each of the respondents' accounts was analysed separately. The second phase included a comparative or horizontal analysis (cross-case analysis) (Miles and Huberman 1994) during which the method of 'constant comparative analysis' (Glaser and Strauss 1967) was used to look for common similarities as well as differences. Coding was carried our according to semantic criteria and emerging categories were identified from the accounts and were validated by both researchers.

Findings

In this section, findings arising from student-teachers' accounts are presented, according to the main emerging themes: (i) student-teachers' perceptions of poverty and its impact on children's well-being; (ii) strategies to deal with poverty at school; (iii) teachers' complex role in a context of crisis: promoting equity and social justice; (iv) ITE and the need to pay attention to the social and cultural dimension of teaching.

Student-teachers' perceptions of poverty and its impact on children's well-being

In their accounts student-teachers spoke of the ways in which they perceived poverty during their practicum in kindergarten and preschools. Most of them talked about situations of poverty which they observed during practicum. They illustrated their perceptions by describing concrete situations that had an impact on them, and they also identified the effects of the economic crisis on children's life and well-being:

> Poverty in schools is actually a very critical issue that worries me because it influences the ways in which children learn and relate to other people. (MEP1CEB 4)
>
> Poverty, in many cases, affects children at school. They lack motivation that may arise from their family context and it can lead to pupils' lack of interest in regard to school. (MEP1CEB 5)
>
> You can see the effects of poverty at school and even in the school atmosphere. Children feel the effects of poverty and they actually talk about that when they are in the playground. This is visible in the ways in which they play and they actually integrate this reality in their role-playings. (MEP2)

Some of the participants stated that they had not observed any situations related to poverty:

> During my practicum I have never come across children with economic difficulties. (MEP1CEB 7)
>
> I have never seen any situation which you could relate to poverty. (MEP1CEB 3)

However, the majority of students did claim that it was possible to identify poverty situations during their practicum, and they highlighted their real effects on children. In their accounts there are abundant examples of the effects of the economic and social crisis at various levels: lack of school material, early dropouts, poor quality of children's clothing, lack of food and so on:

> During my practicum I saw a child with special needs who was going to kindergarten without having had breakfast because her parents had economic difficulties. (MEP1CEB 2)
>
> Many children go to school without having had breakfast and this of course affects their learning. (MEP1)

As a consequence of the economic difficulties that have been exacerbated in Portugal over the last few years, schools have had to open during summer holidays in order to provide meals for pupils. Student-teachers reported situations that articulate the effects of the crisis on children's lives and on their behaviour at school: inadequate clothes, lack of resources, hunger and such like. Some of these situations were not familiar to the student-teachers who expressed surprise at what they had observed at school:

> I did see a child who used to wear the same clothes every single day and the clothes were not adequate to his size. This child had to shower at the school! (MEP11)
>
> When you ask children to bring material to school or money for a school visit, some children are not able to do it at all! (MEP-1CEB-1)

The participants' accounts also pointed to difficulties in doing their job during practicum, not only due to the lack of material and resources but also as a result of children's behaviour and lack of motivation:

> When the school doesn't have the required resources for children to learn, as a teacher you cannot provide them with learning experiences that may challenge them. It becomes difficult to get children motivated to learn if you don't have the materials that you need. (MEP5)
>
> The classroom conditions and facilities don't promote success; if there are no materials in the classroom, as a teacher your work is going to be undermined. (MEP6)

Student-teachers revealed that the lack of resources at school and the lack of funding led them to change their pedagogical activities, with implications for children's learning and development:

> For instance, the lack of material makes you change or postpone some activities. Actually it happened to me. Because of the lack of material, I had to postpone one of the activities during my practicum and it would have been really interesting for children. (MEP1CEB 7)

The lack of material makes your job as a teacher much more difficult. Also, the increasing poverty can be seen in pupils' failure and in their misbehaviour in regard to their colleagues and teachers. (MEP1)

Students' accounts did not just focus on the impact of poverty on pupils' learning and on teachers' work. They also spoke of children's leisure time and the fact that some of them cannot attend some of the activities:

In the kindergarten where I did my practicum, one child was not able to go to the beach because his parents didn't have money to pay for it. (MEP1CEB 2)

I remember that one child has given up from the kindergarten because of economic problems and she went to her grandmother's house. (MEP3)

As this last quotation suggests, one of the consequences of the crisis and growing economic difficulties is the early dropout of children from school:

If children are not motivated due to lack of resources and support they give up after compulsory education. (MEP2)

Being at school is expensive and nowadays parents need to pay much more for school materials and textbooks, which leads to dropout because they cannot afford it. (MEP1)

As previous research has demonstrated, poverty directly affects academic achievement due to the lack of resources available for student success. In other words, low achievement is closely correlated with lack of resources. Empirical work has shown the correlation between low socio-economic status and low achievement (Lacour and Tissington 2011).

Strategies to deal with poverty at school

Student-teachers were asked about the ways in which teachers and schools, and themselves as trainees, deal with poverty and its effects on school. They were asked to describe concrete situations that they had experienced. Most of them highlighted the role of teachers in helping children facing economic difficulties, by providing them with personal and financial support and by creating alternative approaches to responding to shortages of resources:

From what I have heard, for teachers and early childhood carers this situation is very difficult to deal with. They try to come up with alternative solutions in order for children not to drop out. Many of them do even pay for the food for children. (MEP1)

Many times I saw teachers bringing materials from their homes and spending their money on buying stuff for children. (MEP5)

During my practicum I saw that teachers were concerned about situations of poverty and they were offering different sorts of food and trying to find funding to take as many children as possible to the beach during holidays. (MEP4)

Other participants in the study, albeit a minority, refer to some teachers' lack of special attention to poverty issues at school:

In general, I think that schools, especially teachers, think that poverty issues have nothing to do with them... even if it affects children's learning. (EPE1CEB 2)

Teachers' complex role in a context of crisis: promoting equity and social justice

Most of the participants talked about their professional learning during their practicum, and the ways in which they had become more aware of their pivotal role in promoting equity and social justice through acting as facilitators of access to powerful knowledge (Young

2011) for all children. Increasing awareness of poverty issues and children's needs, managing scarce resources, advocating in practice for equity and social justice were at the forefront of their accounts:

> The adaptation to difficult socio-economic contexts makes you reutilise things and materials in order to avoid spending money both in your home and in your workplace. (MEP6)

> To me practicum was very important because it made me reflect upon the current situation, especially about the crisis and how it can affect a child's life. It made me think about possible solutions to deal with these situations. (MEP11)

> It made me realise that as a professional-to-be I need to pay attention to children's needs and help them because they are entitled to education. (MEP1CEB 6)

One of the issues that deserves further attention is the need to update the foundational democratic project of the school, since the principle of 'equal opportunities' has been called into question due to the economic and social crisis. Schools and teachers, and also institutions for ITE, have to ask the question identified by Young (2011) 'what are schools for?'. What is at stake is the democratisation of schooling, but also the democratisation of culture, because social and cultural goods are those that are most affected by austerity. People finding themselves in a critical economic situation start to cut down in these kinds of goods. Teachers as agents of change and workers of knowledge have a key role in promoting the social and cultural dimension of children and their families; and ITE needs to prepare them for that.

ITE and the need to pay attention to the social and cultural dimension of teaching

Looking back on their ITE programme, some study participants stated that poverty issues were discussed in two modules, but the vast majority said nothing about poverty was covered in their ITE programme or stated that these issues were not taken into consideration while at university:

> I haven't discussed these kinds of issues. (MEP7)

> It was not discussed during my ITE programme. (MEP9)

Some could not remember:

> I don't remember, unfortunately, but the discussion of these kinds of issues was minimal. (MEP1CEB 3)

Others did state that they had discussed poverty and its implications during their ITE programme:

> I did discuss these issues in the modules of Sociology of Childhood and Education during my first degree in my second year at university. We did work on that and we read texts about that too. (MEP2)

> This issue was dealt with in the module of Multicultural Education in my Master's degree. It was very superficial though… (MEP4)

> I think it is important to look at these kinds of issues in ITE curriculum, because as a teacher you can see it more and more in kindergarten and pre-school. (MEP1)

Most of the participants identified suggestions and recommendations for ITE in order to include issues related to poverty, social justice and equity in its curriculum:

> Unfortunately, it [poverty] is a theme that is really visible in Portuguese schools. And I think it is necessary to look at how to deal with this situation during your training at university. (MEP1CEB 6)

> It would be useful to include issues of poverty in ITE curriculum as it is more and more present in schools. It would be important to examine how to deal with these situations and, who knows, to actually go to places where poverty is more visible and to see how it is dealt with in practice. (MEP4)
>
> I think it is important that student teachers at basic education are provided with information and strategies that enable them to deal with different contexts, as in the future you may end up teaching in one school where you may find poverty situations. (MEP1CEB 2)

One possibility might be the inclusion in the ITE curriculum of issues related to children's rights, which are far from being a reality, more than two decades after the Convention on the Rights of the Child (1989) was launched. Existing literature suggests that teachers' and head teachers' perceptions and attitudes to social class and poverty in the classroom point to the lack of a critical perspective on context and fall back on deficit models from a middle-class perspective of the norm (see, for instance, Gorski 2012; Lupton and Thrupp 2013).

Discussion and implications for teacher education

> The child should be fully prepared to live an individual life in society, and brought up in the spirit of the ideals proclaimed in the Charter of the United Nations, and in particular in the spirit of peace, dignity, tolerance, freedom, equality and solidarity. (Convention on the Rights of the Child 1989)

This paper set out to reflect on issues of child poverty in the Portuguese context after the financial, economic and social crisis of the last few years. Its aim was twofold: (i) to look at the macro level by examining recent policy documents and other reports on the education sector; and (ii) to analyse the ways in which ITE deals with poverty issues, within the post-Bologna context, through the voices of student-teachers who have finished their practicum at school. Despite the limitations of the study in terms of participants (all volunteers), the findings raise issues related to equity and social justice and highlight the need for teachers to be aware of the social and cultural dimension of their complex and demanding role, particularly in times of crisis.

From the data, three main ideas may be identified. First, the relevant documents about education, as well as existing research, pointed to the deterioration of working conditions at school for teachers and, as a result of the economic and social crisis, greater challenges and pressures have been put into them. Student-teachers participating in this study also reported evidence of increasingly complex demands placed upon schools and teachers who, apart from teaching, have to deal with social issues such as child poverty, lack of motivation and scarcity of resources. Their accounts are illustrative of the difficulties that most teachers have to go through in their work, especially in regard to families in a critical economic situation. Issues of diversity, equity and social justice were also discussed in their accounts. Student-teachers' accounts revealed their perceptions about poverty and its impact on children's well-being and equal opportunities.

Second, the strategies used by teachers to face poverty situations have made student-teachers more aware of their lack of preparedness to deal with teaching in such a demanding context. Being and feeling like a teacher in a real context is seen as an opportunity for student-teachers not only to realise the demanding nature of their work but also its complexity and social dimension. Examples of strategies employed by the teachers included providing individual personal and financial support, and creating alternative approaches to responding to shortages of resources. The findings stress the complex and pivotal role in promoting equity and social justice through acting as a facilitator of access to powerful knowledge for all children. As Young (2011) suggests, there is a need to move beyond the 'knowledge of the powerful' and to take into account the 'powerful knowledge'. In discussions about the school curriculum, it is important to know if the knowledge available at school is powerful, which means, knowledge that enables pupils to understand the world in which they live: 'There is a link between the emancipatory hopes associated with the expansion of schooling and the opportunity that schools provide for learners to acquire "powerful knowledge" that they rarely have access to at home'. (Young 2011, 155).

Finally, the findings also point to the need to reinforce the social and cultural dimension of ITE. Although this topic is seen as a key component for ITE curricula in the Portuguese legal text, it is up to the higher education institutions to make decisions on how to implement it, as there are no compulsory credits allocated to it. The aim is to include the ethical, social and cultural dimension within the other components which have a required number of credits attached to them. ITE plays a key role during these demanding times in Portugal, not only in providing student-teachers with a more complex and broad picture of the teaching profession, but also in terms of a wider and critical debate about education, especially concerning policy, school organisation, curriculum and pedagogy. Talking about the USA context, Zeichner (2010) discusses the commodification of teacher education, its hyper-rationality and increased accountability and attacks on multicultural education. Also, Sleeter (2008) analyses the ways in which equity and democracy have been undermined and she identifies three neoliberal pressures on teacher education: away from explicit equity-oriented teacher preparation, and towards preparing teachers as technicians; away from defining teacher quality in terms of professional knowledge, and towards defining it in terms of testable content knowledge; and towards shortening university-based teacher education or bypassing it altogether. Other existing empirical work suggests that pre-service teachers' attitudes to poverty are often also deeply ingrained and resistant to change (Cox, Watts, and Horton 2012).

The participants in this study were clear about the role of ITE. They highlighted some areas in which ITE needs further improvement. Most of these related to social and cultural issues. Recent trends in ITE tend to emphasise the technical and didactical side to the detriment of other key dimensions (see Flores 2014).

Teachers are agents of change and workers of knowledge and thus they have a pivotal role in promoting the social and cultural dimension of children and their families. ITE needs to prepare them for that. In times of high unemployment, ITE may need to be re-examined and re-invented in order to meet the challenges of a global society and the needs of the schools of the twenty-first century. One way of moving forward is to develop a broader understanding of ITE associated with social and cultural issues, teachers as agents of change and workers of knowledge, and schools as places where culture, leisure and other aspects need to be considered in different ways.

The economic crisis and austerity measures have profoundly affected schools and teachers' lives and brought changes in ITE policy and curriculum in the post-Bologna context. Changes have been towards an accentuation of the academic and didactical perspective, to the detriment of a more humanistic and critical approach open to discussion on social issues with pupils, families and local communities.

This analysis is in line with other research literature which points to the need to reinforce the ethical, cultural, social and political dimension of teaching and teacher education (Tirri 2014; Zeichner 2014; Flores 2016). Tirri (2014, 15), for instance, in Finland identified the need for a set of competencies for 'professional and ethical' teachers in light of the moral dimension of their work in dealing with a rising number of immigrant students and children with learning difficulties. Similarly, in the USA, Zeichner (2014, 560) argued that 'the teacher as a professional view goes beyond providing teachers with teaching and management skills'. More needs to be done in this regard also in the Portuguese context. Children growing up in poverty and disadvantaged contexts are less likely to do well at school, which, in turn, has implications for their later life and it may affect their children too. To move beyond this cycle, ITE can play a pivotal role in addressing the attitudes and experiences that lie behind social differences in education. The project upon which this paper is based aims to make a contribution to the discussion and consideration of the ethical, social and cultural dimension in ITE programmes. Another implication lies in pupil voice. In such demanding times it is more important than ever to pay attention to pupils' voices, through listening to their own views and experiences about the ways in which the school and the curriculum affect their lives, their learning and their motivation.

Disclosure statement

No potential conflict of interest was reported by the authors.

References

Benavente, A., G. Aníbal, J. Martins, L. Salgado, M. Jacinto, M. C. Lino, M. T. Macara, et al. 2014. *O estado da educação num estado intervencionado* [The state of education in a State under intervention]. Portugal, Lisboa . op.edu - observatório de políticas de educação e de formação. Ces . Uc . Ceied.Ulht.

Clandinin, D. J., D. Pushor, and A. M. Orr. 2007. "Navigating Sites for Narrative Inquiry." *Journal of Teacher Education* 58 (1): 21–35.

Convention on the Rights of the Child. 1989. http://www.ohchr.org/en/professionalinterest/pages/crc.aspx

Cox, B. J., C. Watts, and M. Horton. 2012. "Poverty Perceptions of Pre-service Teachers and Social Work Candidates." *Journal of Studies in Education* 2 (1): 131–148.

Ek, A.-C., M. Ideland, S. Jönsson, and C. Malmberg. 2013. "The Tension Between Marketisation and Academisation in Higher Education." *Studies in Higher Education* 38 (9): 1305–1318.

Elliott, J. 2005. *Using Narrative in Social Research. Qualitative and Quantitative Approaches*. Londres: Sage.

EU. 2014. *Social Europe. Many Ways, One Objective*. Annual Report of the Social Protection Committee on the social situation in the European Union. Luxembourg: Publications Office of the European Union. doi:10.2767/60243.

Flores, M. A. 2011. "Curriculum of Initial Teacher Education in Portugal: New Contexts, Old Problems." *Journal of Education for Teaching* 37 (4): 461–470.

Flores, M. A., ed. 2014a. *Profissionalismo e liderança dos professores* [Teacher Professionalism and Leadership]. Santo Tirso: De Facto Editores.

Flores, M. A. 2014b. "Teacher Learning in the Workplace in Pre-service Teacher Education in Portugal: Potential and Limits from A Pre-service Teacher Perspective." In *Workplace Learning in Teacher Education. International Practice and Policy*, edited by O. McNamara, J. Murray, and M. Jones, 243–260. Dordrecht: Springer.

Flores, M. A. 2016. "Teacher Education Curriculum." In *International Handbook of Teacher Education*, edited by J. Loughran and M. L. Hamilton, 187–230. Dordrecht: Springer Press.

Flores, M. A, F. I. Ferreira, and C. Parente. 2014. "Conclusões e recomendações [Conclusions and Recommendations]." In *Profissionalismo e liderança dos professores* [Teacher Professionalism and Leadership], Coord by M. A. Flores, 217–236. Santo Tirso: De Facto Editores.

Flores, M. A., I. Viana, and F. I. Ferreira. 2014. "Liderança e profissionalismo docente: resultados de um inquérito por questionário [Leadership and Teacher Professionalism]." In *Profissionalismo e liderança dos professores* [Teacher Professionalism and Leadership], edited by M. A. Flores, 79–99. Santo Tirso: De Facto Editores.

Flores, M. A., F. Veira, J. L. Silva, and J. Almeida. 2016. "Integrating Research Into the Practicum: Inquiring Into Inquiry-based Professional Development in Post-Bologna Initial Teacher Education in Portugal." In *Redefining teacher education for the Post-2015 Era: Global challenges and best practices*, edited by M. A. Flores and T. Al Barwani, 109–124. New York: Nova Science Publisher.

Glaser, B. G., and A. L. Strauss. 1967. *The Discovery of Grounded Theory: Strategies for Qualitative Research*. Chicago, IL: Aldine.

Gorski, P. C. 2012. "Perceiving the Problem of Poverty and Schooling: Deconstructing the Class Stereotypes that Mis-Shape Education Practice and Policy." *Equity and Excellence in Education* 45 (2): 302–319.

Hollway, W., and T. Jefferson. 2000. *Doing Qualitative Research Differently. Free Association, Narrative and the Interview Method*. London: Sage.

INE-Portugal. 2015. *Inquérito às Condições de Vida e Rendimento 2014* [Survey on working life and income] (dados provisórios). Lisboa: INE.

Lacour, M., and L. Tissington. 2011. "The Effects of Poverty on Academic Achievement." *Educational Research and Reviews* 6 (7): 522–527.

Lupton and Thrupp. 2013. "Headteachers' Readings of and Responses to Disadvantaged Contexts: evidence from English primary schools." *British Educational Research Journal* 39 (4): 769–788.

Miles, M., and M. Huberman. 1994. *Qualitative Data Analysis. An Expanded Sourcebook*. 2nd ed. Thousand Oaks: CA, Sage.

Ministério da Educação. 2007. *Política de Formação de Professores em Portugal* [Policy for Teacher Education in Portugal]. Lisboa: ME/DGRHE.

OECD. 2014. *OECD Economic Surveys*. Portugal: OECD Publishing.

PERA Portugal, Ministério da Educação e Ciência. 2012. *PERA Programa Escolar de Reforço Alimentar 2012/2013 e 2013/2014* [PERA Programme, Food Reinforcement]. Lisboa: Ministério da Educação e Ciência. http://pera.portaldasescolas.pt/Documento_Orientador.pdf

Pires, R. P., C. Pereira, J. Azevedo, and A. C. Ribeiro. 2014. *Emigração Portuguesa. Relatório Estatístico 2014* [Portuguese Emigration: Report on Statistics 2014]. Lisboa: Observatório da Emigração e Rede Migra, Instituto Universitário de Lisboa (ISCTE-IUL), CIES-IUL, e DGACCP.

PORDATA. 2014. *Retrato de Portugal na Europa* [A Picture of Portugal in Europe]. Edição 2014. Lisboa: Fundação Francisco Manuel dos Santos.

Sleeter, C. 2008. "Equity, Democracy, and Neoliberal Assaults on Teacher Education." *Teaching and Teacher Education* 24: 1947–1957.

Tirri, K. 2014. "The Last 40 years in Finnish Teacher Education." *Journal of Education for Teaching* 40 (5): 600–609.

UNICEF. 2014. *Children of the Recession The impact of the Economic Crisis on Child Well-being in Rich Countries*. Florença: UNICEF Office of Research – Innocenti.

Young, M. 2011. "What Are Schools For?" *Educação, Sociedade and Culturas* 32: 145–155.

Zeichner, K. 2010. "Competition, Economic Rationalization, Increased Surveillance, and Attacks on Diversity: Neo-Liberalism and the Transformation of Teacher Education in the US." *Teaching and Teacher Education* 26: 1544–1552.

Zeichner, K. 2014. "The Struggle for the Soul of Teaching and Teacher Education in the USA." *Journal of Education for Teaching* 40 (5): 551–568.

Teacher prep 3.0: a vision for teacher education to impact social transformation

Kerry Kretchmar and Ken Zeichner

ABSTRACT
Teacher education in the USA is composed of both defenders and critics of the current system of teacher preparation. Some critics of college and university-based teacher education who describe themselves as 'reformers' have referred to the non-university programmes as 'teacher preparation 2.0' in order to emphasise the innovativeness they feel these programmes represent. They imply that the programmes existing prior to these new, non-university are teacher education 1.0 programmes, which they see as obsolete. We argue in this paper that many 1.0 and 2.0 programmes are inadequate for meeting the nation's needs to provide high quality, effective teachers for all children in USA public schools, and we present a case for teacher preparation 3.0 programmes. Given the weaknesses in both teacher education 1.0 and 2.0, there exists a need to transform rather than defend or 'reform' the current system.

Introduction

Research demonstrates that out-of-school factors explain most of the variation in student learning. Therefore, schools alone cannot confront the challenges of poverty and effective education reforms must address structural inequity (e.g. Duncan and Murnane 2011; Rothstein 2004). With a majority of public school students in the USA living in poverty (Suitts 2015), teacher education programmes must focus on preparing teachers to understand deeply and value their students' lives and cultures (Warren 2005), and to support broader struggles for justice, such as affordable housing and jobs that pay a living wage (Zeichner et al. 2015). When education reforms focus on 'fixing' teacher education, teachers, or students, without taking into account poverty, such reforms 'justify existing conditions, such as the socioeconomic achievement gap, by identifying the problem of inequality as located within, rather than as pressing upon, poor people' (Gorski 2012, 313). Below, we illustrate the limits of current teacher preparation programmes in addressing poverty, and argue for a transformed Teacher Preparation 3.0 that develops educators who engage in the struggle for educational equity both inside and outside of the classroom.

Teacher education in the USA is composed of both defenders and critics of the current system of teacher preparation, which is dominated by college and university programmes

Table 1. Teacher preparation 1.0, 2.0, 3.0.

Programme	Knowledge emphasised	Knowledge privileged	Pedagogical focus	Assessment	Approach
1.0-Defenders	Professional	Academic ↓ Practitioner	Learner and learning-centred	Holistic, performance-based	Teacher as saviour
2.0-Reformers	Technician	Practitioner ↓ Academic	Classroom management	Measurable outcomes, standardised tests	Teacher as saviour
3.0-Transformers	Community teacher	Integrated community, practitioner, & academic	Learner and learning-centred situated in relation to the specific context	Holistic, performance based with community-based accountability	Teacher in solidarity with communities

that have prepared most USA teachers since around 1960 (Wilson and Tamir 2008). Currently about two-thirds of teachers in the USA are prepared by colleges and universities (National Research Council 2010) despite the rapid increase of non-university programmes that are often fast-track and funded by venture philanthropists (Zeichner and Pena-Sadnoval 2015).

This paper argues that given the weaknesses in all types of teacher education programmes in the United States, there exists a need to transform rather than defend or 'reform' the current system. Some critics of college and university-based teacher education who describe themselves as 'reformers' have referred to new non-university programmes as 'Teacher Prep 2.0' to emphasise the innovativeness they feel these programmes represent. They imply that the programmes existing prior to these new, non-university are teacher education 1.0 programmes, which they see as obsolete (e.g. Gastic 2013). This paper argues that many 1.0 and 2.0 teacher preparation programmes in the United States do not inadequately provide high quality, effective teachers for all children in USA public schools. We present a case and vision for teacher preparation 3.0 programmes (Table 1).

Teacher preparation 1.0 (defenders)

Teacher preparation within and outside of universities varies significantly in quality (Grossman and Loeb 2008), and includes some dismal (Levine 2006), as well as outstanding, programmes (Darling-Hammond 2006). University-based teacher education programmes have long faced criticism for a disconnection between theory and practice, particularly in their failure to prepare teachers for the realities of the accountability-driven context they enter as novice teachers (Clifford and Guthrie 1990; Labaree 2004). Additionally, despite research that documents the importance of a more ethnically and racially diverse teaching force, programmes have struggled to recruit diverse candidates and to prepare teachers who work and remain in low-income schools serving communities of colour (Villegas and Irvine 2010).

University-based programmes have experienced significant challenges in recent years including being constrained by decreasing resources and increasing accountability demands from their institutions, states, and the federal government. Public universities continue to face shrinking budgets (Lyall and Sell 2006). At the same time that state and federal funding is being cut, foundation and government funding has shifted to focus on 2.0 programmes, at the expense of the 1.0 college and university teacher education programmes that require funding to innovate and transform (Zeichner and Pena-Sadnoval 2015).

As Schools of Education lose resources, they also face increased accountability demands from the federal government and states (Cochran-Smith, Piazza, and Power 2013). These include the push for value-added data systems that attempt to tie K-12 students' test scores to the teacher preparation programmes from which their teachers matriculated, despite research from assessment experts that questions the appropriateness of such measures (e.g. AERA 2015; American Statistical Association 2014; Plecki, Elfers, and Nakamura 2012). Although states have made massive investments to create longitudinal data systems (which was one of the criteria in the 'Race to the Top' a competitive grant programme designed to encourage and reward states to create the conditions for education innovation and reform favoured by the US Department of Education) value-added models that evaluate teachers' performance based on test scores have proven to be inconsistent, with teachers' performance varying significantly depending on the statistical model utilised (Darling-Hammond, Wei, and Johnson 2009). In 2015, the USA Education Department released a draft of mandatory federal regulations for teacher education programmes, which would require states to rank programmes yearly using K-12 student assessment data. States would be required to provide technical assistance to failing programmes and eventually cut off state approval and funding and federal financial aid for teacher candidates if those programmes did not show improvement. The students would be forced to find other, non-failing programmes if they wanted to continue to receive the federal aid.

Unsurprisingly, such regulations will impact how teacher education programmes are expected to function (Kumashiro 2010; Zeichner 2010). Under pressure to measure and document everything (i.e. classroom assessment outcomes, hours in the classroom), programmes will be asked to operate in an environment of 'hyperrationality,' (Zeichner 2010) in which the efforts to collect and analyse data and rationalise their work will detract from the actual work of educating teachers (1547).

Teacher preparation 1.0 conceptions of effective teaching

As mentioned above, university-based programmes vary greatly in quality and have not adequately prepared a teaching force that is effective for all students. Yet, strong programmes do exist. Darling-Hammond (2006) and her research team identified common characteristics of exemplary teacher education programmes including a vision of teachers as professionals, a focus on learner and learning-centred pedagogy, and holistic performance assessments. Strong university-based programmes, such as Alverno College and Bank Street College of Education, demonstrate a thoughtful balance between theory and practice. These 1.0 programmes feature coherent curricula, provide carefully structured clinical experiences with partner K-12 schools, and are mostly staffed by full-time faculty who are invested in and study teacher education (Darling-Hammond 2006). Exemplary university-based programmes develop a clear vision and professional practice that draws on complex and varied knowledge, skills, and dispositions related to pedagogy, content, and understanding learners and their development in social contexts. Teachers as professionals draw on this diverse knowledge base to determine the appropriateness of various teaching strategies (Darling-Hammond and Bransford 2005).

Developing teacher candidates' adaptive expertise and their ability to exercise judgement in the classroom requires varied curricula that include developing an understanding of learners and learning in social contexts (human development, learning, language), curriculum and subject matter (educational goals and purposes for subject matter content and skills), and teaching (teaching subject matter, teaching diverse learners, assessment, classroom management) (Darling-Hammond 2006). 'Powerful' teacher education programmes prepare students to be *learning-centred* (that is, supportive of focused, in-depth learning that results in powerful thinking and proficient performance on the part of students) and *learner-centred* (responsive to individual students' experiences, interests, talents and cultural backgrounds)' (Darling-Hammond 2006, 7–8.) For example, at Bank Street students are immersed in pedagogy that merges theory and practice, and that mirrors the approach Bank Street advocates for K-12 students. Students take courses in child development, teaching methods, and 'social foundations' (i.e. schools, society, and culture) while spending significant time in school placements that model Bank Street practices, and cross-reference these experiences to develop their own practice. The learner-centred approach views classroom management as a theme woven throughout coursework and clinical experiences related to 'how to work with children to develop and sustain learner engagement and productive behaviour (Darling-Hammond 2006, 93).' In contrast to the 2.0 emphasis on discrete classroom management techniques, 1.0 programmes examine research on motivation and social dynamics at the same time they are analysing the organisation of effective learning and classroom communities in strong clinical experiences. 1.0 provides techniques and strategies for pre-service candidates, but often focuses on how to use those strategies thoughtfully and appropriately. This rich connection between theory and practice, absent from many Teacher Preparation 2.0 and 1.0 programmes of lesser quality, is critical for using teaching tools effectively.

Further, such programmes view an understanding of the issues of inequity, power and privilege as critical to becoming an effective teacher for all students and consistently ask pre-service teachers to make connections between foundational course work and clinical experience. This social and political frame, however, is typically focused on helping teachers recognise their own privilege and biases in order to provide K-12 students tools to operate inside of a classist and racist system, rather than providing teachers with tools to challenge the system (Gorski 2006). This approach often positions the teacher as a saviour.

1.0 programmes use holistic performance assessments of teacher candidates that address the complex nature of teaching and require teacher candidates to integrate knowledge and theory, which include: (1) focus on teaching through lesson plans, videotapes of teaching, and assessments of K-12 students' learning; (2) integration of knowledge and skills in practice; (3) multiple measures evidenced over time from varied contexts; and (4) opportunities for practice or assessment to provide feedback and help teachers continue to develop, as opposed to just measuring a successful outcome or the ability to raise student test scores (Darling-Hammond 2006, 116–118). Assessments include case studies, analysis of teaching and learning, portfolios, and action research.

Discrepancies exist between 1.0's approach to assessing teachers and the increasing push for value-added assessment and teacher content exams. In response to pressure to address teacher quality, the American Association for Colleges of Teacher Education and Stanford University created a consortium to design a teacher performance assessment tool (edTPA). edTPA is currently in use in 35 states and is used by both 1.0 and 2.0 programmes. Designed as a holistic assessment, the edTPA attempts to capture the complex dimensions of teaching, including planning, instruction, assessment analysis and reflection. Although developed by teacher educators, this assessment has also experienced criticism from within the teacher education community due to its adoption as a high-stakes assessment in many states and its perceived limitations in addressing culturally responsive pedagogy (e.g. Dover et al. 2015).

Teacher preparation 2.0 (reformers)

As states face deeper budget cuts and Schools of Education are subject to reduced resources and increased accountability demands, non-profit and for profit independent teacher preparation programmes operating independently from Universities have prospered, including (i) Master's degree granting programmes that operate independently from Universities, including Relay, and MATCH, and High Tech High (ii) fast-track routes such as Teach For America (TFA), a programme that trains recent university graduates (a vast majority of whom have not studied education) in a five-week summer institute and places them as a teacher for two years in low-income communities. Below we identify key shared characteristics of Teacher Preparation 2.0 programmes, which mostly are 'no-excuses' teacher preparation programmes that primarily prepare teachers for schools serving low-income students of colour with a focus on teaching and learning that contends that poverty is 'no-excuse' for low educational outcomes. We categorise TFA as a 2.0 programme, yet many universities have established partnerships with TFA by creating programmes for TFA teachers to complete certification. Federal law requires teachers in TFA and other 'early entry' programmes to complete a full certification programme during their placement. Some TFA teachers do this through other 2.0 programmes like Relay while others enrol in university-run alternative programmes.

Significant philanthropic and federal funding has created an opportunity for the growth of independent programmes that maintain an exacting focus on preparing teachers to teach using methodologies believed to increase student standardised test scores. In the past 20 years, a number of philanthropies have gained significant power in the educational sector through large contributions to reforms (Scott 2009). These philanthropies, including the Walton, Broad, Gates, Dell, and Fischer Foundations, have joined policy-makers who promote market-based reforms and make exaggerated claims that democratic control is inherently bureaucratic and corrupt. Consequently, they argue that business strategies and principles must be applied to improve our public services (Lipman 2011; Saltman 2010). Reckhow and Snyder (2014) analysed USA grant data from 2000, 2005, and 2010 from the fifteen largest K-12 grant-makers and found that 'most major education foundations increasingly support jurisdictional challengers–organisations that compete with or offer alternatives to public sector institutions' (186), like independent teacher preparation programme and charter management organisations (CMOs) entities that manage two or more charter schools and promote market-based alternatives to public education. They found that the fifteen top funders tend to give money to the same organisations, indicating overlap in their agendas. The convergence of agendas is exemplified by TFA, which received a total of $44.5 million dollars from thirteen of the top fifteen funders in 2010 (191).

In addition, the federal government has increased financial support for alternative programmes while simultaneously decreasing support for university-based teacher preparation. In the USA Department of Education's 2010 Innovation in Education competition, none of the proposals submitted by public universities and colleges were funded, but TFA was awarded $50 million dollars, and The New Teacher Project was awarded $20 million dollars (Zeichner 2014). Financial support from the federal government and foundations has encouraged a significant increase in alternative paths to becoming a teacher (Grossman and Loeb 2008).

This expansion includes Schools of Education operating independently from Universities. Many of these independent Schools of Education focus on preparing teachers for K-12 charter schools. For example, Relay Graduate School of Education is an independent, institution granting Masters degree which was created as a joint effort between three CMOs (Knowledge Is Power Programme (KIPP), Uncommon Schools, and Achievement First) in partnership with TFA. Relay has programmes operating or opening in eight cities with further plans to expand (Relay Graduate School of Education 2014). Many of the teachers trained through Relay go on to work at KIPP, Uncommon Schools or Achievement First Schools. Using a different model, MATCH teacher residency (which places teacher candidates (residents) in a classroom for a full year under the supervision of a veteran teacher, with academic coursework at night and on the weekends. Teacher Residency models are seen in 1.0, 2.0, 3.0 programmes.) trains teachers through a yearlong programme embedded in MATCH Charter Schools (Stitzlein and West 2014). It can be expected that Relay, MATCH and similar programmes will continue expanding since the passage of the 'Growing Achievement Training Academies for Teachers and Principals Act (GREAT)' and related provisions in the Every Student Success Act (ESSA), which allows states to apply for grants to set up 'teacher preparation academies' independent from universities and exempt from the state requirements that other teacher preparation programmes must meet. When the GREAT Act was presented to the Senate, Relay and MATCH were described as the type of innovation needed to close the achievement gap (Zeichner and Pena-Sadnoval 2015).

'No excuses' CMOs share close connections to 2.0 programmes like TFA, Relay and MATCH (Kretchmar, Sondel, and Ferrare 2014). 'No excuses' K-12 charter school, such as KIPP and Achievement First, primarily service low-income students and often feature an extended school year and day, a very strict environment, and an exacting focus on improving standardised test scores (Goodman 2013). These CMOs have been critiqued for creating a highly regulated environment (Goodman 2013) that relies on direct instruction and on curricula with a myopic focus on tested material (Sondel 2015).

Teacher Preparation 2.0's pedagogical approaches and definitions of success outlined below are aligned with those of many 'no excuses' K-12 charter schools (Sondel 2015). Thus, CMOs have 'created their own teacher certification and master's degree programmes after concluding that the teachers who graduate from most traditional teacher education programmes lack the skills needed to teach successfully' (Arnett 2015, 2). Our examples include two teacher preparation programmes that are directly connected to CMOs (Relay and MATCH), although many other similar programmes exist (namely Yes Prep Teaching Excellence Programme, KIPP DC Teacher Residency). Additionally, TFA is placing increasing numbers of what they call 'corps members' in charter schools (Brewer et al. 2016).

2.0 programmes are receiving not only funding for expansion, but financial support for their students that aids their recruitment efforts. Investors like Gates, New Schools Venture Fund, the Schusterman Foundation, and Credit Suisse provide funding to programmes like Relay that significantly reduces tuition costs for students (Kronholz 2012). In Newark, New Jersey, former Superintendent and TFA alumnus Cami Anderson established a relationship between the school district and Relay whereby teachers can receive up to $20,000 for completing one of the approved Relay programmes, a sum not made available to teachers taking classes in university-based teacher education programmes (Relay Graduate School of Education 2015).

Teacher preparation 2.0 conceptions of effective teaching

An analysis of curricular materials, outlines, rubrics, Coursera (MOOC) courses, websites and promotional materials from three of the most prominent 2.0 programmes (TFA, MATCH, and Relay) provides a view of the teacher as a technician, test scores as sole indicators of a teacher's success, and of a teacher-centric approach to family–community involvement. In a model that presents a false choice between theory and practice, 2.0 programmes focus heavily on discrete classroom management techniques and measurable outcomes (Stitzlein and West 2014). On their website, Relay presents itself in opposition to university teacher education, claiming that their faculty are 'exceptional thinkers' who are 'not sitting in ivory towers' (Otterman 2011 in Stitzlein & West, 5). This uncritical glorification of practice and demonisation of educational theory is evident in the structure and content of 2.0 programmes as well as the current reform literature, which characterises university Education Schools as emphasising theory at the expense of preparation in effective teaching practices. Thus, 2.0 programmes are concentrated almost entirely on teaching and practicing discrete skills. For example, Relay describes their programme as a 'breakthrough approach' that 'emphasises the practical, not the theoretical' and focuses on techniques that will 'work on Monday morning' (Relay Graduate School of Education 2014).

Many of the strategies emphasised in Relay, MATCH, and TFA curriculum materials are not inherently flawed. In fact, despite the exclusion of educational research throughout the materials, many of the tools presented in Teacher Preparation 2.0 programmes are strategies that educational researchers have long promoted as best practice (i.e. learning stations, wait time). Thus, our critique of 2.0 programmes is centred less on the strategies advocated and more on the implications of what is excluded by this narrow approach. 2.0 programmes are explicitly preparing teachers to work with low-income populations, yet conspicuously absent is any attention to sociocultural theory, structural critique of poverty, or discussion of race, class and power.

This belief that teaching is merely a technical skill is illustrated in the programme structure. Rather than offering courses, Relay is organised around competency-based modules of varying lengths, with approximately 40% of the content delivered online (Relay Graduate School of Education 2015). At MATCH, teacher residents work full-time in the MATCH charter school in year one while participating in coursework. In year two, MATCH residents work as full-time teachers while taking distance courses, receiving individualised coaching, and having their classroom practices 'evaluated using a battery of assessments' (MATCH Teacher Residency 2015). With the exception of curriculum sessions, four of the five components of the TFA summer institute are practice-based. Structurally, 2.0 programmes greatly favour a narrow technical approach, which reduces teaching outcomes to test scores.

A key example of this teacher-as-technician approach is 2.0's frequent use of Doug Lemov's *Teach Like A Champion: 49 Techniques that Put Your Students on the Path to College* (2010). In particular, Relay's materials are heavily organised around Lemov's work. Lemov, director of Uncommon Schools, codified a set of specific strategies based on observations and conversations with teachers in 'no excuses' charter schools whose students were performing well on assessments. Lemov's 'observable, concrete, and named' strategies (Gatti 2014, 215), such as, '#1 No Opt Out: How to move students from the blank stare or stubborn shrug to giving the right answer every time' (Lemov 2010) primarily frame learning through a behaviourist lens and centralise students' compliance and acquisition of specific skills. The strategies themselves are not inherently good or bad; their effectiveness is dependent on the ways educators take up these tools in their contexts (Gatti 2014, 215). Yet, when classroom management practices like those of Lemov (2010) are used primarily in control-oriented ways, research has indicated they can sometimes have negative psychological effects on students (e.g. Gatti and Catalano 2015). Whether directly referencing Lemov or presenting other practice-based strategies, the foundation of the MATCH, Relay and TFA materials we analysed consisted of observable, concrete, and named strategies for classroom management, assessment and instruction.

This focus on tools without attention to the relational and sociocultural elements of teaching does not provide teacher candidates with sufficient understanding of the multidimensionality of learners required to appropriately select teaching methods. Although the *Relay Instruction Delivery Methods Reader* (2014) states, 'Your job is not just to vary your use of methods, but to choose the right method based on an understanding of the content, your students' learning styles, and their current levels of understanding (Relay Graduate School of Education 2014, 2)' nowhere in the reader is there evidence that teacher candidates are asked to develop the adaptive expertise required by teachers (Hammerness et al. 2005), or provided with the knowledge that would help them truly select an appropriate instructional method for their students. The *Relay Instruction Delivery Methods Reader* (2014) presents a number of typical teaching methods, including 'discussion,' 'discovery learning' and 'stations,' but they are all presented in brief form with an 'overview' and 'how-to' step-by-step guidelines for using a method. This focus on the 'how' defines the function of teaching as 'managing and implementing curricular programmes rather than developing or critically appropriating curricula to fit specific pedagogical concerns' (Giroux 2013, 46). This is at the expense of an opportunity for students to examine social, educational and curricular aims.

The teacher-as-technician approach is also prominent in the MATCH 'process,' which is prescriptive and teacher directed. For example, to learn about a reactive discipline move, teacher candidates: (1) model and discuss the move, (2) practice that move with flashcards, (3) practise with a partner, (4) practise with a group of six, (5) practise in a simulation with real students, in which they must pass an assessment using the move correctly before they are allowed to progress in the programme (MATCH Teacher Residency, 2015). Little room is provided for candidates to draw on pupils' prior knowledge or teachable moments, nor is there space for candidates to question critically the instructional strategies. This uncomplicated, task-oriented approach mirrors the K-12 pedagogy that Relay, MATCH and TFA promote (Stitzlein and West 2014).

While these sorts of concrete strategies are used for all areas of teaching, including lesson planning and instructional methods, a significant portion of the curriculum is devoted to discrete classroom management techniques. A PowerPoint used in recruiting for MATCH states, 'If we can solve Classroom Management issues during our training year, great news – Rookies can proceed to learn other stuff later, from PD [professional development], from colleagues, from administrators (Goldstein 2013a).' Here, classroom management is seen as the backbone of effective pedagogy with the remainder of pedagogical components reduced to 'other stuff' that teachers can learn later. Similarly, the first several modules for

Relay graduate students are centred on 'classroom management and classroom systems' (Relay Graduate School of Education 2014, 8). A core component of 2.0 curriculum revolves around explicit instruction, practice, and assessment of discrete and primarily behaviourist classroom management techniques that emphasise reward and punishment.

2.0 candidates received instruction in areas such as 'reactive moves to misbehaviour', which includes learning how to use gestures for redirection and how to give student demerits (Goldstein 2013a). These include Lemov strategies like SLANT, an acronym for 'behaviours to maximise student attention' (S – Sit Up, L – Listen, A – Ask and Answer Questions, N – Nod Your Head, T – Track the Speaker) and Strong Voice (Relay Graduate School of Education 2014). TFA classroom management templates require corps members to describe their negative and positive behaviour tracking systems. All of these classroom management strategies focus on teacher control and student compliance. Relay, TFA and MATCH value classroom management techniques as among the most, if not *the* most, substantial elements of the curriculum for teacher candidates. Thus, teacher candidates are more likely to adopt transmission methods of teaching by default.

2.0 programmes subscribe to a conception of urban teaching that Haberman (1991) termed a 'pedagogy of poverty', which results in a focus on compliance and an environment 'in which learners can 'succeed' without becoming either involved or thoughtful' (4). Despite the presentation of diverse pedagogies, many 2.0 programmes define teaching by the core acts outlined by Haberman with a focus on compliance rather than authentic learning, which would support cognitive and ethical development. This extreme focus on classroom management is rooted in a deficit perception of students in poverty, in which students are viewed as unable to access the hidden curriculum of school and thus need control-oriented instruction (e.g. Dudley-Marling 2007).

Defining success: measurable student growth

This focus on the teacher as merely a technician reduces teaching outcomes to test scores. Relay, MATCH and TFA define successful teaching as 'measurable student growth', most often tied directly to standardised tests and apparent in the ways programmes evaluate teacher candidates. In order to earn a degree, Relay requires teacher candidates to provide evidence that all of their students perform at 70% mastery on state and Common Core assessments, or 80% for an honours degree. In addition, rather than receiving a traditional grade point average, Relay students receive a number that reflects their 'PK-12 student growth and achievement data' (Relay Graduate School of Education 2014).

Materials in all three programmes present a technocratic approach to understanding assessment. TFA corps members are required to collect data around a 'big goal' and document 'significant gains'. An example of a big goal would be, '80% of students will achieve proficiency on the state exam'. Selected course materials do not include any critical analysis about what constitutes student success or examination of which important skills and dispositions might *not* be evident through quantifiable measures of student achievement, including *civic development, critical thinking and analysis, and aesthetic development*.

Rather than engaging teacher candidates in deep critical thinking/learning experiences, Teacher Preparation 2.0 programmes focus on discrete learning objectives and measurable outcomes, much like the K-12 pedagogy they promote. The definition of successful education for teachers is tied to clear measurable goals that can be checked off a list, rather than the promotion of learning from practice over time. At Relay, students can be exempted from modules if they demonstrate proficiency on summative assessments (Relay Graduate School of Education 2014). Learning how to document and analyse student assessment data is an important skill for teacher candidates, but without theoretical grounding teachers will not learn to ask critical questions about what should be taught and assessed, or consider the important knowledge that is left out of standardised testing materials.

When educators enter the classroom with an exacting focus on standardised assessment data, they often privilege literacy and mathematics and neglect non-tested areas like social studies, science, and the arts (Berliner 2011). Research has shown that this results in K-12 curricula tailored towards testing preparation and away from individual and cultural relevance, decreased opportunities for developing critical thinking skills, pedagogy heavily weighted towards direct transmission as opposed to child-centred teaching, and diminished relationships between teachers and students, particularly for low-income students and students of colour (Lipman 2011; Valenzuela 2005). This intense focus may potentially raise test scores, but may also define and limit the education students in low-income communities receive. 2.0 programmes contend that raising student test scores is the way out of poverty. However, students in middle class and upper middle class communities attend schools where they interact with knowledge in authentic ways (Kozol 2005) and the curriculum is not narrowed and success is not defined by a standardised test score.

Researchers have argued for decades that in order to evaluate fairly the quality of a teacher education programme a broad range of costs and benefits associated with particular programmes needs to be examined (Levin & Long, 1981) rather than only focusing on a narrow set of alleged benefits. Research provides clear evidence of the negative effects of the resultant narrowing of the curriculum associated with a myopic focus on raising test scores (e.g. Berliner 2011) and suggests that a strict emphasis on test scores increases educational inequities and perpetuates a second-class system of schooling for students living in poverty. Rose (2014) characterised this test-driven inequality, noting that students in low-income communities get 'an education of skills and routine, a lower-tier education, while students in more affluent districts get a robust course of study' (51).

Teacher-centric approach to family–community involvement

2.0 programmes view family–community relationships from a teacher/school-centric perspective as technical skills to be developed in order to increase student achievement. The teacher–community interactions emphasised by 2.0 programmes centre around communicating student academic and behavioural progress to families. Perhaps the most striking exclusion from 2.0 programmes is attention to race, power or poverty. For example, issues of power, race, or privilege are not addressed in the 78 page *Phoning Parents*, MATCH's prescriptive guide for calling parents written by founder Michael Goldstein. The single mention of race is included when Goldstein provides strategies for working with the 'resistant' parent and notes, 'You may be called a sexist. A racist. Other – ist (41)'.

Phoning Parents exemplifies the skill-obsessed approach extending beyond the classroom, into the spheres of parental and familial interaction. The book presents discrete strategies to achieve efficient and effective calls with parents alleged to improve students' behaviour and academic achievement. Although Goldstein notes that gaining information from parents is a potential positive, he recommends 2–5 min phone calls that are teacher-centric.

Comparatively, the 2013 TFA Summer Institute materials provide a more complex view through one of the five areas of coursework entitled 'Diversity, Community, and Achievement'. This section of curriculum highlights the needs to listen to and learn from families and students, consider what families and communities value, and tap into student and community resources. However this, too, comes at the exclusion of a greater structural critique of poverty, race, and class. Instead, in the few instances when materials directly address poverty they focus on the role of individuals. An example from a TFA PowerPoint on 'beliefs and habits' states:

> Students with Low Income Backgrounds: My students will make dramatic academic and personal growth that endures beyond my classroom, earning my students the opportunities and choices usually only available to students in higher income communities. (TFA 2013)

Here, providing 'opportunities and choices' to low-income students is emphasised. Often, 2.0 programmes identify college as the main goal for K-12 students in poverty. Yet, the goal of college has limitations. First, as explored by Carr (2014), test preparation, strict behavioural codes, and emphasis on external motivation in 'no excuses' charter schools may not appropriately prepare students for higher education where success relies on the ability to think critically and independently. Further, the college goal misplaces emphasis on personal responsibility without addressing the significant barriers resultant from systemic racism and inequity and the potential lack of career opportunities for students in poverty even with a college degree. Rather than empowering students and tapping into the assets in their own lives and communities, a singular focus on going to college can send an implicit message that success requires leaving your own community.

Using a narrow definition of effective teaching, 2.0 programmes contend they are 'closing the achievement gap'. Yet the absence of a curriculum that requires teacher candidates to understand the structural causes of inequity through an analysis of poverty, race, social class and power limits severely limits the ability of teacher candidates to meet the needs of all learners and continues to position the teacher as a saviour.

Teacher preparation 3.0 (transformers)

It is our contention that many Teacher Preparation 2.0, and 1.0 programmes have not adequately prepared teachers to meet the needs of all learners. We advocate a vision for Teacher Preparation 3.0 that will prepare community teachers to work in solidarity with community and families. These programmes are grounded in school *and* community expertise. The foundation of 3.0 programmes is an understanding that education reform alone is insufficient to address the significant challenges of poverty. Thus, in addition to preparing effective educators for the classroom, 3.0 views the work of teaching as connected to broader social movements for justice, such as struggles for affordable housing and living wages. In its preparation for the classroom, 3.0 programmes include strong elements of 1.0 programmes such as learner, and learning, centred approaches, reciprocal school partnerships, and clinical experiences that ask teacher candidates to authentically connect theory and practice. Yet, equally essential is knowledge of the history and context of a community (Murrell, 2015) as well as a commitment to 'teaching against the grain' and preparing teachers to understand that 'they are a part of a larger struggle' and that they have a responsibility to challenge 'not just replicate, standard school practices' (Cochran-Smith 1991, 280).

Teacher Preparation 3.0 programmes are distinct from 1.0 and 2.0 in the ways that they value community expertise, emphasise place-based learning, and prepare community teachers who are knowledgeable of the communities in which they teach. Together, these components of 3.0 programmes help situate teacher education amid a larger movement for social justice. While this is a vision for a transformed approach to teacher preparation, several existing programmes embody elements of 3.0 including the Illinois Grow Your Own (GYO) Programme, the Community Teaching strand in several University of Washington programmes, and the Schools Within the Context of Community (SCC) Programme at Ball State University.

Community experts

To prepare teachers to teach in a democratic society, Teacher Preparation 3.0 must embody an epistemology that is itself democratic. There must be new hybrid spaces where academic, practitioner, and community-based knowledge respect and interact to develop new solutions to the complicated process of preparing teachers (Zeichner, Payne, and Brayko 2015). These spaces must be less hierarchical and less haphazard in the ways they support teacher learning. Further, 3.0 programmes must offer more than just critiques of structural inequities; they must actually shift power and knowledge to value community and family members (Zeichner et al. 2015). This means that community members and parents play an integral role in the development of a teacher preparation programme, including curriculum development, defining accountability measures, and the day-to-day preparation of teachers. The value of community activists and parents is demonstrated through their inclusion as paid staff in teacher education programmes. For example, several teacher education programmes at the University of Washington have hired community members to serve as mentors of teacher candidates (Zeichner et al. 2015). Using a different approach, The Illinois GYO programme recruits non-traditional teacher education students from within communities, including parents, who demonstrate capacity to be effective educators. GYO is developed and implemented through a collaboration of community members and organisations, University partners, and school districts (Skinner, Garreton, and Schultz 2011).

3.0 programmes also value community expertise in the assessment process. They add an additional layer onto the holistic performance assessment approach of strong 1.0 programmes by including community members and parents in the process of determining outcomes, and in the evaluation of teacher candidates. This could mean that a teacher candidate receives feedback not only from Education faculty on a performance assessment or portfolio, but also from a parent or community member.

Place-based learning

3.0 programmes provide teacher candidates with a nuanced and deep understanding of the context and history of a particular place, and the varied facets of structural inequality that impact that place, which shapes their approach to teaching. For example, a programme at Ball State University called SCC immerses teacher candidates in a low-income, African American neighbourhood for a full semester course load. Courses, held at a local community centre, include readings, discussion, and speakers related to the culture, language, history, and narratives of the neighbourhood. Concurrently, students complete a practicum in a neighbourhood school and are paired with a community mentor who facilitates authentic participation in the neighbourhood through attendance at family dinners, church, neighbourhood activities and sporting events (Zygmunt and Clark 2015). These sorts of place-based learning courses promote contoured understandings of inequities and poverty, so that as teacher candidates move onto learning how to teach (i.e. methods courses) they can consider whether their practice is based in real understandings of individuals in poverty or stereotypes (Gorski 2012, 314). This situates their work amid related struggles for justice. This analysis of inequity undergirds the mediated methods courses candidates take later in their programme, which is co-taught with University faculty and K-12 teachers at partner schools, and emphasise the consistent connections between theory and practice also seen in exemplar 1.0 programmes.

Community teacher

According to Murrell (2001), community teachers:

> Draw on richly contextualized knowledge of culture, community, and identity in their professional work with children and families in diverse urban communities ... Community teachers have a clear sense of their own cultural, political, and racial identities in relation to the children and families they hope to serve. This sense allows them to play a central role in the successful development and education of their students. (4)

By learning from and about the families and communities of their students (e.g. the hopes and dreams of parents for their children's education, the funds of knowledge within communities), community teachers develop a perspective of their role as working with and for communities as opposed to the common missionary perspective within many 1.0 and 2.0 programmes wherein teachers see themselves as working to save students from their communities.

Community teachers see themselves as a part of a larger constellation of effort to work in solidarity with community members to help realise the conditions that allow better access to the social preconditions for learning in school, preconditions such as affordable housing, transportation, jobs that pay a living wage, high quality and affordable early child care, nutritious food and quality healthcare.

Teachers who see themselves as working in solidarity with their students' families and community members can recognise how community knowledge supports their work as teachers and can help students learn. For example, two teacher candidates at the University of Washington who were part of a teacher education programme where community members served as mentors (Zeichner et al. 2015) said the following about how being a community teacher supports their work:

> I'm now thinking of the role of teacher as something less than an expert. There's so much wisdom coming from other places in my students' lives that I'm really their secondary or tertiary educator. My role is not to transmit my knowledge and expertise, but to help develop them in tandem with all of the other parts of their lives. I'm not the sole steward of their learning. (ibid., 30)

> It gives power to the students and the families in the community, but I also feel empowered as a teacher... to have all these other ways to try and navigate and try to find a solution... it opens up so many doors and just stops that feeling of helplessness. (ibid.)

This work to develop community teachers in their preparation programmes often results in a disruption of negative perspectives of families and communities, particularly in communities highly impacted by poverty, a perspective that is prevalent in many 1.0 and 2.0 programmes where teachers often see themselves as missionaries helping to lift students out of their communities. For example, oftentimes teacher candidates in both 1.0 and 2.0 programmes assume that parents do not really care about their children if they are not present at school-designed events to receive knowledge about the school and/or their students from school staff. Community teachers reach out to their students' families to develop trusting relationships and work together with students' parents or other caregivers to support students' learning and development. A teacher candidate at the University of Washington shared with researchers how her view of parents had changed when she was able to interact with community mentors who were helping her prepare for teaching in communities unlike the ones where she had lived:

> I think unfortunately I always had the feeling that they really didn't care about their kids, that they weren't there and maybe they wouldn't come in because they didn't care about their kids, really care. Maybe it's because they had a bad experience in school, maybe they didn't get along well with their teachers or they can't come because they have all of these jobs they have to work. I think that there's been a really big shift in my thinking, just hearing stories from people who are in those positions. (Zeichner et al. 2015)

Community teachers use the knowledge that they gain about and from community members to teach in ways that attempt to build on the cultural capital that students bring to school (Gay 2010) and the funds of knowledge that exist in their communities. There is a substantial literature that demonstrates the value to student learning of teaching in ways that are informed by community knowledge (Hammerness et al. 2005).

Conclusion

The USA is experiencing rapid growth and increased investment in Teacher Preparation 2.0 programmes. Despite rhetoric and programme marketing that often claims 2.0 Teacher Preparation is working to 'close the achievement gap,' the narrow focus on teaching as a technical skill and test scores as a primary indicator of a good education does little to address the impact of poverty on education. Public discourse has focused on the (supposed or exaggerated) failures of 1.0 or University-based teacher preparation programmes and has presented the purported innovations of 2.0 programmes as the only alternative. Yet if teacher preparation has any hope of influencing issues of equity in the United States, it must develop ways to prepare teachers to work with and for communities to educate students with aims than go far beyond increased test scores and to see this work as connected to broader struggles to address poverty. Teacher preparation 3.0 programmes begin to move teacher education in this direction.

Disclosure statement

No potential conflict of interest was reported by the authors.

References

AERA. 2015. AERA Statement on the Use of Value-Added Models for the Evaluation of Educators and Education Preparation Programs. *Educational Researcher*. Accessed February 28, 2015. http://edr.sagepub.com/content/early/2015/11/10/0013189X15618385.full.pdf+html

American Statistical Association. 2014, April. *American Statistical Association Statement on Using Value Added Models for Education Assessment*. Accessed May 10, 2014. http://www.scribd.com/doc/217916454/ASA-VAM-Statement-1

Arnett, T. 2015. Start-up Teacher Education: A Fresh Take on Teacher Credentialing. Redwood City, CA: Christensen Institute.

Berliner, D. 2011. "Rational Responses to High Stakes Testing: The Case of Curriculum Narrowing and the Harm That Follows." *Cambridge Journal of Education* 41 (3): 287–302.

Brewer, T. J., K. Kretchmar, B. Sondel, S. Ishmael, and M. Manfra. 2016. "Teach for America's Preferential Treatment: School District Contracts, Hiring Decisions, and Employment Practices." *Education Policy Analysis Archives* 24: 15. Retrieved on July 29, 2016 from http://epaa.asu.edu/ojs/article/view/1923.

Carr, S. 2014. *Hope against Hope: Three Schools, One City, and the Struggle to Educate America's Children*. London, UK: Bloomsbury Publishing.

Clifford, G. J., and J. W. Guthrie. 1990. *Ed School: A Brief for Professional Education*. Chicago, IL: University of Chicago Press.

Cochran-Smith, M. 1991. "Learning to Teach against the Grain." *Harvard Educational Review* 61 (3): 279–311.

Cochran-Smith, M., P. Piazza, and C. Power. 2013. "The Politics of Accountability: Assessing Teacher Education in the United States." *The Educational Forum* 77 (1): 6–27. Taylor &Francis Group.

Darling-Hammond, L. 2006. *Powerful Teacher Education: Lessons from Exemplary Programs*. San Francisco, CA: John Wiley & Sons.

Darling-Hammond, L., and J. Bransford. 2005. *Preparing Teachers for a Changing World: What Teachers Should Learn and Be Able to Do*. Hoboken, NJ: John Wiley &Sons.

Darling-Hammond, L., R. C. Wei, and C. M. Johnson. 2009. "Teacher Preparation and Teacher Learning: A Changing Policy Landscape." *Handbook of Education Policy Research* 613–636.

Dover, A., B. Schultz, K. Smith, and T. Duggan. 2015. "Embracing the Controversy: EdTPA, Corporate Influence, and the Cooptation of Teacher Education." *Teachers College Record*. Retrieved on July 29, 2016 from www.tcrecord.org.

Dudley-Marling, C. 2007. "Return of the Deficit." *Journal of Educational Controversy* 2 (1): 5. Retrieved on July 29, 2016 from http://cedar.wwu.edu/cgi/viewcontent.cgi?article=1028&context=jec.

Duncan, G. J., and R. J. Murnane, eds. 2011. *Whither Opportunity?: Rising Inequality, Schools, and Children's Life Chances*. New York: Russell Sage Foundation.

Gastic, B. 2013. *Closing the Opportunity Gap: Preparing the Next Generation of Effective Teachers*. Washington, D.C: American Enterpise Institute.

Gatti L. 2014. "Negotiating Conflicting Frames of Experience: Learning to Teach in an Urban Teacher Residency." In *Learning Teaching from Experience: Multiple Perspectives and International Contexts*. London, UK. 207.

Gatti, L., and T. Catalano. 2015. "The Business of Learning to Teach: A Critical Metaphor Analysis of One Teacher's Journey." *Teaching and Teacher Education* 45: 149–160.

Gay, G. 2010. *Culturally Responsive Teaching: Theory, Research, and Practice*. New York, NY: Teachers College Press.

Giroux, H. A. 2013. *America's Education Deficit and the War on Youth: Reform beyond Electoral Politics*. New York, NY: NYU Press.

Goldstein, M. 2013a. Phoning Parents. Boston, MA: Match Education.

Goldstein, M. 2013b. "Match Teacher Residency." Accessed May 25, 2015. http://www.teachingworks.org/images/files/MATCH_Teacher_ResidencyMichael_Goldstein.pdf

Goodman, J. F. 2013. "Charter Management Organizations and the Regulation Environment: Is It worth the Price?" *Educational Researcher* 42 (2): 89–96.

Gorski, P. 2006. "The Classist Underpinnings of Ruby Payne's Framework." *Teachers College Record* 12322. Retrieved on July 29, 2016 from www.tcrecord.org.

Gorski, P. C. 2012. "Perceiving the Problem of Poverty and Schooling: Deconstructing the Class Stereotypes That Mis-Shape Education Practice and Policy." *Equity and Excellence in Education* 45 (2): 302–319.

Grossman, P., and S. Loeb, eds. 2008. *Taking Stock: An Examination of Alternative Certification*. Cambridge, MA: Harvard Education Press.

Haberman, M. 1991. "The Pedagogy of Poverty versus Good Teaching." *Phi Delta Kappan* 73 (4): 290–294.

Hammerness, K., L. Darling-Hammond, J. Bransford, D. Berliner, M. Cochran-Smith, M. McDonald, and K. Zeichner. 2005. *How Teachers Learn and Develop. Preparing Teachers for a Changing World: What Teachers Should Learn and Be Able to Do*. New York: John Wiley & Sons.

Kozol, J. 2005. *The Shame of the Nation: The Restoration of Apartheid Schooling in America*. New York, NY: Random House LLC.

Kretchmar, K., B. Sondel, and J. J. Ferrare. 2014. "Mapping the Terrain: Teach for America, Charter School Reform, and Corporate Sponsorship." *Journal of Education Policy* 29 (6): 742–759.

Kronholz, J. 2012. "A New Type of Ed School." *Education Next* 12 (4). Retrieved on July 29, 2016 from http://educationnext.org/a-new-type-of-ed-school/.

Kumashiro, K. 2010. "Seeing the Bigger Picture: Troubling Movements to End Teacher Education." *Journal of Teacher Education* 61 (1–2): 56–65.

Labaree, D. F. 2004. *The Trouble with Ed Schools*. New Haven, CT: Yale University Press.

Lemov, D. 2010. *Teach like a Champion: 49 Techniques That Put Students on the Path to College (K-12)*. San Francisco, CA: Jossey-Bass.

Levin, T., and R. Long 1981. *Effective Instruction*. 225 North Washington Street, Alexandria, VA 22314: Association for Supervision and Curriculum Development.

Levine, A. 2006. Educating School Teachers. Princeton, NJ: Education Schools Project.

Lipman, P. 2011. *The New Political Economy of Urban Education: Neoliberalism, Race, and the Right to the City*. New York: Routledge.

Lyall, K. C., and K. R. Sell. 2006. "The De Facto Privatization of American Public Higher Education." *Change: The Magazine of Higher Learning* 38 (1): 6–13.

MATCH Teacher Residency. 2015. Accessed August 30, 2015. http://www.matcheducation.org/join/match-teacher-residency/

Murrell Jr., P. C. 2001. *The Community Teacher: A New Framework for Effective Urban Teaching*. New York: Teachers College Press, Columbia University.

National Research Council. 2010. *Preparing Teachers: Building Evidence for Sound Policy*. Center for Education. Washington, DC: National Academies Press.

Otterman, S. 2011. "Ed Schools' Pedagogical Puzzle." *The New York times*, July 21. http://www.nytimes.com/2011/07/24/education/edlife/edl-24teacher-t.html?pagewanted=all.

Plecki, M. L., A. M. Elfers, and Y. Nakamura. 2012. "Using Evidence for Teacher Education Program Improvement and Accountability an Illustrative Case of the Role of Value-Added Measures." *Journal of Teacher Education* 63 (5): 318–334.

Reckhow, S., and J. W. Snyder. 2014. "The Expanding Role of Philanthropy in Education Politics." *Educational Researcher* 43 (4): 186–195.

Relay Graduate School of Education. 2014. *Relay New Orleans Curriculum Materials and Readers*. New York, NY.

Relay Graduate School of Education. 2015. Accessed May 26, 2015. http://www.relay.edu/programs/houston-mat/details

Rose, M. 2014. *Why School?: Reclaiming Education for All of Us*. New York, NY: The New Press.

Rothstein, R. 2004. *Class and Schools: Using Social, Economic, and Educational Reform to Close the Achievement Gap*. Washington, DC: Economic Policy Institute.

Saltman, K. J. 2010. *The Gift of Education: Public Education and Venture Philanthropy*. London: Palgrave Macmillan.

Scott, J. 2009. "The Politics of Venture Philanthropy in Charter School Policy and Advocacy." *Educational Policy* 23 (1): 106–136.

Skinner, E. A., M. T. Garreton, and B. D. Schultz. 2011. *Grow Your Own Teachers: Grassroots Change for Teacher Education. Teaching for Social Justice*. New York: Teachers College Press.

Sondel, B. 2015. "Market-Based Pedagogies: Assessment, Instruction, and Purpose at a 'No Excuses' Charter School." In *Only in New Orleans*, edited by L. F. Miron, B. R. Beabout and J. L. Boselovic. 109–128.

Stitzlein, S. M., and C. K. West. 2014. "New Forms of Teacher Education: Connections to Charter Schools and Their Approaches." *Democracy and Education* 22 (2). Retrieved on July 29, 2016 from http://democracyeducationjournal.org/cgi/viewcontent.cgi?article=1146&context=home.

Suitts, S. 2015. *A New Majority Research Bulletin: Low Income Students Now a Majority in the Nation's Public Schools*. Atlanta, GA: Southern Education Foundation.

Teach For America 2013. *Teach For America Summer Institute Training Materials. First 8 Weeks. Teach For America*. New York, NY.

Valenzuela, A. 2005. *Leaving Children behind: How "Texas-Style" Accountability Fails Latino Youth*. Albany, NY: Suny Press.

Villegas, A. M., and J. J. Irvine. 2010. "Diversifying the Teaching Force: An Examination of Major Arguments." *The Urban Review* 42 (3): 175–192.

Warren, M. 2005. "Communities and schools: A new view of urban education reform." *Harvard Educational Review* 75 (2): 133–173.

Wilson, S. M., and E. Tamir. 2008. "The Evolving Field of Teacher Education: How Understanding Challenge (R) S Might Improve the Preparation of Teachers." *Handbook of Research on Teacher Education: Enduring Questions in Changing Contexts* 3: 908–936.

Zeichner, K. 2010. "Competition, Economic Rationalization, Increased Surveillance, and Attacks on Diversity: Neo-Liberalism and the Transformation of Teacher Education in the U.S." *Teaching & Teacher Education* 26 (8): 1544–1552.

Zeichner, K. 2014. "The Struggle for the Soul of Teaching and Teacher Education." *Journal of Education for Teaching* 40 (5): 551–568.

Zeichner, K., M. Bowman, K. Napolitan, L. Guillen, D. Bennett, K. Cooly-Strom, and J. Gardner. 2015. "Engaging Local Communities in Preparing the Teachers of Their Children." Paper presented at the American Educational Research Association Annual Meeting, Chicago, IL.

Zeichner, K., K. A. Payne, and K. Brayko. 2015. "Democratizing Teacher Education." *Journal of Teacher Education* 66 (2): 122–135.

Zeichner, K., and C. Pena-Sadnoval. 2015. "Venture Philanthropy and Teacher Education Policy in the U.S.: The Role of the New Schools Venture Fund." *Teachers College Record* 117 (6): 1–44.

Zygmunt, E., and P. Clark. 2015. *Transforming Teacher Education for Social Justice*. New York, NY: Teachers College Press.

The impact of adopting a research orientation towards use of the Pupil Premium Grant in preparing beginning teachers in England to understand and work effectively with young people living in poverty

Katharine Burn, Trevor Mutton, Ian Thompson, Jenni Ingram, Jane McNicholl and Roger Firth

ABSTRACT

The introduction in England of the Pupil Premium Grant (PPG) provided a stimulus to ensure that beginning teachers understand the nature of poverty and critically examine strategies used by schools seeking to overcome the barriers to academic achievement that it presents. This article explores the effects of asking student-teachers within a well-established initial teacher education partnership to adopt a research orientation towards the use of PPG funding. It focuses on the student-teachers' experiences and developing thinking as they engaged in small-scale investigative projects and on the perspectives of their school-based teacher educators (professional tutors). Whole-course evaluation data suggest that most projects operated successfully, with the student-teachers encouraged to ask critical questions about current practices, drawing on different kinds of evidence. Three case studies illustrate the diversity of approaches adopted towards the project, reflecting the views of individual professional tutors and the complex interplay between the competing object motives of different participants.

Introduction

The strength of the relationship between pupils' socio-economic status and their educational outcomes has long been a matter of concern in education, with increasing attention focused on raising the attainment of the most disadvantaged pupils. The strong correlation between economic disadvantage and low educational outcomes is well established (e.g. ESRC 2011; Hills et al. 2010; Horgan 2007; Raffo et al. 2007). Researchers and commentators have highlighted the impact that socio-economic disadvantage can have on young people's life chances (Buras 2014; Gorski and Landsman 2014; Payne 2005). Gorski (2012) and Dudley-Marling and Lucas (2009) have argued that popular stereotypes of people living in poverty affect both individual preconceptions and policy. The resultant deficit model is used to direct blame onto the perceived shortcomings of the poor, rather than on structural inequalities in the educational system, and can lead to stereotypical views about pupils and their families

(Rank, Yoon, and Hirschl 2003). With such views widely accepted by teachers and teacher educators (Ullucci and Howard 2015), it is unsurprising that recent UK research (Thompson, McNicholl, and Menter 2016) suggests that this deficit model is also accepted by many beginning teachers. Since beginning teachers' pre-existing beliefs are known to shape their experience and professional learning (Pajares 1992; Richardson 1996; Wideen, Mayer-Smith, and Moon 1998), there is a strong social justice imperative for ITE programmes to address student-teachers' understanding of, and attitudes towards, people living in poverty (Cochran-Smith 2004; Darling-Hammond and Bransford 2007; Zeichner 2009).

In England, the Pupil Premium Grant (PPG), introduced by the Coalition Government in 2011 (DFE 2015), has provided a new opportunity to examine some of these issues. The grant comprises additional payments made to schools, which in 2014–2015 (the year in which the research was conducted) ranged from £300 for each child from a family in the armed services to £935 for secondary age and £1300 for primary age pupils eligible for Free School Meals (at any point in the last six years) and £1900 for children in local authority care or adopted from care (DFE 2014). Specific consideration of how schools use this funding can act as a focus for beginning teachers' explorations of the impact of poverty on young people's learning and attainment. As responsibility for teacher education in the UK is increasingly passed to schools (DFE 2011), it is particularly important to understand how school staff conceive of the issues and how they encourage beginning teachers to respond to them.

The aim of our research was to explore the effects of an intervention that prompted student-teachers, within an established one-year postgraduate certificate in education (PGCE) programme, to examine the relationship between young people's socio-economic status and their attainment and to explore school practices intended to remove the barriers to learning often created by poverty. The intervention, jointly designed by the university and its partnership schools, required all student-teachers to undertake a small-scale collaborative research project within their second placement school, investigating use of PPG funding in any way that they and the school's professional tutor (the teacher responsible for coordinating their learning within their placement school) chose. In researching the operation and outcomes of this project, we had two objectives:

(1) To explore the ways in which poverty and its effects were presented to the student-teachers in school, including the kinds of research aims and methods advocated in relation to this issue, and the kinds of outcome and evaluative perspectives encouraged; and
(2) To explore student-teachers' responses to issues of poverty and the opinions they expressed in reflecting on their investigations about the most effective ways of overcoming socio-economic barriers to pupils' learning.

Using three case studies as exemplars, we begin by exploring the perspectives of the professional tutors: both their own conceptions of poverty and its impact on pupils' learning and their decisions about the most appropriate kinds of research for student-teachers to conduct within the particular school context. We then focus on the perspectives of the student-teachers, examining their responses to the particular project in which they were engaged in the light of their prior knowledge and experience.

Our research framework is informed by a sociocultural analysis of the situated social and cultural interaction between the student-teachers and their professional tutors, as well as of the impact of the university-initiated project. Beginning teachers face a multi-layered social situation of development (Vygotsky 1987) that involves a complex interplay between individual, social and institutional histories. In the context of the school/university partnerships, there are multiple object motives in play (Edwards 2010) for each participant. The student-teachers need to learn to teach effectively and to demonstrate achievement of the teachers' standards within their particular school context, while simultaneously responding to the project's emphasis on the relationship between poverty and educational attainment. The professional tutors are concerned not only with the student-teachers' learning but also with the school's reputation and current development priorities. In some institutional and personal contexts, these motives align, but this is not always the case. A case study approach allows us to examine these complex intersecting social situations of development, identifying how they influence the preparation of student-teachers to teach young people from impoverished backgrounds.

Conceptions of professional learning

One of the many challenges inherent in ITE is the need not only to develop beginning teachers' classroom competence but also to situate their developing knowledge and understanding in a wider context. The ITE curriculum needs to be 'oriented around the intellectual and practical tasks of teaching and the contexts of teachers' work' (Feiman-Nemser 2001, 1048), with an acknowledgement that we need to understand more about the role that such contextual factors play in teacher education programmes more generally (Grossman and McDonald 2008). This task becomes more complex if we expect beginning teachers to learn how to engage critically with policy initiatives about which there may be little, or no, established research, even more so in the context of performative systems that make it particularly difficult to raise critical questions about practices and their underlying assumptions. Existing theories of teachers' professional learning do not necessarily address fully the question of how to promote learning about aspects of practice which are in the early stages of development, nor the way in which experienced teachers can learn 'through their engagement with novices' in cases where 'part of the process of legitimate peripheral participation for many novices is to help other workers to learn' (Fuller et al. 2005, 64).

McIntyre, Hagger, and Burn (1994), aware of the risks of restricting beginning teachers' learning to the practices of the particular school in which they are placed, advocate an approach that encourages beginners to question the rationales for these practices, leading to a critical examination of the alternatives. The success of such an approach depends, however, on sustained engagement with the issue in question through a carefully planned programme that operates within an agreed framework. Borko's (2004) model of a 'professional learning system', based on what she refers to as 'a situative perspective', identifies the key elements of such a system as:

- The professional development programme;
- The teachers, who are the learners in the system;
- The facilitator, who guides teachers as they construct new knowledge and practices; and
- The context in which the professional development occurs (2004, 4).

Within such a system, it is important not only to acknowledge the need for a sustained and integrated approach to learning but also to recognise the influence of beginners' individual preconceptions about what it is they need or expect to learn and the kinds of learning they believe to be of value (Hammerness et al. 2005; Hobson et al. 2006; Younger et al. 2004) as well as their particular orientations towards learning from experience (Hagger et al. 2008).

The Pupil Premium Grant

Relatively little research into the use of PPG funding had been published before the student-teachers were invited to carry out their investigative projects. The studies then available included one government-commissioned evaluation (Carpenter et al. 2013) and annual reports from the government inspectorate (Ofsted 2012, 2013, 2014), all obviously premised on the assumption that appropriate educational interventions could indeed overcome social inequalities. These reports identified that the PPG was commonly used to provide increased staffing (both teachers and teaching assistants) and to support the participation' of disadvantaged children in extra-curricular activities. While the most recent Ofsted report claimed that the 'pupil premium was making a positive difference in many schools' (2014, 9, para. 5), it also identified poor leadership and ineffective use of performance data as the key problems in schools judged to require improvement in this area. The implicit emphasis is thus on blaming schools rather than acknowledging the social realities of poverty. Carpenter et al. (2013) highlight a number of tensions in schools' use of the PPG, not least 'between what they believed they were expected to do by external authorities, and what they understood to be in the best interests of their pupils' (99) and discuss the need for schools to draw on both local contextual knowledge, as well as externally validated evidence, to inform their decision-making. In the absence of a substantial body of research into the effectiveness of the use of the PPG, many schools were drawing, essentially uncritically, on the Education Endowment Foundation/Sutton Trust Toolkit (Higgins et al. 2014) which offered a research synthesis of a range of interventions, evaluating each of them in relation to effect size, degree of confidence in the evidence and cost. Little attention tended to be paid to the ways in which the Toolkit's exclusive reliance on quantitative evidence (drawn from randomised control trials and large-scale experiments) might have constrained the kinds of insight that it could provide.

Research design

We adopted a mixed-methods design for the research, allowing us to examine the experiences and views of the participants in a range of different contexts and on different scales. In order to explore the professional tutors' perspectives and choices about the project within their distinctive school settings and to examine the student-teachers' developing thinking *in relation to* their experiences within those particular contexts, detailed case studies were conducted within six partnership schools. Each involved an interview with the professional tutor, participant observation of the student-teachers' presentations in school (or examination of the material presented where attendance was not possible) and individual interviews with three of the student-teachers.

The case study schools were chosen to include three in large urban areas and three in predominantly rural areas, each with differing proportions of pupils eligible for PPG funding. While we confined our selection to those schools with experienced professional tutors, we ensured representation of a range of views in terms of the professional tutors' level of enthusiasm for the investigative project and included student-teachers from across all subject disciplines within the PGCE programme.

The final element of the research, which allows us to contextualise each of the case studies and gives some indication of their typicality, was a series of questions asked of all student-teachers (within their whole-course evaluation) about their experience of the investigative project and their perceptions of its value to them. Permission to use their responses to these questions as research data was given by 140 student-teachers, representing 84% of those who completed the PGCE programme. Likert scale responses (in addition to more open reflections) allowed for some quantitative analysis of their perspectives which is used to frame the three case studies that are presented below.

Most of the methods of data collection had been trialled the previous year when the project was implemented as a pilot study in a number of partnership schools. An inductive, iterative approach was developed with two of the researchers initially working together on the pilot data, generating codes that were compared and successively refined to elaborate the key themes in relation to the participants' views of the impact of poverty on educational outcomes, their perceptions of PPG as a policy response and their reflections on different kinds of interventions that might operate on different scales (school, the classroom and the individual). These themes were reviewed and refined by the research team as they were applied to the case study data, which included the professional tutors' perspectives, with new themes added to encompass their conceptions of the student-teachers' professional learning. In reporting the findings, each case study is presented separately, making it possible to examine the different kinds of interplay that shaped outcomes: the interaction, for example, between the professional tutors' views of the substantive issues and their conceptions of beginning teachers' professional learning; between the professional tutors' understanding of the impact of poverty and the student-teachers' developing ideas; and between the student-teachers' very diverse existing ideas of poverty as an issue of social justice and their developing thinking as they engaged with different sources of evidence.

Findings

Questionnaire data

In presenting our findings, we report first on analysis of the data from the whole-course evaluation (see Table 1), noting the proportion of student-teachers who were actually given the opportunity to carry out an investigative project, the value that they attributed to it and any specific concerns that were raised about it. Detailed accounts of the operation of the projects in three different schools are then provided by the case studies.

The questionnaire data presented in Table 1 reveal that over 90% of the 140 respondents had the opportunity to carry out the PPG investigation in their second placement school and that most regarded it as a valuable learning experience (74%). Most claimed that it had enabled them to develop a better understanding of both the PPG and the government policy underpinning it, as well as of the ways in which individual schools were using the funding and any difficulties associated with it.

When asked to provide further details, many of the student-teachers were positive about the experience, although three kinds of concerns were also raised. The first related to presentation of their findings in the school, with some student-teachers disappointed that they

Table 1. Summary of questionnaire data.

	Strongly agree (%)	Agree (%)	Neither agree nor disagree (%)	Disagree (%)	Strongly disagree (%)	Not applicable (%)
The PDP programme in school helped me understand the nature of the Pupil Premium	25	42	19	11	4	0
The programme in school helped me understand the way in which my S2 school was implementing various aspects of the Pupil Premium	18	50	15	13	4	0
The programme in school helped me understand better the issues (including any difficulties) around the implementation of the Pupil Premium in my S2 school	21	47	13	14	4	0
We, as a group, had the opportunity to carry out our own investigations related to the Pupil Premium in our S2 school	40	51	4	3	3	0
We had the opportunity to present our findings to colleagues in the S2 school	46	38	4	8	4	0
I think that the Pupil Premium work carried out by the student-teachers in my S2 school made a contribution to the school's knowledge and understanding of the issues.	22	31	23	12	12	0
I found it valuable to learn more about the current government policy	31	39	11	2	2	14
I found it valuable to learn more about the school's policy and practices	28	50	12	1	3	6
I found it valuable to discuss the issues with relevant school staff	31	44	9	6	2	9
I found it valuable to carry out my (or our) own investigations in the school	28	46	10	8	4	5

had not been asked to report to members of the senior leadership team or others with direct responsibility for PPG policy:

> We were not given the opportunity to report our findings to senior colleagues within the school, merely the other student-teachers and our professional tutor. [Science student-teacher, School 1]

It seemed important to many student-teachers that the school should affirm their work and they particularly valued the project where this was the case:

> Our school definitely used us to try and fix the problem of a Pupil Premium black hole. They were aware that last year's project had highlighted their lack of provision for PP and had recently hired someone to be in charge of provision but had yet to do anything else. Our presentations seemed to have had an immediate effect as the school has now hired heads of PP for each key stage and seems to be planning more interventions and provision. [English student-teacher, School 17]

Second, where student-teachers felt that they were working on the project in isolation from the rest of the school, they were generally less happy than others about conducting an investigation. There were also tensions about the degree of independence entrusted to them. In some cases, there was resentment that the school had sought to influence the nature of the project too directly or had intervened inappropriately (for example, by framing the questions that the student-teachers should ask). It was sometimes implied that the school had not really encouraged investigative approaches that might have prompted closer critical examination of its policy and practice.

Third, in several cases, it had been difficult for professional tutors to achieve an appropriate balance between giving the student-teachers sufficient guidance and preserving the scope for them to act autonomously. Nearly a sixth of student-teachers commented on the need either for more structure or for better communication (between the university and the school or within the school itself), as summarised in the following observation:

> The project was valuable; however, I feel that there could have been a greater communication between S2 schools and the university department. The rules and rubric for the project were not always reflected by our professional tutor, which caused a general air of confusion with the student-teachers. [English student-teacher, School 25]

Only a small proportion (2%) of the student-teachers felt that the project had detracted from the need to focus on their classroom teaching. Overall, the most positive comments came from those who found it valuable in terms of their own learning *and* of demonstrable use to the school:

> We were given a clear structure and something the school wished for us to investigate, making it far more purposeful and a worthwhile task. [Science student-teacher, School 4]

Case study 1: Church Green academy

Church Green, a Church of England converter academy, with just over 1000 pupils, is situated in a small market town serving an essentially rural catchment area. In 2013–2014, the school received PPG funding of approximately £90,000 for 112 eligible pupils. The school's website reported that the largest items of expenditure were related to teaching assistants engaged in various one-to-one and small group initiatives focused on literacy and maths, and to the work of an attendance officer. Funding was also used for holiday revision courses and a late bus service, allowing pupils to attend after-school revision sessions. A strong emphasis was also placed on ensuring access to trips and to the whole-school extra-curricular enrichment programme.

The professional tutor, Frances, takes it for granted that poverty creates many different barriers to learning, but treats it as axiomatic that young people eligible for PPG funding do not represent a single group with shared characteristics. Their individual circumstances have to be understood and appropriately addressed. While many needs are material ones, such as a lack of food and clean clothing, to which the school provides a very practical response, Frances also notes high levels of isolation within the school's rural catchment area. She seems particularly aware of the various kinds of neglect from which some young people suffer and of their need to build trusting relationships. While she is concerned about the school's limited contact with some parents, her focus is always on what the school could do to improve those relationships: building bridges, rather than identifying 'failings' in what parents or carers are offering.

Having been expressly prohibited by the head teacher from undertaking the investigative project the previous year, Frances embraced it enthusiastically (under a new head teacher) in 2015. She chose to involve all nine of the student-teachers on placement in the school (including two from a different ITE partnership), presenting them with three different group projects, identified in collaboration with the teacher to whom specific responsibility for Year 11 PPG pupils had recently been assigned:

(1) A Year 6–7 transition project involving visits and conversations with key staff in three feeder primary schools to investigate their use of PPG funding, particularly to support Year 6 pupils preparing to move to Church Green.
(2) A small-scale intervention undertaken by the student-teachers with designated Year 8 pupils, withdrawn from their weekly Personal, Social, Citizenship and Health Education lesson. The student-teachers were asked to focus particularly on developing pupils' meta-cognition.
(3) An investigation of 'best practice' in two nearby city schools, one of which had received a DFE award for the quality of its PPG provision. The student-teachers were expected to visit both schools and 'to go well beyond the information available on their websites' in seeking to understand the effectiveness of their policies.

Frances met a different group each week to support their work. She ensured that the student-teachers' presentations were attended by the deputy head, an assistant head and the special needs coordinator (SENCO), and was thrilled that the deputy head stayed behind to discuss how they might act on particular recommendations relating to nurture groups. Although the head teacher could not attend, he read the student-teachers' presentations and subsequently met with them, specifically to invite them to 'talk through their findings in additional meetings with the staff'.

The student-teachers' response, as expressed within the whole-course evaluation, was almost universally positive. The only uncertainty, expressed by one of them, related to the scope to 'discuss the issues with relevant school staff' (perhaps reflecting the fact that two of the projects were examining practices elsewhere). While all agreed that the project had been valuable to their learning, they were even more emphatic about its value to the school.

Two of the three student-teachers interviewed claimed to have been well informed *before* their PGCE about how poverty can impact young people's educational outcomes. Anna, training to teach Modern Foreign Languages, cited her reading of Sutton Trust research reports, while Izzy, a historian, recounted personal experience mentoring individuals who had no space at home to work or limited experience of positive relationships with adults. Miriam, who taught geography, described her conversations with Year 6 teachers as a 'revelation', alerting her both to the challenges that certain young people face and also to the difference that particular strategies could make. While the student-teachers who led the Year 8 intervention – a series of cookery sessions designed to enhance pupils' experiences of competency, belonging, usefulness and potency – spoke passionately in the light of their experience and interviews with the pupils involved, they also made repeated reference to research they had read, as did the group investigating pupils' experience of primary–secondary transition.

Frances expressed some regret about asking one group simply to report on practice elsewhere, suspecting that this option had allowed them to avoid personal engagement. However, Izzy, who admitted to taking that option precisely because she was cynical about what could be learned through the direct intervention, was not only won over by her peers' experiences, but also profoundly impressed by what the teachers elsewhere had shared with her. The teachers' arguments were based on different kinds of evidence: both individual anecdotes demonstrating the impact of appropriately targeted support and research evidence (gradually being confirmed in the schools' experience), highlighting the influence of particular approaches within mainstream teaching. While all the student-teachers felt that they had offered specific and valued advice to the school, they also identified key ideas to take forward themselves, particularly relating to the value of detailed knowledge about each of the individuals within their own classes.

Case study 2: Hilltop academy

Hilltop, another converter academy with just over 1000 pupils, is similarly located in a rural market town, and received approximately £150,000 for 136 eligible pupils in 2014–2015. The school's website reported that their grant was used in a number of different ways, including provision of one-to-one or small group support, private tutors, subject-specific resources, extra-curricular opportunities and expenses for volunteer mentors.

While Grace, the professional tutor, acknowledges that some pupils eligible for PPG funding have difficult home circumstances or face additional caring responsibilities which make it difficult to focus on school work, she essentially attributes the 'huge link' between pupils' socio-economic background and academic achievement to parental attitudes: 'I think the parental value and importance of education isn't there, or as strong as it might be in other families'. She cites the case of individual PPG pupils who seem well provided for ('they've got Sky TV and he's got iPads'), suggesting that the real problems derive from low aspirations and poor parenting. It is a 'poverty of relationships' that she believes exerts the most powerful influence on young people's motivation. Grace is essentially pessimistic about what can be done for young people 'by the time they get to us'. In pointing to high levels of trial and error in use of PPG funding nationally and acknowledging that the school's own approaches have not been effectively evaluated, she questions whether 'throwing money at the problem is necessarily the best way to deal with it'.

In setting up the investigative project for the three student-teachers undertaking their second placement in the school, Grace was particularly concerned not to create further work for her colleagues. She therefore provided quite tight direction, asking the student-teachers to 'audit' the school's current use of its funding before exploring evidence of provision elsewhere in order to offer the school further specific recommendations. She hoped that this would benefit both the school and the student-teachers and she ensured that members of the senior leadership team attended the presentation of their findings.

The project was implemented very much as Grace had intended. The student-teachers drew mainly on the Education Endowment Foundation/Sutton Trust Toolkit (Higgins et al. 2014), although they also referred to practices in their first placement schools. After evaluating Hilltop's current provision in the light of the Toolkit's research summaries, they proposed other 'low-cost/high impact' strategies of potential benefit.

Data from the whole-course evaluation suggest that the student-teachers valued the project highly, particularly the opportunity to discuss their findings with each other. Doubts were only expressed in response to two of the questions, with one student-teacher 'uncertain' whether the programme had helped in understanding issues associated with the implementation of the PPG in the school, and another unsure as to whether it had been valuable to discuss the issues with relevant staff in the school.

In reflecting in interview on the barriers to learning that PPG pupils may encounter, the student-teachers at Hilltop all noted the overlap between PPG pupils and those identified as having some kind of special educational need. Their explanations of this link tended to focus less on the impact of material deprivation (although they acknowledged this), and more on early cultural deprivation, namely a 'lack of opportunity for reading or talking or socialising' and on pupils' emotional and relational needs. When the student-teachers referred to a lack of parental support for their children's schooling, it is notable that they sought to *explain* such attitudes, suggesting, for example, that they might derive from a perception that the school system had previously 'failed' them.

All the student-teachers claimed that the project influenced their thinking and practice, although this was refracted in different ways through their prior experiences. John, a scientist, admitted that he 'hadn't really encountered poverty' before embarking on the PGCE and had been surprised by how prevalent it is. He suggested that the project had increased his awareness of the need to address literacy barriers, reducing the amount of reading and writing that he sets and providing writing scaffolds or scope for pupils to use laptops (although he stressed that this would be his response to *all* pupils with such difficulties). Sally, teaching Modern Foreign Languages, was prompted to review her own educational experience in the light of the differences in pupil engagement and motivation that she had seen between different sets. The project highlighted the importance of understanding the particular personal circumstances of each individual within her class, enabling her to appreciate their emotional and relational needs. Evan, a Religious Education student-teacher, who had lived for some time in disadvantaged communities in South America, arrived with strong views about the impact of poverty, arguing that it is 'not just a concept that involves money' but has to be understood in wider societal and political terms. Engagement with the project confirmed his conviction that data alone are insufficient to address the issues, which require personal commitment. Indeed, while he had originally seen the PPG as a means of addressing disadvantage at school level (by securing access to key resources), he came to recognise that it required his engagement with pupils at an individual level: 'No two pupils are the same so each one has to be transformed in a different way'.

Case study 3: Midway City School

Midway City School, another converter academy, is located within an ethnically diverse and rapidly growing city. The school is similarly diverse in terms of pupils' ethnicity and socio-economic background. Of almost 1400 pupils on roll, nearly 400 qualify for PPG (generating an income of £406,264). The school website reported that PPG funds were used to help with the cost of uniforms, trips and other educational essentials. One-to-one tuition was provided with a specialist Education Inclusion Tutor along with some pastoral support for disadvantaged pupils and their families. The report also cited use of 'evidence -informed' group interventions (with reference to the Education Endowment Foundation /Sutton Trust Toolkit).

The professional tutor, James, explicitly endorses views expressed in *The Spirit Level* (Wilkinson and Pickett 2009) that 'there are all types of symptoms of an unequal society' and suggests that poverty may give rise to a range of pupil characteristics: 'lack of resilience; lack of self-esteem; a reluctance to try anything so they don't engage in learning'. James links problems of parental security and upbringing with social disadvantage and is keen not to subscribe to a deficit model. It is the 'hidden' barriers that schools struggle most to overcome, such as pupils' self-selection (their decisions that 'this is not for me'). Tackling such barriers requires determination and commitment: 'You've got to engage. There is no short term fix. You've got to have long-term goals to address poverty and lack of stable upbringing'. James thinks that Midway recognises the importance of the issue, but acknowledges that it is struggling, like other city schools, to make a difference for PPG pupils. He urges a more proactive approach, 'We have to engage students with the way we view things as well as be reactive', and regards staff training as 'a key issue'.

James' distinctive approach to the investigative project was intended to help the student-teachers reflect on their own attitudes and to avoid a 'tick-box' mentality that simply required them to identify existing knowledge within the school about disadvantage or how the funding was spent. Rather than focus exclusively on PPG pupils, he also asked the nine student-teachers involved in the project to investigate the experiences of pupils from black and minority ethnic backgrounds (BME) and those with English as an additional language (EAL). Their task was to interview pupils in each category about their experiences in school in order to create a series of short videos (using the pupils' voices but not their images) to help future student-teachers and new staff prepare for the diversity that they would encounter at Midway. In the task briefing, James explained that 'we all have preconceived ideas about different groups [that] need continual challenging' and expressed the hope that the videos would 'provoke deeper thought in all staff about the needs and school experience of our students'.

James sought explicit permission from the head teacher to undertake the project in this way and she was involved, along with the deputy head, SENCO and subject mentors in selecting pupils for interview and in ensuring that the videos were sensitively made. James recognised the student-teachers' anxieties that their project was different from investigations elsewhere, but thought that it helped promote significant changes in some of their views. He suggested that its strength lay in 'trying to put things into context' and that it had worked well to provoke 'self-awareness and self-reflection', though he would try to take that further in future years.

The student-teachers' anxieties about the unorthodox nature of their project were clearly reflected in their responses to the whole-course evaluation. More than two-thirds of them claimed that the project had not helped develop their understanding of PPG funding or knowledge of how it was used in school. While they presented their work (the videos they had created), few thought that it had contributed to the school's own understanding of specific issues associated with the PPG. In responding to questions about the value of being able to discuss issues with each other and with relevant school staff, opinions were more evenly balanced. Overall, while about a third of the student-teachers gave positive responses about how much they and the school had learned, a third gave negative responses to all questions and the remainder were positive about some aspects while clearly recognising that their task did not fit the brief followed in other schools.

The three student-teachers who were interviewed clearly recognised the link between poverty and educational attainment. David, a mathematician, attributed this to the influence of a wide range of factors, specifically citing material resources and educational experiences within the family. Sam, who acknowledged that his view of 'what it means to be disadvantaged' turned out to be 'inaccurate', stressed the importance both of checking the data and of looking beyond the classroom. Jane, the only one of the three who had specifically worked with pupils eligible for PPG funding, was most insistent that while some degree of generalisation inevitably occurs, any serious attempt to close the gap has to be 'about individual provision' responsive to individual needs.

Jane reported that her group was extremely positive about the nature and value of their interactions with the PPG pupils. While they had approached the task with particular assumptions, such as the idea that PPG pupils 'were often tired or struggled with homework', they quickly realised that being identified as eligible for PPG is inevitably somewhat 'arbitrary' and that you simply 'can't pigeon-hole'. While they saw a 'wide range of need', the key messages that they took away were about good teachers who 'listen, help and don't get annoyed' and the pupils' appreciation of routine, stability and strong, sustained relationships.

However, the student-teachers who had focused on the experience of black or minority, ethnic (BME) or EAL pupils were somewhat aggrieved that they had not found out more about the use of the PPG funding, complaining as David did, that 'we were never given the information about the interventions'.

Discussion

In seeking to interpret these findings, our attention is focused on three themes of particular significance in the context of school-based (and increasingly 'school-led') initial teacher education. One of the main challenges of locating initial teacher education predominantly in school is that of ensuring that alongside opportunities to learn from current practices, beginners are also given the chance and the resources with which to examine those practices critically. Another is the extent of variation in the experience of any cohort of student-teachers even within the structures provided by a jointly planned programme. We therefore focus on the extent to which schools were prepared to promote a research orientation and thus to permit critical examination of their own practices; the ways in which the institutional histories of the individual schools and the distinctive perspectives and personal agendas of the professional tutors interacted with those of individual student-teachers to shape their learning experiences; and on the nature of the project's impact, given this complex interplay between the object motives of different participants.

The scope to adopt a research orientation

As these case studies reveal, there was considerable variation in the nature of the projects undertaken by the student-teachers and in their complex social situations of development. However, both the individual cases and the whole-course evaluation data suggest that the project was effectively implemented in the vast majority of schools, enabling the students-teachers to engage, albeit in different ways, with issues of poverty and its relationship to young people's educational experiences and outcomes. The fact that some student-teachers were *not* given the opportunity to carry out an investigation hints at the range of constraints that professional tutors faced and at the challenges for schools inherent in encouraging beginners to adopt such an open and potentially critical orientation towards a high-profile and rapidly evolving aspect of professional practice. Permission was only given at Church Green after the arrival of a new head teacher, prepared to acknowledge that the school could be doing better, who therefore welcomed insights from elsewhere. Grace at Hilltop deliberately sought to contain the project, anxious that it might generate difficult questions that the school was ill-equipped to address. It is difficult to know how far Grace's reported anxieties about overloading other staff may simply have served to justify the restricted investigation that she proposed, but it is true that all professional tutors were constrained by the time that other teachers could give to the project and by their willingness to respond to the student-teachers' questions. Given these contextual factors, the project's success owed much to the gradual way in which it was introduced, with an initial year of piloting and examples from that work made available to all the professional tutors to illustrate the kind of possibilities open to them.

The lack of prescription about the project's design was also crucial in allowing professional tutors to shape and contain it in ways that they thought would be acceptable within their specific context (McIntyre, Hagger, and Burn 1994). Such flexibility, however, also proved unsettling as student-teachers compared their experiences across schools and the extent of the student-teachers' anxiety at Midway City serves to demonstrate just how powerful the performative agenda remained, at least partially undermining the most radical attempt to encourage the student-teachers to focus on the lived experiences and perspectives of young people themselves.

Competing object motives and the complex interplay of personal and institutional histories

Contrasts across the schools highlight the complex interaction between different players within the partnership, shaped in part by different conceptions of teachers' professional learning and by the different object motives (Edwards 2010; Vygotsky 1987) towards which their actions were oriented. They thus confirm Hodkinson and Hodkinson's (2004) findings about the interplay between individual teachers' dispositions towards their own learning and the school cultures in which they are working. Not only does each affect the other and in turn affect teacher learning 'but national policy and organisational regulatory practices' – such as the PPG funding and schools' accountability for it – 'operate as an overlying third determinant of that learning' (2004, 120).

In some cases, participants' object motives were well aligned, as at Church Green where the professional tutor's conviction that the student-teachers would learn most productively through tightly focused, detailed investigative work with teachers and pupils supported her ambitions (and those of the new head teacher) for the school to learn as much as possible from effective practices elsewhere. In other cases, as at Hilltop, the tensions were more evident, although the project was still productive because of the in-built enquiry process. Grace, who was sceptical both about the extent and influence of poverty on young people's learning and about the capacity of secondary schools to impact pupils' established trajectories, seemed more concerned to minimise the demands on other staff than to promote particular kinds of student-teacher learning. Nonetheless, the relatively simple processes of investigating the school's use of the funds and comparing their choice of strategies with the claims of published research summaries about cost-effectiveness and impact (a comparison that they reported to members of the senior leadership team) provided sufficient scope and stimulus for the student-teachers to engage with the realities of some young people's experience.

While James' commitment at Midway City to helping student-teachers engage with those realities was undoubtedly profound, his assumptions about the most effective way of doing so clashed with the student-teachers' expectations about what and how they should be learning. This clash prompted most of them to question the value of the project, despite the range of things that they reported learning from it. James' determination that they should hear the pupils' voices rather than focus on official expectations or school policies here conflicted with their concerns as student-teachers to demonstrate mastery of the knowledge they believed was expected of them.

The impact of the project and its interaction with other sources of learning

In every case, the project *designs* were shaped by the professional tutors' views of poverty and by their conceptions of beginning teachers' professional learning. The *outcomes* of each project, however, were never simply shaped by those views since the process of enquiry built into the investigation gave the student-teachers access to other perspectives, including those of the pupils. The student-teachers' prior experiences (within the PGCE and before joining the programme) also shaped the attitudes with which they responded to the new information and ideas that they encountered. Thus, while the student-teachers at Hilltop did echo some of the professional tutors' concerns about unhelpful parental attitudes, they sought to understand how those attitudes might have arisen and draw on their prior experience to explain how material deprivation can destroy young people's confidence. Frances may have deliberately steered some of the student-teachers to report on the role of nurture groups, that she already knew featured prominently in the primary schools to which she sent them; but those who investigated secondary school practices elsewhere returned fully persuaded of the importance of particular in-class teaching strategies.

While some student-teachers were already well informed about the material and psychological effects of poverty on young people, others were surprised by what they encountered, regarding their new insights as a real 'revelation'. They applied this idea of revelation not just to what they learned about the effects of poverty, but also to insights into particular practices that could make a profound difference for individual pupils. In all cases, even where the original design of the project seemed to direct them towards data *about* young people, rather than towards the young people themselves, the student-teachers all reflected on what they had learned about the needs and experiences of particular individuals and on the importance of that knowledge. Even where their professional tutors had articulated pessimistic or sceptical views, the student-teachers expressed a more positive and carefully nuanced understanding. All of them claimed that what they now understood, even if not entirely new to them, would have an impact on their classroom practice and claimed that it is obviously important to investigate in future research.

In some cases, the development of more nuanced views and the emphasis on individuals' experiences were derived from student-teachers' conversations with pupils. The importance of this direct experience was stressed by some of the most enthusiastic professional tutors, like Frances and James. It is interesting to note, however, that the student-teachers also claimed to have been powerfully influenced by more indirect insights, such as those that Izzy gained from the work of her peers and from tightly focused conversations with experienced teachers, referring in detail to individual children and tailored forms of support.

Engagement with particular issues through the project also prompted many student-teachers to turn to the research literature with renewed interest, supporting McIntyre's (2005) claim that enquiry-based approaches enhance teachers' engagement with existing research. While this source was obviously built into those projects that steered student-teachers (often uncritically) towards the Education Endowment Foundation/Sutton Trust Toolkit (Higgins et al. 2014), several student-teachers engaged in other projects, most notably at Church Green, drew explicitly on reading encountered within their curriculum programme or undertaken for earlier professional development assignments. It is likely that the student-teachers' interest in research reflected the need to defend their claims and recommendations to members of the school's senior leadership team, but it also appeared to be driven by genuine interest in the options presented to them and the evidence advanced in their support.

Conclusion

The research reported here reaffirms the importance of the distributed expertise (Edwards 2010) that student-teachers encounter in school/university partnerships. Student-teachers are engaged in a multi-layered social situation of development within the specific social and cultural contexts of both their placement schools and their university environment. From a sociocultural theoretical perspective, the findings reported here suggest that if ITE programmes are to engage meaningfully with wider issues of social justice, then more attention needs to be paid within such programmes to the conflicting object motives of professional tutors, beginning teachers and mentors and to the mediating role of individual, social and institutional histories and experiences. The findings also confirm that in areas of educational complexity, such as working with pupils living in poverty, contextualised intervention may be needed to disrupt previously held professional assumptions and positions.

The flexibility of the project and its phased introduction, carefully negotiated with the professional tutors, were essential in encouraging the schools to permit the student-teachers to adopt a research orientation: an orientation that prompted them to engage with young people's lived experiences and made it possible to articulate critiques of existing practice. The status of the investigation was also crucial in convincing the student-teachers of its value, prompting them to invest seriously in the work. It was in those schools where the student-teachers believed that the project was of genuine value to the staff and senior leadership that they claimed to have learned most from it themselves, while it may seem counter-intuitive for schools to entrust learning about a new and important initiative to the most junior members of the profession, investing that responsibility in beginners and demonstrating a commitment to their own continued professional learning by listening to the 'expert' knowledge that those beginners then develop serves as a powerful tool for professional learning for all those involved.

Disclosure statement

No potential conflict of interest was reported by the authors.

References

Borko, H. 2004. "Professional Development and Teacher Learning: Mapping the Terrain." *Educational Researcher* 33 (8): 3–15.

Buras, K. L. 2014. "There Really is a Culture of Poverty: Notes on Black Working-class Struggles for Equity and Education." In *The Poverty and Education Reader: A Call for Equity in Many Voices*, edited by P. C. Gorski and J. Landsman, 60–75. Sterling, VA: Stylus Publishing LLC.

Carpenter, H., I. Papps, J. Bragg, A. Dyson, D. Harris, K. Kerr, L. Todd, and K. Laing. 2013. *Evaluation of Pupil Premium: Research Report*. Department for Education. http://dera.ioe.ac.uk/18010/1/DFE-RR282.pdf.

Cochran-Smith, M. 2004. *Walking the Road – Race, Diversity and Social Justice in Teacher Education*. New York: Teachers' College Press.

Darling-Hammond, L., and J. Bransford, eds. 2007. *Preparing Teachers for a Changing World: What Teachers Should Learn and Be Able to Do*. New York: Wiley.

DFE (Department for Education). 2011. *Training Our Next Generation of Outstanding Teachers*. London: DFE. Accessed September 15, 2015. https://www.gov.uk/government/publications/training-our-next-generation-of-outstanding-teachers-implementation-plan

DFE (Department for Education). 2014 *Pupil Premium 2014–2015 Conditions of Grant*. Accessed September 15, 2015. https://www.gov.uk/government/uploads/system/uploads/attachment_data/file/283193/Pupil_Premium_CoG_2014-15.pdf

DFE (Department for Education). 2015. *Policy Paper: 2010 to 2015 Government Policy: Education of Disadvantaged Children* (First published 2013, updated 8 May 2015). Accessed September 15, 2015. https://www.gov.uk/government/publications/2010-to-2015-government-policy-education-of-disadvantaged-children/

Dudley-Marling, C., and K. Lucas. 2009. "Pathologizing the Language and Culture of Poor Children." *Language Arts* 86 (5): 362–370.

ESRC (Economic and Social Research Council). 2011. Child Poverty Casts a Long Shadow over Social Mobility. *ESRC Evidence Briefing*. Accessed September 15, 2015. http://www.esrc.ac.uk/files/publications/evidence-briefings/child-poverty-casts-a-long-shadow-over-social-mobility-pdf/

Edwards, A. 2010. *Being an Expert Professional Practitioner: The Relational Turn in Expertise*. Dordrecht: Springer.

Feiman-Nemser, S. 2001. "From Preparation to Practice: Designing a Continuum to Strengthen and Sustain Teaching." *Teachers College Record* 103 (6): 1013–1055.

Fuller, A., H. Hodkinson, P. Hodkinson, and L. Unwin. 2005. "Learning as Peripheral Participation in Communities of Practice: A Reassessment of Key Concepts in Workplace Learning." *British Educational Research Journal* 31 (1): 49–68.

Gorski, P. C. 2012. "Perceiving the Problem of Poverty and Schooling: Deconstructing the Class Stereotypes That Mis-shape Education Practice and Policy." *Equity & Excellence in Education* 45 (2): 302–319.

Gorski, P. C., and J. Landsman, eds. 2014. *The Poverty and Education Reader: A Call for Equity in Many Voices*. Sterling, VI: Stylus Publishing LLC.

Grossman, P., and M. McDonald. 2008. "Back to the Future: Directions for Research in Teaching and Teacher Education." *American Educational Research Journal* 45 (1): 184–205.

Hagger, H., K. Burn, T. Mutton, and S. Brindley. 2008. "Practice Makes Perfect? Learning to Learn as a Teacher." *Oxford Review of Education* 34 (2): 159–178.

Hammerness, K., L. Darling-Hammond, J. Bransford, D. Berliner, M. Cochran-Smith, M. McDonald, and K. Zeichner. 2005. "How Teachers Learn and Develop." In *Preparing Teachers for a Changing World: What Teachers Should Learn and Be Able to Do*, edited by L. Darling-Hammond and J. Bransford, 358–389. San Francisco, CA: Jossey-Bass.

Higgins, S., M. Katsipataki, D. Kokotsaki, R. Coleman, L. E. Major, and R. Coe. 2014. *The Sutton Trust-education Endowment Foundation Teaching and Learning Toolkit*. London: Education Endowment

Foundation. Accessed September 15, 2015. https://educationendowmentfoundation.org.uk/uploads/toolkit/EEF_Toolkit_-21st_November_2014.pdf

Hills, J., M. Brewer, S. P. Jenkins, R. Lister, R. Lupton, S. Machin, C. Mills, T. Modood, T. Rees, and S. Riddell. 2010. *An Anatomy of Economic Inequality in the UK: Report of the National Equality Panel*. London: Centre for Analysis of Social Exclusion, London School of Economics and Political Science.

Hobson, A., A. Malderez, L. Tracey, and G. Pell. 2006. "Pathways and Stepping Stones: Student Teachers' Preconceptions and Concerns about Initial Teacher Preparation in England." *Scottish Educational Review* 37: 59–78.

Hodkinson, P., and H. Hodkinson. 2004. "The Complexities of Workplace Learning: Problems and Dangers in Trying to Measure Attainment." In *Workplace Learning in Context*, edited by H. Rainbird, A. Fuller and A. Munro, 259–275. London: Routledge.

Horgan, G. 2007. *The Impact of Poverty on Young Children's Experience of School*. York: Joseph Rowntree Foundation.

McIntyre, D. 2005. "Bridging the Gap Between Research and Practice." *Cambridge Journal of Education* 35 (3): 357–382.

McIntyre, D., H. Hagger, and K. Burn. 1994. *The Management of Student Teachers' Learning: A Guide for Professional Tutors in Secondary Schools*. London: Routledge.

Ofsted. 2012. *The Pupil Premium. How Schools Are Using the Pupil Premium Funding to Raise Achievement for Disadvantaged Pupils*. Accessed September 15, 2015. https://www.gov.uk/government/publications/the-pupil-premium-how-schools-used-the-funding

Ofsted. 2013. *The Pupil Premium: How Schools Are Spending the Funding Successfully to Maximise Achievement*. Accessed September 15, 2015. https://www.gov.uk/government/publications/the-pupil-premium-how-schools-are-spending-the-funding-successfully

Ofsted. 2014. *The Pupil Premium: An Update*. Accessed September 15, 2015. https://www.gov.uk/government/publications/the-pupil-premium-an-update

Pajares, M. F. 1992. "Teachers' Beliefs and Educational Research: Cleaning up a Messy Construct." *Review of Educational Research* 62 (3): 307–332.

Payne, R. 2005. *A Framework for Understanding Poverty*. Highland, TX: Aha! Process, Inc.

Raffo, C., A. Dyson, H. Gunter, D. Hall, L. Jones, and A. Kalambouka. 2007. *Education and Poverty: A Critical Review of Theory, Policy and Practice*. York: Joseph Rowntree Foundation.

Rank, M. R., H.-S. Yoon, and T. A. Hirschl. 2003. "American Poverty as a Structural failing: Evidence and Arguments." *Journal of Sociology and Social Welfare* 30 (4): 3–29.

Richardson, V. 1996. "The Role of Attitudes and Beliefs in Learning to Teach." In *Handbook of Research on Teacher Education*, edited by J. Sikula, 102–119. New York: Macmillan.

Thompson, I., J. McNicholl, and I. Menter. 2016. "A Failure to Learn? Student Teachers' Perceptions of Poverty and Educational Achievement." *Oxford Review of Education* 42 (2): 214–229.

Ullucci, K., and T. Howard. 2015. "Pathologizing the Poor: Implications for Preparing Teachers to Work in High-poverty Schools." *Urban Education* 50 (2): 170–193.

Vygotsky, L.S. 1987. "Thinking and Speech." In *Collected Works*, edited by L. S. Vygotsky, Vol. 1, 39–285. New York: Plenum Press.

Wideen, M., J. Mayer-Smith, and B. Moon. 1998. "A Critical Analysis of the Research on Learning to Teach: Making the Case for an Ecological Perspective on Inquiry." *Review of Educational Research* 68 (2): 130–178.

Wilkinson, R., and K. Pickett. 2009. *The Spirit Level: Why Equality is Better for Everyone*. London: Allen Lane.

Younger, M., S. Brindley, D. Pedder, and H. Hagger. 2004. "Starting Points: Student Teachers' Reasons for Becoming Teachers and Their Preconceptions of What This Will Mean." *European Journal of Teacher Education* 27 (3): 245–264.

Zeichner, K. 2009. *Teacher Education and the Struggle for Social Justice*. New York: Routledge.

Rethinking initial teacher education: preparing teachers for schools in low socio-economic communities in New Zealand

Lexie Grudnoff, Mavis Haigh, Mary Hill, Marilyn Cochran-Smith, Fiona Ell and Larry Ludlow

ABSTRACT
Differential student achievement has particular significance in New Zealand as it has one of the largest gaps between high and low achievers among all OECD countries. Students from low socio-economic status (SES) communities, who are often Māori and Pasifika, are heavily over-represented in the low achieving group, while students from wealthier communities, mainly European and Asian, are over-represented in the high achieving group. This article reports a predominately qualitative study, which investigated student teacher perceptions of how their programme, specifically designed to put equity front and centre, prepared them for teaching in low SES communities. Overall, the findings indicated that the student teachers perceived their programme did prepare them to work in such contexts. However, the study also highlighted ways in which the programme could be strengthened, including the need for a more direct focus on the effects of poverty on children's learning, and the implications of this for teaching.

Introduction

Over the last two decades many countries have grappled with the persistent problem of differential achievement between groups of students related to ethnicity, gender, language, and culture. More recently, poverty has entered the discourse around educational underachievement accompanied by concerns for the lifelong consequences of growing up poor (UNICEF Innocenti Research Centre 2012). Hence, greater policy attention is being paid to addressing increasing disparities in educational opportunities and outcomes for students from high- and low-income families (Hills et al. 2010). The international policy discourse highlights improving teacher quality, including the quality of teacher preparation, as being key to addressing these increasing disparities (OECD 2016).

Researchers in a number of countries have also grappled with how to address the problem of inequitable outcomes for disadvantaged learners in terms of teaching and teacher education. In the USA, for example, some scholars have focused their work on social justice issues (e.g. Cochran-Smith 2010), while others have specifically addressed issues related to race and racism (e.g. Milner and Self 2014) and preparing teachers for high poverty schools in urban areas (e.g. Anderson and Stillman 2013). In the UK and Australia specific attention is being paid to preparing teachers to work with children who live in poverty (e.g. Burnett and Lampert 2015; McIntyre and Thomson 2015) and in Australia an additional focus has been on teaching indigenous Aboriginal populations (e.g. Munns, Martin, and Craven 2008).

The co-authors of this article are members of Project Rethinking Initial Teacher Education for Equity (RITE), a six-member, two-country research team comprising researchers at the University of Auckland in New Zealand and Boston College in the United States. We are also grappling with how to address the problem of inequitable outcomes for disadvantaged learners. As members of Project RITE our work over time has been based on two main assumptions. First, that the goal of initial teacher education (ITE), as a values-oriented enterprise, is to prepare teachers who challenge inequities by enacting practice that promotes all students' learning, defined broadly to include academic achievement as well as social, emotional and critical learning. Second, learning, teaching, and learning to teach are complex processes. This assumes that a complex approach to teacher education not only takes account of what student teachers know and can do, but also attends to the complex and multi-layered contexts, school and policy environments in which student teachers learn to teach, and the larger structures of advantage and disadvantage that intersect with these (Anderson and Stillman 2013; Cochran-Smith et al. 2016).

This article reports an exploratory study, which examines student teacher perceptions of how their postgraduate ITE programme (Master of Teaching, Primary: [MTchg]) prepared them to work in primary schools located in low socio-economic status (SES) communities. In the following sections we provide an overview of the New Zealand context, describe the conceptual underpinnings and key features of the MTchg designed to place 'equity front and centre' (Nieto 2000, 180) of ITE and, following our methods and findings, conclude with a discussion and considerations for programme refinement and further research.

The New Zealand context

New Zealand education policy documents are explicit in their expectation that all teachers have an obligation to ensure that the diverse range of New Zealand students are successful learners. For example, the New Zealand Registered Teacher Criteria (New Zealand Teachers Council 2010) states that an effective teacher in New Zealand, across the career stages, has a responsibility to advance the social, emotional and cognitive growth of all learners. Given New Zealand's status as a bicultural nation, founded on the partnership established between Māori and the Crown by the Treaty of Waitangi in 1840, it is not surprising that policy documents also assume that teachers need to be culturally competent and responsive. The need for teachers to have knowledge, understanding and skills to teach students with different needs and backgrounds is reinforced by the increasingly diverse nature of New Zealand's population in terms of ethnic, religious and linguistic make-up. The 2013 Census data show that over 25% of New Zealanders were born overseas while Auckland, where the MTchg is located, is the most diverse city with approximately 40% of its population born overseas, mainly from the UK, the Pacific Islands (the Cook Islands, Niue, Tonga and Samoa) and from Asia, particularly China, India and Korea. Auckland has the largest Pasifika population (those of Pacific Island descent) in the world, with many Pasifika living in poorer communities.

International educational comparisons reveal a significant achievement gap in New Zealand: while students appear to do well overall, aggregate results mask one of the largest gaps between high and low achieving students among OECD countries (OECD 2011). The data reveal that students who are Māori (New Zealand's indigenous population) and Pacific Island, often from poor communities, are over-represented in the low achieving group, while Pākeha (NZ European) and Asian students, often from wealthier communities, are over-represented in the high achieving group (Snook and O'Neill 2014). For many years New Zealand policy initiatives have been aimed at addressing Māori and Pasifika students' inequitable educational outcome. However, it is only fairly recently that the word 'poverty' has figured prominently in the discourse around differential achievement. While it has long been recognised that Māori and Pacific ethnic groups have poverty rates that are around double those of the European/Pākeha ethnic group (Perry 2013), the policy discourse is starting to acknowledge the strong link between parents' SES and a child's educational outcomes.

New Zealand researchers such as Carpenter and Osborne (2014) claim that compulsory schooling has a significant role to play in addressing education's outcome inequalities. Wylie (2013) further asserts that inequality and poverty are among the greatest challenges for New Zealand's education system where, for example, schools in poor communities face greater challenges in attracting and retaining teachers compared to schools in wealthy areas that can select from a larger pool of applicants and have lower staff turnover. Wylie suggests that this problem is exacerbated by New Zealand's self-managing schools environment. Since it is the responsibility of each school to find and employ teachers there is no systemic mechanism to ensure that low SES schools recruit and retain teachers with the knowledge, skills and attitudes needed to enhance disadvantaged students' learning outcomes and opportunities.

New Zealand's policy direction is aligned with the international reform discourse that identifies educational underachievement as a problem of teacher quality. The assumption is that if the quality of teaching is improved then student achievement gains will follow and New Zealand will become a high achievement *and* high equity nation. Improving the quality of ITE is therefore a key policy strategy for improving teacher quality in order to lift educational achievement (New Zealand Government 2010). Thus, in 2013, the Ministry of Education initiated a competitive tendering process for 'exemplary post-graduate ITE programmes' (New Zealand Ministry of Education 2013) aimed at lifting the quality of graduating teachers' practice in order to raise the achievement of priority learners (i.e. Māori and Pasifika students and those from low socio-economic communities). The aim was to incentivise providers through the provision of additional funding to develop new approaches to ITE. Programmes were to be more intellectually demanding (i.e. used higher entrance criteria and resulted in a postgraduate degree), more practice-focused (i.e. they involved rich partnerships with schools and more time on practicum), and increase beginning teachers' expertise in working with priority learners.

The University of Auckland's proposal for a Master of Teaching Primary was one of two programmes contracted in the first round of the highly competitive tendering process. This process provided an opportunity for the University to design a new programme that put equity at the centre of ITE. The programme was informed by the work of Project RITE, in particular the development of the *facets of practice for equity* as outlined in the following section.

Putting equity at the centre of ITE

We construe equity as related not only to concepts of equality but also to concepts of fairness and justice. As such, equity within educational systems encompasses notions consistent with distributive justice (Fraser and Honneth 2003), for example equal access to resources such as good teachers, *and* recognises and challenges society's systemic inequalities, coherent with the notion of justice as recognition (Honneth 2003). Putting equity at the centre of ITE means preparing teachers who have the knowledge, skills and dispositions to enhance the learning of students historically disadvantaged by the system, including those from lower socio-economic groups, *and* are able to challenge the systems that reproduce inequity. In this section, we exemplify one aspect of what we mean by putting equity at the centre of ITE by describing the concept of *facets of practice for equity* developed by the Project RITE team. These facets became the centrepiece of the University of Auckland's MTchg programme.

Facets of practice for equity

To identify teaching practices that have a positive effect on disadvantaged and other learners, the Project RITE team searched for programmes of empirical research that linked teaching practice to broadly defined student learning outcomes, and took a complex view of learning and teaching. Because Project RITE includes researchers from New Zealand and the United States, we were particularly interested in drawing on research from these two countries. However, we also intentionally considered research syntheses or large programmes of empirical research undertaken in a range of other countries and that were different from one another in purpose, scope and format. We engaged in a process of systematic review to see whether, despite differences in political and policy contexts, we could find similarities that could inform our work as researchers and teacher educators who were concerned about equity-centred teacher education (Grudnoff et al. 2015). We ultimately identified five key sources of research evidence from different international jurisdictions, each of which had been originally compiled for a different purpose: three 'Best Evidence Syntheses' (BES) conducted by New Zealand researchers using international research (Alton-Lee 2003; Anthony and Walshaw 2007; Aitken and Sinnema 2008); the 'Teaching and Learning Research Programme' (TLRP) carried out over more than a decade in the UK (James and Pollard 2011); and the 'Measures of Effective Teaching' project in the USA (MET Project 2013). All of these large-scale programmes of research or syntheses met the criteria we had set: student outcomes were broadly conceived; teaching and learning was viewed as complex and non-linear; empirical evidence used to substantiate the practices could be traced; and, they provided evidence that the identified practices had a positive influence on diverse learners, including those in low SES communities.

Using directed qualitative content analysis procedures (Hsieh and Shannon 2005) and iterative 'cross-case comparison' (Wong et al. 2012, 93) we identified themes and interconnections among the practices within and across the five reviews listed above. We searched for similarities and differences in terms of key ideas about teaching practice that made a positive difference to all learners. We found that, despite the different origins and purposes of the above syntheses, we could identify strikingly similar themes across them that were consistently associated with positive student outcomes, broadly defined. Based on these identified commonalities, we developed the concept of *facets of practice for equity* initially including: (1) selecting worthwhile content and designing and implementing learning opportunities aligned to valued learning outcomes; (2) connecting to students' lives and experiences; (3) creating learning-focused, respectful and supportive learning environments; (4) using evidence to scaffold learning and improve teaching; (5) and, adopting an inquiry stance and taking responsibility for professional engagement and learning. As we noted earlier, BES, TLRP and MET were all motivated by a desire to address inequitable outcomes for diverse students within their own contexts but did not specifically focus on practices shown to enhance educational outcomes for socio-economically historically disadvantaged students. We therefore examined two additional frameworks: the 'Te Kotahitanga Effective Teaching Profile,' intended to improve outcomes for Māori students in New Zealand (Bishop, Berryman, and Wearmouth 2014); and, the work of the Centre for Research on Education, Diversity and Excellence (CREDE) in the USA, which focused on effective practice for Native Hawaiian and other minority students (Dalton 2007). While both Te Kotahitanga and CREDE were smaller in scale than our main data sources, the key ideas from both aligned with the facets of practice we had distilled from BES, TLRP and MET. Additionally, and significantly, they strongly emphasised the critical role that teachers play in improving disadvantaged students' opportunities by challenging inequities in terms of their practice. To take account of these additional insights, we added a sixth facet: *Recognising and challenging classroom, school and societal practices that reproduce inequity*.

We have elaborated these *facets of practice for equity* in Grudnoff et al. (2015). The first four facets with their classroom practice focus link directly to notions of equity as equality, that is equity considered from a redistributive perspective. The second, fifth and sixth speak additionally to the moral foundations of teaching and thus more directly link to equity as social justice by taking a recognition perspective. It is important to emphasise, however, that all six interconnected facets are grounded in the overarching assumption that schools and society, including their policy and political environments, are structured by pervasive systems of inequality. At the same time, however, we also hold that teachers, as human agents, have the opportunity and responsibility to enact patterns of practice that generate positive outcomes for disadvantaged learners and to work with others to challenge inequities (Cochran-Smith et al. 2016).

The evidence distilled from the seven selected syntheses/frameworks indicated that the six *facets of practice for equity* are context dependent in relation to classroom and school cultures and relationships with particular students and the resources they bring to school. The six facets are therefore general principles of practice, not specific strategies, behaviours or actions. They should be interpreted and applied in ways that are appropriate to specific contexts, content, and points in time. The facets are also interconnected. Because each facet is in relationship with other facets, it would be difficult to enact one of these practices without enacting many of the others.

An example of an equity-centred ITE programme

In this section we outline key features of the MTchg, a new one-year primary ITE programme, which was intentionally designed to be equity-centred. In line with the Ministry of Education's contractual requirements, the overarching goal is to prepare teachers who engage in practice that promotes equitable outcomes for students from priority learner groups, that is, Māori and Pasifika and those from low socio-economic communities in urban areas. The MTchg however, takes a broader view of student outcomes to include emotional and social as well as academic achievement. The programme also addresses issues to do with inequity and inequality up front, including understanding teachers' roles in challenging the systematic and structural aspects of inequality as well as addressing these issues in their own classrooms. Recognising the challenging nature of these concepts about which many student teachers bring little prior understanding, we designed the programme so that the MTchg students' first collective experience focused on the Māori world view and New Zealand's history of Māori socio-economic and educational disadvantage. The *Te Ao Māori* course (which means 'the Māori world' and addresses the language, practices and spiritual dimensions of Māori) started on the second day of the programme and involved the cohort staying overnight on a *Marae* (a communal place that serves spiritual and social purposes in Maori society) and visiting urban *Marae* to meet with Maori activists, elders and youth to hear their stories and aspirations for Māori learners. During the six-month *Te Ao Māori* course the MTchg students began to learn the Māori language and develop cultural competencies for teaching Māori learners. The student teachers also examined their own cultural locatedness in relation to Māori learners and broader issues of equity and equality.

The MTchg is taught over three semesters in collaboration with 12 Auckland primary schools with very diverse populations in terms of student ethnicity, culture, language and socio-economic status. The student teachers work intensively in two different schools over the programme. In their first six months, a group of four to six student teachers work in a high SES and culturally diverse school for two days a week and undertake a three-week full-time practicum in the same school. In the final six months of the programme, a different mix of four to six student teachers are deliberately placed in a low SES school with a high proportion of priority learners. In addition to being in the second school for two days a week, the MTchg students undertake a nine-week full-time practicum in this low SES school, three weeks at the beginning of the school year and a culminating six weeks.

As noted above, the six *facets of practice for equity* form the centrepiece of the MTchg and provide programme coherence. The facets inform the curriculum that the MTchg students experience and underpin how they learn. The new courses in the MTchg were co-constructed by interdisciplinary teams and combine university and school-based teaching and learning in order to help make explicit the links between theory and practice, and to support candidates to teach in ways that promote equitable outcomes for priority learners. The *facets of practice for equity*, which are embodied in the content, teaching and assessment of each course, prompted a move away from the traditional curriculum areas of primary school teaching (and ITE) and the development of courses that combined curriculum in different ways.

The placement of different curriculum areas in juxtaposition to each other was intended to make the *facets of practice for equity* clearer and more relevant to the MTchg students. For example, mathematics and literacy were intentionally integrated and taught by cross-discipline teams in three courses across the programme. The goal was to support student teachers to examine concurrently the two disciplinary areas in which primary school students are often grouped by ability and tested frequently, the outcomes of which primary teachers are most often held accountable. The three courses focus on teaching to promote equity, including questioning the consequences for learners of particular strategies such as ability grouping, which is commonly used for these curriculum areas in New Zealand primary schools.

Making explicit connections between literacy and mathematics teaching and learning and using the facets to question the discourses of ability/lack of ability opened up critical analysis about the adverse consequences of widespread teaching practices on disadvantaged students (Rubie-Davies 2014).

The *facets of practice for equity* also infuse the work in schools and the university. Course lecturers and partner school staff use the facets when designing learning activities and in professional conversations. The facets provide a common language and set of ideas that those involved in the programme, including student teachers, use to explicitly examine and discuss practice and to make changes that could improve outcomes for disadvantaged learners. There is also an explicit focus on modelling the facets. For example, school and university staff work together to create a safe learning environment, which is learning-focused, respectful and supportive. Establishing norms of respect and openness with the MTchg students involves careful leadership and facilitation by staff in both school and university settings, and a focus on supporting student teachers to understand and work productively in environments that are very different from what they are accustomed to.

Adopting an inquiry stance and taking responsibility for professional learning is a *facet of practice for equity* that is explicitly woven through the whole programme. The notion of 'inquiry as stance' (Cochran-Smith and Lytle 2009) shapes the processes by which the MTchg students learn to teach in university and school settings. The inquiry orientation of the programme is made explicit through course titles like *Promoting Learning through Inquiry: Understanding our Communities*, which includes the curriculum areas of social studies and health/physical education. The inquiry focus culminates in a teacher inquiry research project that MTchg students undertake during their final six-week practicum in a low SES school. They develop their focus for inquiry through their combined work in the university and schools. For example, in the three mathematics and literacy courses the MTchg students draw on teacher mentor feedback, reflections on their own teaching, student observations, and evidence of student learning to identify the focus for their inquiry. They justify this focus in terms of their students' learning requirements, their own strengths and needs as teachers, relevant research literature, and in relation to the *facets of practice for equity*. As a capstone activity, the student teachers show how their understandings and enactment of practice for equity has changed in response to evidence of students' learning through their inquiry project. Teachers in the partner schools work with the student teachers on their inquiries, and in many cases co-inquire into learning with the MTchg students. In this way inquiry as stance serves to integrate further the university and in-school experiences of the MTchg students.

In summary, the *facets of practice for equity* underpin the MTchg curriculum and the notion of inquiry informs the ways in which student teachers learn to teach at the university and in partner schools. Explicitly addressed in all ten courses and in school and university settings, the facets and inquiry approach became part of a shared language between MTchg students, course lecturers and partner school staff.

Method

The research question posed for this exploratory study is *What are MTchg student teachers' perceptions of how their programme prepared them for teaching in schools in low SES communities?* We have prioritised student teacher voice in this study to take account of critiques of

ITE research that do not pay sufficient attention to student teacher perspective when investigating ITE programmes (Korthagen, Loughran, and Russell 2006). To answer the research question we accessed two main sources of data: (i) programme exit survey data and (ii) assignment material.

Twenty-five student teachers completed the first iteration of the MTchg programme. All submitted the two assignments we analysed and 12 answered the programme exit survey. The demographics were broadly similar across the group of 25 and the group of 12. For both groups the majority of respondents were female; the median age group was 21–25; and English was the first language for most.

The survey measured perceptions of graduating student teachers' preparedness to teach. It was developed by the Teacher Education Forum of Aotearoa New Zealand (TEFANZ) (Grudnoff et al. 2013) for use by TEFANZ members to gather information about their ITE programmes. The items were designed generically to apply across programmes, that is, the survey items are not programme specific. However, the MTchg students who responded to this exit survey were asked to answer in relation to their perceptions of all aspects of their MTchg experiences. By completing the survey the student teachers provided consent for the anonymised data to be used for research purposes.

We received Ethics Committee approval and participant consent to access all student teacher assignments as data for research purposes. Data from two sets of assignments were used for this exploratory study: the teacher inquiry milestone reports and the post-practicum reflections. As per ethics requirements these had been anonymised. As part of the milestone reports the student teachers were asked to comment on their understandings about learners developed through doing their teacher inquiry research in a low SES school; questions, issues or concerns that had been raised through engagement in this inquiry; and what new understandings and/or insights had they developed about the *facets of practice for equity* from undertaking this inquiry. The post-practicum reflection required the students to reflect on their six-week practicum in a low SES school that occurred during the final semester of their ITE programme. The student teachers typically wrote 2–3 A4 pages of reflection.

Two members of the research team individually analysed the milestone reports and practicum reflections thematically (Braun and Clarke 2006). These two analyses were then compared and six strong themes were identified across both sets of data. The survey data were analysed using simple descriptive statistics, and the findings considered against the themes identified from the qualitative data. First we report on the findings from the qualitative data using examples from the student teachers' reflective statements, and then consider the findings from the survey.

Findings

Qualitative data

The six key themes identified from both the student teacher inquiry milestone reports and their reflections following a practicum in a low SES school were: (1) Knowing learners as individuals; (2) Building relationships and reciprocity; (3) Setting high expectations across broad learning domains; (4) Challenging assumptions and stereotypes; (5) Taking an inquiry stance; and (6) Using facets of practice as a philosophical and practice frame. Four of these six key themes relate to student teachers' engagement with the individuals in their class

(*Knowing learners as individuals; Building relationships, reciprocity; Setting high expectations across broad learning domains and Challenging assumptions and stereotypes*). Two of the six key themes arise from, or relate to directly to, programme philosophy, structure and practice (*Taking an inquiry stance;* and *Using facets of practice as a philosophical and practice frame*).

Considering first the four key themes associated with engagement with school students, these arose directly from the deliberate practicum placement in low SES school. As described earlier, the MTchg students' placement in low SES school for the final six months of the programme provided many opportunities for them to thoroughly get to know the individuals in their class. This is revealed in their post-practicum reflections where there were more references to the importance of *Knowing learners as individuals* than any other of the identified key themes. Included in this key theme were notions of knowing the students' interests and contexts, consideration of who is a priority learner, recognition of diverse cultures, accommodating special needs students and the need to build inclusive classroom communities. Comments from half of the MTchg students suggest that they believed knowing their students strongly influenced their students' learning, for example:

> Connecting with students' lives and experiences has been one of the most important aspects within my teaching. Understanding who the students are, where they come from physically, emotionally and mentally has been integral in creating trust and engagement in learning. (Post-practicum reflection – S13)

All but four of the MTchg students had begun to understand the complexity of the factors influencing a student's approach to learning across academic and other outcomes:

> I have come to recognise just how complex and influential outside factors can be on a child's ability to learn. This all impacts on the academic development of the child, but more importantly, it impacts on their physical, emotional and social development. (Post-practicum reflection – S02)

All had realised how unique each learner was and thus the need to capture the learner's interest through identifying contexts for learning that were significant for the learner:

> Each child learns in their own unique way that needs to be identified and catered to in order for them to achieve to the best of their abilities. I find students are more engaged in learning when the content is relevant to their interests, lives and experiences. (Post-practicum reflection – S07)

Linked to the first theme of *knowing learners as individuals,* is the second theme of *building relationships and reciprocity.* Included within this are ideas related to making connections with the community, with parents, and two-way sharing of information between teachers and students. All the MTchg students commented on the importance of building relationships with the children, for example:

> Relationships are one of the most significant factors in teaching and learning, without [positive] relationships with the students they would not feel comfortable enough to take risks in class. (Post-practicum reflection – S06)

They understood that for children to learn well they needed to be assured that their teachers had a genuine interest in their well-being and achievement and believed that 'building positive relationships founded in trust and respect was most important' (Post-practicum reflection – S06) as this was facilitated by teachers 'showing genuine interest in each child so that they were aware that we cared for them and their learning' (Post-practicum reflection – S06).

The value of reciprocally sharing aspects of themselves with their students to facilitate building relationships was also identified, for example:

> All of the relationships that I built with students were as genuine as I could make them. I endeavoured to share real-life stories about my heritage, my family ... sharing these experiences opened me up as a person to the students and, in return, many of them opened up to me about their lives and stories. (Post-practicum reflection – S24)

Building relationships with the parents was also perceived as important with one student teacher commenting 'it was also important to build relationships with parents so that they felt comfortable discussing their child's learning' (Post-practicum reflection – S13).

With regard to theme 3, a third of the student teachers mentioned the importance of setting high expectations and building an environment where success is expected. The MTcgh students saw *setting high expectations for the students across broad learning domains* as being significant in enhancing student learning 'regardless of their level of achievement, socioeconomic status, ethnicity or gender' (Post-practicum reflection – S19). They believed, for example:

> It is essential to maintain high and realistic expectations of all students in the classroom, to offer continuing support and positive praise for their efforts and to provide a range of rich and meaningful learning experiences that draw on a variety of skills in different contexts. (Post-practicum reflection – S03)

Working with children who had different cultural backgrounds from themselves enabled the MTcgh students to reconsider and broaden their own understanding of learning and success:

> I have come to realise that learning does not happen in a one way, western-world view of learning. Challenging students to excel is the key because regardless of where they come from or what background education they have, all children learn through motivation, challenge and excitement. (Post-practicum reflection – S12)

The deliberate placement of MTchg students in low SES schools also *challenged their assumptions and stereotypes* (theme 4) around the provision of education for school students in low SES schools. Half of the student teachers specifically commented on this, for example:

> I assumed that maybe being at a low SES school, learners might not have access to rich resources and therefore be disadvantaged in learning – however, I learnt very quickly that this was not the case. (Post-practicum reflection – S09)

The MTchg students learned to aim high for all students regardless of their home and community background and to accept the responsibility for capturing and releasing students' potential. They believed that 'students are always capable of great things and within every student there is a key to help them learn, it is the teacher's job to find this' (Post-practicum reflection – S17).

We now discuss the two key themes that relate more directly to the intentional design of the MTchg programme. First, theme 5, *taking an inquiry stance*, a key feature of the MTchg, was recognised by all of the student teachers as being critical to both their development as teachers and to their continuing professional practice, for example:

> Teaching as inquiry is crucial to my future teaching and learning, as it will ensure that I continue to develop my own teaching practice to remain in tune with the fast changing pace of how children are learning and adapting to the world. (Post-practicum reflection – S02)

Inquiry as stance was viewed as being of importance for testing and challenging their own preconceptions in the interest of enhancing student learning and the role that teacher inquiry could play in this:

> As a teacher and a human being, it is a given that I come with my own pre-conceived ideas. I now know the value of 'constant teacher inquiry', to help challenge these ideas. As a teacher I am a life-long learner, meaning I need to constantly inquire, adjust and improve my practices to meet the various learning needs of the priority students [I am working with]. (Post-practicum reflection – S22)

As noted above, the MTchg students' conducted a teacher inquiry research project alongside their mentor teachers during their final six-week block practicum. Many of the student teachers commented on the value of this, with one stating that:

> Through completing an inquiry I learned the value of bringing an outside critical eye to looking at my class for the purpose of improving my practice and therefore learning outcomes for the children. I plan to find a critical friend once I start teaching my own class and engage in a similar form of teacher inquiry. (Post-practicum reflection – S10)

Finally we address the sixth theme, *using the facets of practice as a philosophical and practice frame*. The facets of practice, around which their programme had been built, appeared to be very influential in their learning, and a third used these to structure their post-practicum reflection. Three of the six themes identified above are embodiments of three of the facets (knowing students, building relationships and taking an inquiry stance). The deliberate framing of all aspects of the programme around the *facets of practice for equity* appeared to open the MTchg students' minds to the value of using these as a philosophical and practice frame. As one noted:

> I realise now that the facets of practice are fundamental principles that should be embraced by all teachers. Not only does teacher inquiry combined with the facets promote best practice to challenge inequities, they place a focus on the teacher rather than students. They make us accountable for student learning. They make us step back and look at our teaching pedagogy. They make us teachers as inquirers. (Post-practicum reflection – S10)

Those students who used the *facets of practice for equity* to frame their reflections indicated that three facets presented the most challenge. These were:

- identifying outcomes as valued (facet 1):

  > I have struggled with what valued outcomes really mean. I have come to understand that it is important to balance national standards with everyday struggles the children are dealing with. This is something I need to think about on a day-to-day basis and individual case. (Post-practicum reflection – S09)

- using evidence (facet 4):

  > I always considered this one of my weaker areas – however, I feel this has improved. I can now utilize assessment data to select a group and use informal assessment to create steps moving forward in each session. This is a really important part of my practice, which needs to be developed further. (Post-practicum reflection – S05)

- challenging inequities (facet 6)

Having sufficient agency to challenge perceived inequities seemed to be difficult for these student teachers, especially when they observed practice contrary to what they believed to be good practice. The student teacher quoted below did not report taking any action following the situation she describes:

> There were times when some decisions made by a teacher involved deficit thinking that I did not agree with whole heartedly, to the point where I could feel my whole body heating up and I had to take deep breaths to control my wanting to react. (Post-practicum reflection – S18)

Table 1. MTchg student perceptions of opportunity provided during practicum and other in-school experiences.

Item	Mean score	Link with qualitative theme
Teaching learners from different cultural backgrounds	5.0	Knowing learners as individuals
Reflecting on your practice with mentor teachers in ways that supported your professional learning	4.75	Taking an inquiry stance
Planning and developing authentic learning experiences based on learner's interests and abilities	4.67	Knowing learners as individuals
Teaching Pasifika learners in culturally responsive ways	4.33	Knowing learners as individuals; building relationships
Determining ways to meet individual learner needs	4.25	Knowing learners as individuals; setting high expectations
Using Te Reo (Māori language) in teaching and learning	3.92	Knowing learners as individuals; building relationships
Teaching Māori learners in culturally responsive ways	3.5	Knowing learners as individuals; building relationships

Survey data

The exit survey also enabled us to access the MTchg students' views of how the design of the programme had enabled their learning to teach students from low socio-economic communities. The exit survey responses suggest that the design of the MTchg, which required student teachers to work intensively and over lengthy periods in two schools (one high and one low SES), was influential in the learning of these student teachers. The respondents were asked to indicate their level of opportunity to engage with, or do, a range of things during the placement, using a positively skewed six-point scale (from 1 = none/negligible to 6 = extreme). The mean level of opportunity across the 25 items in this question ranged from 5.00 (a lot) to 2.67 (some). We show in Table 1 those items that most closely align with the principles and aims of the MTchg and their link with the qualitative themes identified earlier in Section 6.1. However, we note that despite the programme focus on working successfully with Māori learners, the mean scores for related items were among the lowest recorded.

The 12 students completing the exit survey also indicated that they felt 'highly confident' to begin their teaching (on a six-point scale their mean was 4.01 with a standard deviation of .701). When asked to indicate what features of the MTchg had contributed to this confidence level, the respondents reported that, most strongly, it was the way course based work and practicum reinforced and supported each other.

Discussion

This article reported MTchg student teachers' perceptions of how their programme prepared them to work in low SES primary schools. Notwithstanding the limitations of this exploratory study, including a reliance on 'perception data' and small numbers of participants, the findings indicate that the programme, which was designed to put equity 'front and centre' (Nieto 2000), provided the student teachers with knowledge and skills that enabled them to support the learning of students from low SES communities. The study suggests that the intentional placement of MTchg students in schools in poor communities was critical to the student teachers' enactment of the key elements of the programme: the *facets of practice for equity and inquiry*.

The findings show that the facets, which infused course content and assessments across all settings, were utilised by the student teachers in their extended placement in low SES schools. The facets were evident in the data both as drivers for practice and through being recognised by the student teachers as crucial organising principles for their teaching. The most utilised facets related to knowing and building relationships with the learners in their class. These interconnected facets were evident in both the qualitative and survey data. However, the low mean scores in the survey data relating to Maori learners point to the need for the programme to pay more attention to this important aspect of teaching in New Zealand. As Powell and Kusuma-Powell (2011) argue, knowing one's students is often difficult and challenging as it involves understanding the unique sets of background experiences and learning preferences that children bring to the classroom. While getting to know students is fundamental to building professional relationships to enhance educative engagement (Margonis 2004), knowing learners and building relationships becomes particularly challenging when teachers are very different from their students in terms of their lived experiences (Bishop, Berryman, and Wearmouth 2014).

This was the case for the MTchg students as they were predominately Pākeha with limited previous connection with low SES communities, which is a reality of ITE internationally (Sleeter 2001). Through working with children who had different backgrounds from themselves it appeared that the MTchg students were able to reconsider their own assumptions about the diverse learning capabilities and potential of the individual children they taught. As Gorski (2012) argues, teachers need to recognise that diversity exists among low-income groups and that such learners must be academically challenged. This study suggests that seeing learners as individuals had enabled the student teachers to set realistic, yet high, academic expectations for them (Rubie-Davies 2014).

The findings also reveal that some facets were more evident than others. The facets reported on least frequently were *selecting worthwhile content* (facet 1), *using evidence* (facet 4) and *challenging inequities* (facet 6). Furthermore, when reported they were identified as being problematic. One explanation for this may be that the student teachers had, unsurprisingly, not yet developed a strong experiential base from which to draw, which as Hagger et al. (2008) argue points to the importance of ITE programmes providing a strong foundation to support teachers' continued professional learning and development. Nevertheless, given the goal of the MTchg we need to investigate further why these facets do not appear to be utilised/connected with as frequently as other facets and why the student teachers appeared to find them particularly challenging.

The MTchg was designed to provide opportunities for student teachers to consider their beliefs and understandings about priority learners in both university and school settings. The study suggests that the MTchg students did examine their attitudes, beliefs and assumptions and modified their perceptions of low SES schools and their students. A number of researchers have argued that popular stereotypes of people living in poor communities can result in deficit thinking whereby disadvantaged students and their families are blamed for their perceived underachievement, rather than structural inequalities in the education system (e.g. Rank, Yoon, and Hirschl 2003). While the MTchg students did not engage in blaming the children or their parents, they did not make any significant reference to recognising and challenging classroom, school and societal practices that reproduce inequity, the focus of Facet 6. This seeming failure to recognise and take agency to challenge inequity needs further exploration and attention in the programme.

While the findings overall suggest that the MTchg prepared the student teachers to work productively with priority learners they also indicate that more programme emphasis needs to be given to socio-economic influences on underachievement. This must be done with care, however, as there is a tension between believing that teachers have a responsibility to challenge inequities in their classrooms, schools and wider society, and recognising that teachers and schools cannot by themselves mitigate the impact of historical societal inequities (Snook and O'Neill 2014). Teacher preparation programmes should support student teachers to be clear about the challenges that children living in poverty face, while at the same time not making them feel helpless in the face of such challenges. One concern is that graduates may become overwhelmed by the prevailing discourse that blames inequitable student outcomes mainly on schools and teachers and eventually leave teaching, which is problematic given the challenges of recruiting and retaining effective teachers for schools in low SES communities (Wylie 2013).

Although the student teachers recognised inequities they did not challenge deficit thinking of others, resulting in a limited application of Facet 6. Power relationships may be one reason for recognising but not challenging inequities arising from other teachers' deficit thinking. Although the schools working in the MTchg have collaborative and inclusive professional cultures, it would be unrealistic to expect that the student teachers did not experience issues to do with power and status. For example, Groundwater-Smith, Ewing, and Le Cornu (2015) discuss how student teachers can be caught up in micro-politics of the school related to competing demands and affiliations. Indeed, Kelchtermans and Ballet (2002) have long argued that because micro-politics are pervasive in schools, explicit attention should be given to the politics of schools in ITE programmes. This aspect of learning to teach needs further attention in the MTchg.

Another key element of the MTcgh was the focus on teacher inquiry. The findings indicated that the student teachers had adopted an inquiry stance (Cochran-Smith and Lytle 2009) that had guided and arguably improved their practice. It will be interesting, as we follow them into their teaching careers, to see if they continue to use inquiry to further their professional learning. The data also indicated that the teacher inquiry research project the MTchg student teachers carried out was important in their development as teachers in low SES schools. Equipping teachers with the skills necessary to conduct their own research has been identified as being important by Burn and Mutton (2015) as this enables them to adopt a research-orientation towards their own practice. In line with Tatto and Furlong (2015) we believe that a coherent inquiry-based approach to preparing teachers can provide the glue that feeds and binds an ITE programme.

Conclusion

In New Zealand, as in other countries, schools in poor communities are challenged to attract and retain teachers who have the knowledge, skills and dispositions to promote the learning of disadvantaged learners. This exploratory study investigated the first iteration of an ITE programme specifically designed to more effectively prepare teachers for working with priority learners in low SES schools (Cochran-Smith et al. 2016). We will continue to examine the alignment between the aims of the MTchg and student teachers' enactment of these aims in order to strengthen the programme. In particular, we need to more directly address the effects of material poverty on children's learning, and the implications of this for teaching.

We intend to follow MTchg graduates into full-time teaching to examine whether and to what extent the programme has influenced their long-terms beliefs and practice as a teacher. Thus, the MTchg will continue to be a strategic research site for studying equity-centred ITE to advance Project RITE's overall aim of building theory about how, why, to what extent, and under what conditions student teachers learn to enact practice for equity.

Disclosure statement

No potential conflict of interest was reported by the authors.

ORCID

Mary Hill ⓘ http://orcid.org/0000-0001-9552-8112

References

Aitken, G., and C. Sinnema. 2008. *Effective Pedagogy in Social Sciences/tikanga a iwi*. Wellington: Ministry of Education.
Alton-Lee, A. 2003. *Quality Teaching for Diverse Students in Schooling: Best Evidence Synthesis*. Wellington: Ministry of Education.
Anderson, L., and J. Stillman. 2013. "Student Teaching's Contribution to Preservice Teacher Development: A Review of Research Focused on the Preparation of Teachers for Urban and High-needs Contexts." *Review of Educational Research*. 83 (1): 3–69.
Anthony, G., and M. Walshaw. 2007. *Effective Pedagogy in Mathematics/pangarau*. Wellington: Ministry of Education.
Bishop, R., M. Berryman, and J. Wearmouth. 2014. *Te Kotahitanga: Towards Effective Education Reform for Indigenous and Other Minority Students*. Wellington: New Zealand Council on Education Research Press.
Braun, V., and V. Clarke. 2006. "Using Thematic Analysis in Psychology." *Qualitative Research in Psychology* 3 (2): 77–101.
Burn, K., and T. Mutton. 2015. "A Review of 'Research-informed Clinical Practice' in Initial Teacher Education." *Oxford Review of Education* 41 (2): 217–233.
Burnett, B., and J. Lampert. 2015. "Teacher Education for High-poverty Schools in Australia: The National Exceptional Teachers for Disadvantaged Schools Program." In *Teacher Education for High Poverty Schools*, edited by J. Lampert and B. Burnett, 73–94. New York: Springer Press.
Carpenter, V., and S. Osborne, eds. 2014. *Twelve Thousand Hours: Education and Poverty in Aotearoa New Zealand*. Auckland: Dunmore Publishing.
Cochran-Smith, M. 2010. "Towards a Theory of Teacher Education for Social Justice." In *International Handbook of Education Change*. 2nd ed, edited by M. Fullan, A. Hargreaves, D. Hopkins, and A. Lieberman, 445–467. New York: Springer Press.
Cochran-Smith, M., F. Ell, L. Grudnoff, M. Haigh, M. Hill, and L. Ludlow. 2016. "Initial Teacher Education: What Does It Take to Put Equity at the Center?" *Teaching and Teacher Education*. 57: 67–78.
Cochran-Smith, M., and S. Lytle. 2009. *Inquiry as Stance: Teacher Research for the Next Generation*. New York: Teachers College Press.
Dalton, S. S. 2007. *Five Standards for Effective Teaching: How to Succeed with All Learners*. San Francisco, CA: Wiley.
Fraser, N., and A. Honneth. 2003. *Redistribution or Recognition: A Political-philosophical Debate*. London: Verso.
Gorski, P. 2012. "Perceiving the Problem of Poverty and Schooling: Deconstructing the Class Stereotypes that Mis-Shape Education Practice and Policy." *Equity and Excellence in Education* 45 (2): 302–319.
Groundwater-Smith, S., R. Ewing, and R. Le Cornu. 2015. *Teaching: Challenges and Dilemmas*. 5th ed. Melbourne, Australia: Cengage Learning.

Grudnoff, L., M. Haigh, M. Hill, M. Cochran-Smith, F. Ell, and L. Ludlow. 2015. "Teaching for Equity: Insights from International Evidence." Paper presented at the annual meeting of the American Educational Research Association, Chicago, IL, April 2015.

Grudnoff, L., L. Ward, J. Ritchie, B. Brooker, and M. Simpson. 2013. "A Collaborative Multi Institutional Approach to Evidence Gathering: Graduating Student Teachers' Perceptions of Their Teacher Preparation Programmes." Paper presented at the European Educational Research Association Conference, Istanbul, Turkey, September 2013.

Hagger, H., K. Burn, T. Mutton, and S. Brindley. 2008. "Practice Makes Perfect? Learning to Learn as a Teacher." *Oxford Review of Education* 34 (2): 159–178.

Hills, J., M. Brewer, S. Jenkins, R. Lister, R. Lupton, S. Machin, C. Mills, T. Modood, T. Rees, and S. Riddell. 2010. *An Anatomy of Economic Inequality in the UK: Report of the National Equality Panel*. London: Centre for Analysis of Social Exclusion, London School of Economics and Political Science.

Honneth, A. 2003. "Redistribution as Recognition: A Response to Nancy Fraser." In *Redistribution or Recognition: A Political-philosophical Debate*, edited by N. Fraser and A. Honneth, 110–197. London: Verso.

Hsieh, H.-F., and S. Shannon. 2005. "Three Approaches to Qualitative Content Analysis." *Qualitative Health Research* 15 (9): 1277–1288.

James, M., and A. Pollard. 2011. "TLRP's Ten Principles for Effective Pedagogy: Rationale, Development, Evidence, Argument and Impact." *Research Papers in Education* 26 (3): 275–328.

Kelchtermans, G., and K. Ballet. 2002. "The Micropolitics of Teacher Induction: A Narrative-biographical Study on Teacher Socialization." *Teaching and Teacher Education* 18 (1): 105–120.

Korthagen, F., J. Loughran, and T. Russell. 2006. "Developing Fundamental Principles for Teacher Education Programs and Practices." *Teaching and Teacher Education* 22 (8): 1020–1041.

Margonis, F. 2004. "From Student Resistance to Educative Engagement: A Case Study in Building Powerful Student–teacher Relationships." *Counterpoints* 259: 39–53.

McIntyre, J., and P. Thomson. 2015. "Poverty, Schooling, and Beginning Teachers Who Make a Difference: A Case Study from England." In *Teacher Education for High Poverty Schools*, edited by J. Lampert and B. Burnett, 153–170. New York: Springer.

MET Project. 2013. *Ensuring Fair and Reliable Measures of Effective Teaching: Culminating Findings from the MET Project's Three-year Study*. Bill and Melinda Gates Foundation. Accessed March 5, 2014. http://www.metproject.org/downloads/MET_Ensuring_Fair_and_Reliable_Measures_Practitioner_Brief.pdf

Milner, H. R., and E. A. Self. 2014. "Studying Race in Teacher Education: Implications from Ethnographic Perspectives. " In *Researching Race in Education: Policy, Practice and Qualitative Research*, edited by A. Dixson, 3–28. Charlotte, NC: Information Age Publishing.

Munns, G., A. Martin, and R. Craven. 2008. "To Free the Spirit? Motivation and Engagement of Indigenous Students." *The Australian Journal of Indigenous Education* 37: 98–107.

New Zealand Government. 2010. *A Vision for the Teaching Profession: Education Workforce Advisory Group Report to the Minister of Education*. Wellington: Ministry of Education. Accessed December 10, 2010. http://www.beehive.govt.nz

New Zealand Ministry of Education. 2013. *Request for Application for Provision of Exemplary Post Graduate Initial Teacher Education Programmes*. Accessed July 20, 2013. www.minedu.govt.nz/.../EducationInitiatives/QualityOfITEProvision.asp.

New Zealand Teachers Council. 2010. *Registered Teacher Criteria*. Wellington: New Zealand Teachers Council.

Nieto, S. 2000. "Placing Equity Front and Center: Some Thoughts on Transforming Teacher Education for a New Century." *Journal of Teacher Education*. 51 (3): 180–187.

OECD (Office of Economic Cooperation and Development). 2011. *Society at a Glance: Key Findings New Zealand*. Accessed March 20, 2012. http://www.oecd.org/dataoecd/38/35/47573309.pdf

OECD (Office of Economic Cooperation and Development). 2016. "Who Are the Low-performing Students?" *PISA in Focus*, No. 60. Paris: OECD Publishing. Accessed February 20, 2016. doi: 10.1787/5jm3xh670q7g-en

Perry, B. 2013. *Household Incomes in New Zealand: Trends in Indicators of Inequality and Hardship 1982 to 2012*. Wellington: Ministry of Social Development.

Powell, W., and O. Kusuma-Powell. 2011. *How to Teach Now: Five Keys to Personalized Learning in the Global Classroom*. Alexandria, VA: ASCD.

Rank, M., H. Yoon, and T. Hirschl. 2003. "American Poverty As a Structural Failing: Evidence and Arguments." *Journal of Sociology and Social Welfare* 30 (4): 3–29.

Rubie-Davies, C. 2014. *Becoming a High Expectation Teacher: Raising the Bar*. New York: Routledge.

Sleeter, C. 2001. "Preparing Teachers for Culturally Diverse Schools: Research and the Overwhelming Presence of Whiteness." *Journal of Teacher Education* 52 (2): 94–106.

Snook, I., and J. O'Neill. 2014. "Poverty and Inequality of Educational Achievement." In *Twelve Thousand Hours: Education and Poverty in Aotearoa New Zealand*, edited by V. Carpenter and S. Osborne, 19–43. Auckland: Dunmore Publishing.

Tatto, M., and J. Furlong. 2015. "Research and Teacher Education: Papers from the BERA-RSA Inquiry." *Oxford Review of Education* 41 (2): 145–153.

UNICEF Innocenti Research Centre. 2012. *Measuring Child Poverty: New League Tables of Child Poverty in the World's Rich Countries*. Innocenti Report Card 10. Florence: UNICEF Innocenti Research Centre.

Wong, G., T. Greenhalgh, G. Westhorp, and R. Pawson. 2012. "Realist Methods in Medical Education Research: What Are They and What Can They Contribute?" *Medical Education* 46 (1): 89–96.

Wylie, C. 2013. "Schools and Inequality." In *Inequality: A New Zealand Crisis*, edited by M. Rashbrooke, 134–144. Wellington: Bridget William Books.

Discussing poverty with student teachers: the realities of dialogue

Hanneke Jones

ABSTRACT
This paper is based on my own practice as a teacher educator at a university in the north-east of England and focuses on the effectiveness of dialogue as a tool for teaching the topic of socio-economic disadvantage in initial teacher education (ITE). The research was triggered by questions which had emerged within my work, about the compatibility of the liberal procedures of dialogic enquiry on the one hand, with the aims of critical teacher education on the other. Using critical realism as a theoretical framework, this article explores these tensions in a case study which follows dialogic enquiries across four consecutively taught groups of student-teachers. Results indicate that dialogic enquiry *can* be used as a powerful tool in social justice teaching in ITE, but that critical teacher educators have a duty to support students in identifying false understandings and the workings of inequality. Neutrality on the part of the teacher educator and notions of equal validity of the students' responses were thus found to be of secondary importance to the aims of social justice education. More widely, this article argues that critical realism can shed light on our understanding of the teaching of contentious and politically sensitive issues.

Introduction

Much has been written in this JET Special Edition about the need to educate student-teachers in relation to socio-economic disadvantage. According to Wegerif (2010), dialogic enquiry can be a powerful tool for criticality and transformation; hence, dialogic enquiry has the potential to be an important and innovative approach in the teaching of social justice in initial teacher education (ITE). However, this potential has hitherto been under-researched. This study, which is based on my own practice, focuses on the effectiveness of dialogic enquiry in the education of student-teachers on the topic of poverty. Alongside likely benefits, there are also potential tensions between the liberal procedures of dialogic enquiry on the one hand (Gregory 2014), and the aims of critical teacher education on the other (Apple 2013). This article explores such issues within dialogic enquiry as: variation in participant opinion; the risk that harmful prejudices are exacerbated (Gorski 2012); reciprocity;

the stance and role of the critical teacher educator; and, the extent to which dialogic enquiry is purposeful (Alexander 2006). Critical realism is used as the theoretical framework for this reflexive, iterative case study and its value in this context is, implicitly, also investigated. In the background section of this article, the themes of social justice teacher education and dialogue are introduced and three aims of ITE in relation to poverty are proposed. This is followed by the methodology section, in which the aims of the research, the critical realist perspective, the context and the methods are presented. The findings section is structured according to four themes and followed by a discussion, before the conclusions and recommendations of this research are presented.

Background

Social justice and ITE in England

Student-teachers in England become educators in a deeply unequal society (Wilkinson and Pickett 2010; Hughes 2012), but the terms *social justice*, *equality* and *equity* are absent from the English Teachers' Standards (Department for Education 2011). This is in contrast to, for example, the Standards for Registration in Scotland, where *Social Justice* is the first point mentioned as part of the Professional Values and Personal Commitment (The General Teaching Council for Scotland 2013). Although student-teachers in England are not required to engage with social justice issues such as poverty in order to gain qualified teacher status (or perhaps because of this (Apple 2013)) a discussion of poverty should, arguably, be an important element of ITE programmes in England, for three reasons which are presented below. The ensuing three aims inform my practice as a critical teacher educator, and are referred to in later sections of this article as aims of critical teacher education.

First, according to the government's Department for Work and Pensions (2015, 4), 19% of children in the UK were living in 'absolute low income' families in 2013–2014, and this percentage is expected to stay at least constant for some time (Brewer, Browne, and Joyce 2011; Browne, Hood, and Joyce 2014). It is thus highly likely that student-teachers will teach many children from socio-economically disadvantaged backgrounds during their career. Because for many of these student-teachers there can be a discrepancy between their pupils' disadvantaged backgrounds and their own (often) more privileged backgrounds, it is important to raise student-teachers' awareness of the needs many families face (Wrigley 2012). Aim 1 can thus be formulated as 'to increase understanding of the difficulties faced by pupils living in poverty whilst avoiding the use of deficit discourses in portraying underprivileged families' (Rogalsky 2009; Grainger 2013; Wrigley 2012).

The second reason relates to the impact of socio-economic disadvantage on pupils' educational outcomes. Income is the single most significant determining factor of educational achievement in the UK, and the devastating impact of poverty has been well-documented (Reay 2006; Hatcher 2012; Cooper and Stewart 2013; Smyth and Wrigley 2013). Student-teachers need, therefore, to understand the reasons for this 'attainment gap' between pupils from less and more affluent backgrounds. They need to know how schools and teachers can aim for equity through maximising learning opportunities for pupils from disadvantaged backgrounds. They also need to know how much harm can be done by teachers' prejudices, labelling practices and lowered expectations (Gorski 2012), and to become aware of their own views (Cochran-Smith 2003). We can thus formulate Aim 2 as 'to develop student teachers' knowledge of the reasons for any educational underachievement of disadvantaged pupils and the ways in which teachers can either minimise or exacerbate this'.

However, they also need to develop an understanding that education alone cannot be expected to solve structural problems such as poverty and systemic inequality. So, finally, if one subscribes to Apple's view (2011, 229) that education is a political act, student-teachers should also be engaged in a critical analysis of the structural inequalities which exist and the mechanisms which sustain it. This includes the development of an awareness of the deeply harmful effects of deficit discourses towards disadvantaged people which are prevalent in some sectors of British society, including in large sections of the media (Rogalsky 2009; Hatcher 2012; Jones 2012); in other words, to 'construct and deconstruct issues of poverty' (Cochran-Smith 2003). Aim 3 can thus be formulated as 'to develop an understanding of the structural nature of poverty and the limited powers of education to compensate for it'.

These three arguments, and ensuing aims, are complementary. A deeper understanding of the structural mechanisms of inequality, for example, can help to avoid a sense of alienation which some student-teachers might experience on placement in schools with high numbers of pupils from disadvantaged backgrounds.

Within the sociopolitical context in England it should also be pointed out that this study was carried out against a backdrop in which, following government policy, ITE provision led by higher education providers is being severely threatened. As a result, student-teachers may have minimal input from higher education providers, which risks side-lining deeper social understandings in ITE in favour of a greater emphasis on the pragmatics of classroom practice. The implications of this in relation to dialogue and social justice will be explored in the discussion section of this paper.

Dialogue

The value of dialogue in democratic and progressive education has long been recognised (Dewey [1916] 1966; Freire [1970] 2000; Burbules 1993; Hess 2004; Alexander 2006). Hess argues that discussions of controversial issues in education can develop democratic thinking (2004, 257), and Wegerif (2010) has explained how transformation can take place within the 'dialogic space'. Dialogue could thus be assumed to have the potential to be a transformative tool in the teaching of social justice in ITE.

Burbules (1993, 7) describes dialogue as being marked by a climate of open participation and a spirit of discovery. He goes on to say that it involves, amongst other things, an attitude of reciprocity and respect, even though disagreements may arise. Alexander (2006, 28) also mentions reciprocity, in the sense that ideas are shared by teachers and students on a reciprocal basis. Alongside this, Alexander (ibid.) specifies that dialogue is collective (referring to the collaborative nature of dialogue), supportive (referring to the absence of anxiety), cumulative (referring to ideas being linked and constructed) and purposeful (referring to dialogue fulfilling its educational aims). The concepts of reciprocity (Burbules 1993) and purpose (Alexander 2006) provide two of the main themes explored in this study.

In relation to dialogic education on controversial topics such as poverty, Warnick and Smith (2014) propose four types of dialogic directive teaching: explicit directive teaching, steering, soft-directive teaching and school ethos endorsement. Gregory (2014, 636), rejects these in favour of what he calls the 'procedurally directive approach', present in such dialogic enquiry methods as Philosophy for Children (Haynes 2002; Lipman 2003; Chandley and Sutcliffe 2010). In this method educators do not take a stance, but use 'epistemic authority' (Gregory 2014, 637) to regulate the procedures of the enquiry in order to help participants make reasonable interferences and avoid fallacies in the enquiry (ibid.). A form of dialogue which is related to the Philosophy for Children approach, named the Community of Enquiry (Baumfield and Mroz 2002; Jones-Teuben 2013), features specifically in this study. In this form of dialogic enquiry participants generate and choose a question as the focus for the enquiry, in which the educator's stance is that of a neutral facilitator (Gregory 2014).

Dialogic enquiry is not without its critics. Despite its claims to reciprocity, collectivity and support, Burbules (2000, 2001) and Lefstein (2006) have argued that, on the basis of competition and power which are frequently occurring elements (Lefstein 2006, 6), dialogue can be experienced as discriminatory by participants, and, in fact, restrict self-expression and communication (Burbules 2000; 1). Chetty (2008) has made this point with specific reference to the use of the Community of Enquiry. Efforts were therefore made to identify incidents of marginalisation within the study.

Methodology

It must be pointed out that I am both the researcher in this study and, as the teacher educator, one of its subjects; my standpoints in both roles will be presented later in this section. To maximise clarity the first person is used primarily in relation to my role as practicing teacher educator.

Aim and research questions

The aim of this study was to investigate the suitability of the liberal (rather than critical) practice of the Community of Enquiry, with its focus on a question chosen by the participants, its supposed facilitator neutrality and its inter-student reciprocity, for the critical teaching of social justice. The study explored the following questions:

- To what extent might this liberal practice risk creating an environment in which negative stereotypes of people living in poverty could be expressed and exacerbated (Gorski 2012), rather than disrupted?
- Was it appropriate for me as facilitator to take a neutral stance? And if not, would this lower the degree of *supportiveness* (Burbules 2000; Alexander 2006; Chetty 2008)?
- What was the potential for student-teachers to discuss any contentious views in dialogue or *reciprocity*, given the power differentials between them and myself as the teacher educator (Burbules 2000; Alexander 2006)?
- Is dialogic enquiry an efficient use of the very limited amount of time available on this ITE course: in other words, is dialogue *purposeful* (Alexander ibid.) enough?

Critical realism

Critical realism provides the theoretical framework for this study. This is particularly relevant in relation to teaching about poverty as, in contrast to 'strong' social constructionism, it acknowledges that a world exists which is independent of people's perceptions and constructions, whilst going beyond the descriptive analysis which positivism provides (Sayer 2000, 90; O'Mahoney and Vincent 2014). Critical realists 'seek to identify what exists' (Sayer, 12) and aim to uncover the mechanisms and connections between phenomena in order to provide explanations.

Reality in this perspective is stratified into three elements: the real, the actual and the empirical (Bhaskar 1975, in Sayer, 11). The *real*, according to Sayer (ibid.), is what exists, either natural or social, and independently of whether we have knowledge of it. The *real* contains objects, but also their structures, power and potential. The *actual* refers to what happens when those powers are activated, whereas the *empirical* is the domain of observable experience. Thus, in relation to poverty, we can say that at the *empirical* level 19% of children in the UK live in absolute low-income families, in the *actual* domain we could consider the experiences of these children, whereas when we consider the *real* we know that there are social, economic and political mechanisms at work which cause poverty, and the potential structural impact of poverty.

This ontological stratification can also be used as a methodology to discuss the concept of dialogue in this study. At the *empirical* level we can analyse the data gathered; and at the *actual* level we have to acknowledge that much of what is experienced and thought during dialogues exists, but is not expressed or recorded. In the domain of the *real*, we can discuss what educational, psychological, social and philosophical drivers appear to have caused the development of the dialogues held, and what the potential is of dialogue in ITE (Easton 2010, 121). Italics are used for the terms *empirical*, *actual* and *real* in this article where they are used in this specific critical realist sense (Sayer 2000).

A final argument for the use of critical realism as a framework for this study is its critical approach, not only towards other theories but also towards social practices. Based on Bhaskar's view on the emancipatory potential of social science (1986, in Sayer 2000, 18), this is the identification of shared meanings which are 'false':

> If social scientific accounts differ from those of actors then they cannot help but be critical of lay thought and action. Furthermore, as Bhaskar argues, to identify understandings in society as false, and hence actions informed by them as falsely based, is to imply that (other things being equal) those beliefs and actions ought to be changed. (Sayer 2000, 19)

This statement has implications not just for critical realist researchers, but clearly also for critical educators, as will be discussed. Critical realism is thus not only used as a tool for data analysis in this study, but, more widely, may be able to shed light on our understanding of dialogue in the teaching of contentious and politically sensitive issues.

Context

The context of this study is a 10-month long Master's level PostGraduate Certificate of Education (PGCE) ITE course for primary teachers at a university in the north-east of England, to which I contribute as a teacher educator. In particular, the study focuses on one day which I teach on the links between poverty and education. This day, titled 'Income and Outcomes: Challenging Inequality' (the content of which is described in a later section), forms part of the reflective practitioner module on this programme, which comprises four rotational taught days. In this module a range of critical, theoretical and social perspectives relevant to education is explored: another one of the days, for example, is based on critical whiteness studies, as discussed by Smith (2013). With regards to the discussion of poverty, a day's teaching is, of course, extremely limited but this reflective practitioner module day is one of a number of elements of the course which focuses on this issue. Other elements of the course, which are specifically related to socio-economic disadvantage, include a placement task investigating schools' perspectives of the pupil premium (DfE 2015). This is followed up in a seminar at the university, in which I support the students critically to compare and discuss their findings. School placements also provide opportunities for students to work with pupils from disadvantaged backgrounds and to reflect on these experiences. The day's teaching which forms the focus of this paper is thus situated within a contextual framework of the teaching of social justice on our PGCE programme. However, time available to spend on this issue is limited, due to the many other requirements of the course. This was the reason why this research studied if the use of dialogue in this context is *purposeful* (Alexander 2006), as mentioned earlier in this section.

Other features of the course are the use of enquiry, enquiry-based learning and dialogue. Student-teachers are introduced to aspects of sociocultural theory (Wells 1999), and a range of dialogic teaching methods is used throughout the programme, both by the teacher educators and the student-teachers themselves whilst on placement. One of the other contributions I make to the PGCE programme is a training course in the Philosophy for Children (P4C) method (Lipman 2003; Chandley and Sutcliffe 2010). Once the student-teachers are acquainted with the procedures of the Community of Enquiry, which is inherent in P4C, it is a potentially useful dialogic method which I use in other elements of the ITE course, such as the 'Income and Outcomes: Challenging Inequality' day.

Methods

This is a small-scale, qualitative, practitioner research case study (Cochran-Smith and Lytle 2009; Thomas 2011). It explores the development of my use, as teacher educator, of dialogue across four groups (A, B, C and D), each of 20–25 student-teachers (89 students in total), on the income and outcomes: challenging inequality day. The study is iterative in the sense that it explores data from four days across four consecutive weeks, during which I made changes to the content of each day, based on my reflections of the previous days. The study is based on four data sets, the main one being of my own observations and reflections. These are socially constructed (Sayer 2000, 90) and dialogic (Bakhtin 1986; Wells 1999) in nature: shared reflections with team colleagues, who were simultaneously teaching 'their' Reflective Practitioner days to the other three groups (on a rotational basis), helped to focus, deepen and analyse my thoughts. A second data-set consists of audio recordings of the dialogues held, which were used to clarify specific discourse sequences during analysis. A third data-set emanates from the reflective diaries, in which all students were asked to identify which aspects of this day had most shaped their views. It is acknowledged that the validity of this data-set may have been impaired by the fact that the diaries were part of an assessed piece of course work. Thus, as not all students will have written down their *actual* views, the *actual* domain must be assumed to be far greater than, and not necessarily congruent to, the *empirical* domain of this data-set. A final data-set is provided by the reflective practitioner course evaluations of the day, in which student-teachers were asked to summarise how it had developed their understanding of the issues discussed.

The data were analysed iteratively in relation to the four different groups and the changes I made to the structure and content of the day over the four weeks, and in relation to four themes which emanated from the questions outlined earlier in this section: stigmatisation, facilitator neutrality, reciprocity and the degree to which the enquiries were purposeful. The main data-set was mostly reflective in nature, but rigour and consistency of analysis and explanation was provided by the use of the critical realism framework. Although this is a qualitative study, a very brief quantitative analysis of the reflective diaries was also carried out (see findings section, Table 1).

Ethical considerations and standpoints

All students were informed of the aims and methods of this research, and all gave explicit permission for me to gather observational and audio data. All but one also gave written consent for the use of their reflective diary for this study. A number of ethical issues need to be acknowledged, however, and the first of these relates to my relationship with the student-teachers. As one of their teacher educators, my role was not only to support their professional development, but ultimately also as a gatekeeper towards their accreditation with qualified teacher status: the ensuing power differential, combined with their knowledge of my commitment to both dialogic enquiry methods and social justice may have impacted on the data. Second, as this was an enquiry into my own practice, it is essential that my standpoint is acknowledged (Edwards 2014). The research was driven by my commitment as a teacher educator to both dialogic enquiry and social justice, and I felt professionally compelled to resolve the questions I had posed, in order to improve my practice. Whereas, this has provided my study with a large degree of authenticity (Thomas 2011), the risk of bias is not ruled out.

'Income and Outcomes: Challenging Inequality': a brief overview of the day

In preparation for the day, students were required to read a number of set texts (Kershner and Northen 2010; Hatcher 2012; Smith 2012; Wrigley 2012; Smyth and Wrigley 2013), which were referred to and discussed during the day. There were three sessions in each day, each of which was informed by the aims outlined earlier in the Methodology section of this article. The first two sessions included, amongst a number of other activities, a dialogic enquiry. The focus of the first session was on perspectives of social justice, and inequality. As part of this session, students watched two video fragments of 'Poor Kids' (Neumann 2011), a documentary in which a number of British children from severely disadvantaged backgrounds are filmed in their homes. These film clips were discussed in both small-group and whole-group dialogue, which will be referred to in the findings section as Dialogue 1. The focus of the second session was on the links between educational achievement and poverty, and a whole-group dialogic enquiry session, referred to as Dialogue 2, was held on this topic as part of this session. The third part of the day, which focused on the potential of schools and teachers to support pupils from poorer backgrounds, did not involve any explicit whole-group dialogue, and is therefore not discussed in this study. Although this study focuses on dialogue, it must be emphasised that the day also included a range of other pedagogical methods to address the teaching content.

Findings

This section presents the study findings in relation to the analytic themes mentioned earlier: stigmatisation (Smyth and Wrigley 2013); facilitator neutrality (Gregory 2014); reciprocity (Alexander 2006); and the degree to which the dialogues had been purposeful (ibid.).

Stigmatisation: exacerbated or disrupted?

After watching the film clips, the student-teachers were asked to discuss their observations in small groups. In Group A, a female student in one of these groups commented on the fact that one of the families in the film clips appeared to have a dog. She argued that it was 'unjustifiable', that people on benefits spent 'her and her parents' hard-earned tax-payers' money' on dog food, comments similar to those which Jones (2012) refers to as demonisation of the poor. When I heard and questioned these views in her small group, the student rejected my perspective, and expanded on her views several times. However, when I asked for comments in the whole group plenary, no one from that small group mentioned the issue of the dog, which may have been the result of this student feeling marginalised by my intervention (Lefstein 2006). Aware that this might be the case, I did not raise it either, and thus (as I later saw it) missed the opportunity to disrupt these views. As a result of this reflection, I explicitly asked the following groups (B, C and D) if anyone had noticed the dog, and invited discussion of this issue. During the small group discussions in group B, a male student-teacher argued that the wide-screen television which had been visible in one of the clips was, like the dog, 'unjustifiable' in a family which is dependent on benefits. The phrases 'taxpayer's money' (Dorling 2011) and 'bad parenting' (Jones 2012; Gorski 2012, 309) were brought up. In contrast to Group A, these comments were, however, expressed in the whole group discussion, and matched by counter-arguments from other students in the group, ranging from children's comfort via social capital and the limited options of high-interest loans to human rights, all of which led to a heated discussion with the student who had expressed these opinions. By contrast, in group C no stigmatisation of disadvantaged families came to my attention. Finally, in group D some negative views related to the dog and the television set were expressed by a number of female students in one of the small groups, expressed in the large group and repudiated in the whole group discussion.

A critical realist analysis of this theme would suggest that the *empirical* appearance of the dog and the television set had led some students to share their *actual* thoughts in the small group. Bringing these out in the whole group allowed these comments to be disrupted and identified as 'false' by other students (Sayer 2000).

Facilitator neutrality

As a Community of Enquiry facilitator, I was initially prepared to challenge all views but reluctant to favour any over others (Chandley and Sutcliffe 2010). I asked questions; encouraged students to identify inferences, evidence and assumptions; and attempted to elicit counter arguments (Gregory 2014) in all discussions. However, after my experiences with Dialogue 1 in Group A, I realised that as a critical educator I had to challenge negative stereotyping of disadvantaged people in particular. Although I did not *explicitly* support some students' opinions over others', it can be assumed that my own views were *implicitly* known to most students (Bakhtin 1986, 166).

In Dialogue 2 a development in facilitator neutrality took place, related to the enquiry question. Group A had generated and selected 'Is it the place of Education to solve social problems?'. This question had led to a discussion of a wide range of problems, such as obesity and alcoholism, which were not directly related to socio-economic disadvantage. As I did not feel that this was an effective enough use of the limited time, I presented an enquiry question to the following groups. In Groups B and C this question was: 'In what ways does education perpetuate inequality?'. Although this had led to a productive discussion in Group B, in Group C the same question led to a fairly consensual dialogue based on the literature set. I therefore presented Group D with a potentially more challenging question: 'Why does poverty exist?'. However, Dialogue 2 in Group D was possibly the least productive and cumulative (Alexander 2006, 28), as relatively few students took part and relatively few ideas were linked to each other. This was perhaps related to the fact that I had deliberately chosen a more philosophical and political, *real* domain-related question, which may have rendered this dialogue less collective (Alexander 2006, 28) than some of the other discussions held. One student in group D mentioned the following in his reflective diary: 'This session was fairly demoralising as debate was curtailed by the personal agenda of the session leader' (QH, male student). In all the data-sets this was the only comment which was explicitly critical of my role in the enquiries.

A critical realist analysis of this theme would suggest that whereas my views were not *empirically* apparent during Dialogues 1 and 2, they may have been *actually* detected by many students. It appears that once I became less overtly neutral in my facilitation, it became easier in many discussions to discuss *real* domain issues of poverty. However, for some dialogues such as Dialogue 2 in Group D, and for QH in that group, this may have led to a lowered degree of motivation.

Reciprocity

This theme is based on the mutual respect and sharing of ideas identified by Burbules (1993, 7) and Alexander (2006, 28). The female student in Group A who had not wanted to talk about the dog in the whole group wrote this in her reflective diary:

> Taking on board other people's views showed me that I have very different views to them on the same subject. I believe that the video that we watched showing how children of deprived areas lived caused an awful lot of discussion that took it from the teaching of the children to a more political discussion. (SF, female student)

The 'awful lot of discussion' referred to here had taken place in her small group only and in my presence, and may, as mentioned before, point to a perceived lack of reciprocity, exemplifying the sometimes 'un-dialogic' nature of dialogue (Burbules 2001; Lefstein 2006). A comparison between the female student in Group A and the male student in Group B (who commented on the wide-screen TV in the whole-group plenary) reveals the power of group dynamics and the role which confidence plays in driving dialogue. Gender may have been a factor here.

A conceptualisation of inequality was greatly helped by the personal account of poverty shared by one of the female participants in Enquiry 2 in Group B. Despite, or perhaps as a result of, the heated debate held in Dialogue 1, the level of *supportiveness* (Alexander 2006, 28) in the group was such that this student felt willing to share her highly personal narrative. The male student-teacher who, during enquiry 1, had given his strong negative views on people living on benefits, took part much less vocally in this discussion and commented on the following aspects in his reflective diary:

> The session was very useful in developing my own awareness of how social factors such as poverty and the level of parental education can affect a child's development. (HM, male student, Group B)

Although it is not certain whether this student had changed his views on 'poor parenting', or the use of benefits, his comments here express a much more considered view than those which he had expressed in Dialogue 2. A clear majority of students (12 out of 20) in this group mentioned in their reflective diaries that the discussions had been a positive factor in shaping their view during this day, and particularly Dialogue 1, such as CR:

> The open debate allowed me to take in other people's ideas and experiences and allowed me to develop a deeper understanding of my own thoughts (CR, female student, Group B)

A critical realist analysis shows that a perceived lack of reciprocity may lessen the chances of an *empirical* discussion of certain issues. On the other hand, deliberatively *not* leaving issues undiscussed may, at least in Group B, *actually* have furthered reciprocity and have stimulated a student to share a very personal account. The discussion of this student's *empirical* and *actual* situation, enabled by a degree of reciprocity and supportiveness (Alexander 2006), appeared to have led to a *real* understanding for a number of others.

How purposeful were the dialogues?

Following Group A's day, I made two changes to the format of the following days, in order to make the dialogues more *purposeful* (Alexander 2006, 28), both of which were described in the previous sections: I drew out the issue of the dog in Dialogue 1, and presented Groups B, C and D with a question instead of having this generated by the group, in Dialogue 2.

An overall measure of the degree to which dialogues had been purposeful was the fact that, on average, 46% of students indicated in their evaluations that dialogue (or 'discussions') had shaped their views during the day, as is shown in Table 1.

As is clear from Table 1, the impact of dialogue was mentioned by a greater number of student-teachers than that of any other aspect. Although it cannot be ascertained from the data that student views had been shaped in accordance to my aims, it can be concluded that overall the students perceived the dialogues as purposeful. However, it can also be pointed out that two of the three groups which I had presented with a question (groups C and D), rated the impact of dialogue less highly than the first two groups.

A number of students mentioned in their reflective diaries that the *diversity* of opinions expressed was a particularly strong feature of the dialogic enquiries:

Table 1. Aspects of the day which were mentioned by student-teachers in their Reflective Diaries as having shaped their views.

	% of Group A	% of Group B	% of Group C	% of Group D	Average % for cohort
Dialogue	55	60	35	35	46
'Poor Kids' video	23	20	25	45	28
Creating a poster	5	0	0	0	1
Opinion triangle	14	5	25	5	12
Pre-session reading	18	20	15	5	15
Research findings	5	10	35	10	15
Reflection	5	10	5	5	6

The most interesting thing in this session was the range of opinions around the room with regard to economic inequality. The opinions of some students about people on benefits was astounding to me, and was useful to think about as there may well be people with the same opinions in schools I work whether they are overtly expressed or not (DP, female student Group B, reflective diary entry)

Although I had not identified the development of understanding of the range of opinions on this issue as an aim of my teaching, students such as DP (above) clearly appreciated the opportunities that dialogue had provided them with to get an understanding of this.

Discussion

The aim of this study was to investigate to what extent dialogic enquiry, and in particular the liberal practice of the Community of Enquiry, with its focus on questions generated and chosen by the participants, its facilitator neutrality and its emphasis on reciprocity might be compatible with critical teaching for social justice. As I explained in the previous section in relation to Dialogue 2, I had deemed the discussion of enquiry questions which had been chosen by the participants as insufficiently purposeful (Alexander 2006, 28). Although this would have heightened the students' ownership of the enquiries (Haynes 2002), I felt it was necessary to avoid discussions which were not directly related to my aims, within the limited time available. However, this may have been a factor in the lower evaluations in the last two groups, and in Group D the question presented appeared not to have led to an entirely successful dialogue. It could thus be argued that the enquiry question needs to be chosen *with* rather than *by* or *for* the participants: it needs to be in line with the social justice ITE aims, but it also needs to be relevant to the needs and interests of the participants.

As described in the section on facilitator neutrality, I aimed, as Community of Enquiry advocate Gregory (2014, 637) suggests, to regulate the procedure by asking critical questions and supporting students to identify inferences, evidence and assumptions, and eliciting counter arguments. Gregory argues that, when this is carried out consistently and in great depth, it leads to a *true* (Sayer 2000) understanding of the topic. However, limited amounts of time available, group dynamics and limits to my facilitation prowess produced *empirical* and *actual* dialogues which regularly fell short of this ideal: 'things could go in many different ways' (Sayer 2000, 15).

There is a reason, however, why Gregory's procedurally directive dialogue is, in itself, less than ideal for critical and critical realist teacher educators. He points out that in his method there should be 'neither overt endorsement of a favoured position nor guidance for the students to accept one'. However, educating teachers in an unequal education system within an unequal society is, as Apple (2013) has said, not value-free. According to Bakhtin (1986, 93), everything that is expressed in dialogue relates to other utterances and must be seen within its wider cultural dialogic context. In discussing poverty therefore, all comments should be seen in relation to currently prevailing 'underclass' discourses (Jones 2012; Gorski 2012; Smyth and Wrigley 2013). Not only are such discourses of stigmatisation (Smyth and Wrigley 2013) extremely harmful in education (Gorski 2012), but they also tend to focus on *empirical*, rather than *real* (Sayer 2000) features of inequality. Neutrality is thus not an ideal to aspire to in this context, as critical educators are led by a moral imperative to question and disrupt stigmatising discourses and to discuss the real domain disenfranchisements of the poor (Gorski 2012, 314). It follows that in this context, Burbules' notion of Dialogue as

Instruction would be more appropriate than Dialogue as Inquiry (1993), and Alexander's notion that dialogues should have *purpose* conflicts with, and overrides, that of dialogues being *collective* (2006, 28). It became clear during the study that by being overly concerned about being perceived as neutral, I could, paradoxically, obstruct more open discussions, in which a deeper level of reality (Sayer 2000) was able to be discussed: the most productive dialogues were those in which empirical issues were used as a starting point to explicitly bring out students' *actual* views, but where a multitude of real reasons and consequences could also be discussed, and some identified as 'false' (ibid.). From a critical teacher education viewpoint, educators must thus create opportunities for specific 'false' opinions and misunderstandings to be expressed, identified and interrogated (Sayer 2000, 18). In this, they can draw on the expertise of participants in the group to create opportunities for counter arguments to be posed, and for *real* explanations to be explored (Sayer 2000): some views in the dialogue will thus be favoured over others.

However, it is important to protect reciprocity, as this was identified as a crucial element of successful dialogue in this study. A solution is to make it clear to student-teachers that opinions are discussed rather than the persons expressing them. Sayer argues in this respect that:

> The principle of equality applies to the moral worth of persons, not to the epistemological status of their empirical beliefs: although we might properly regard sociologists and chemists as equals as people, a sociologist's knowledge of chemistry is not equal to that of a chemist [...]. Thus social and moral equality does not entail epistemological equality. (Sayer 2000, 48)

Although it must be acknowledged that concepts held by critical realist teacher educators are fallible too (Bakhtin 1986, 93; Sayer 2000, 60), it is thus crucial that the actions of facilitators are led by their aims. With critical teacher educators, these are to guard the overriding commitment towards educational equity and the well-being of disadvantaged pupils, and to guide dialogic processes in order to help student-teachers understand the *real* connections between phenomena related to this topic.

A day's teaching on the topic of socio-economic disadvantage is of course extremely limited, and it could well be argued that more time should be allocated to this in ITE programmes such as that discussed in this article. However, in a context in which ITE in England is being moved increasingly to school-led provision, we also need to ask what spaces will remain for dialogue when ITE is primarily carried out in schools, where the main focus must be on the development of pupils. Higher education institutions are, intrinsically, best resourced to explore and explain issues in the domain of the *real*. As ITE is moved away from higher education, we must thus not only ask what the spaces are for genuine dialogue, but also what opportunities there will be for student-teachers to access the domain of the *real* in order to understand and explain the issues they will meet in their empirical and actual practice. Without this there is a serious risk that many student-teachers will notice impacts of inequality and disadvantage on their pupils, without the ability to understand these structurally. Importantly, they will thus also lack an awareness of their own role in these processes which perpetuate inequality.

Conclusions and recommendations

This was a small-scale case study (Thomas 2007), based largely on my own observations and reflections as a practitioner researcher (Stenhouse 1981; Lofthouse, Hall, and Wall 2012).

Although this has enabled me to gain a deep understanding of the data, implications drawn from it must be cautious. A greater degree of generalisability could be achieved in further studies of this kind in other contexts, or in larger scale studies. Nonetheless, the findings from this study indicate that dialogic enquiry, alongside other pedagogical interventions, has an important role to play within the teaching of social justice in relation to socio-economic disadvantage within ITE.

A number of conclusions and recommendations for further practice can be made on the basis of this study. To begin, I have suggested three aims for social justice ITE in relation to socio-economic disadvantage: these would be first to increase understanding of the difficulties faced by pupils living in poverty whilst avoiding the use of deficit discourses in portraying underprivileged families; second to develop student-teachers' knowledge of the reasons for any educational underachievement of disadvantaged pupils and the ways in which teachers can minimise or exacerbate this; and third to develop an understanding of the structural nature of poverty and the limited powers of education to compensate for it.

I have argued that, whilst reciprocity is an important aspect of effective dialogue, these aims of social justice education should be prioritised over facilitator neutrality and epistemological equality between participants. Where dialogue is based on enquiry questions, these have to be both related to the aims of social justice, and relevant to the participants in order to lead to successful dialogue.

The study has shown that it can be very useful to draw on *empirically* shared experiences, such as film fragments, or students' *actual* experiences as a focus for dialogic enquiry. However, it is only by leading the enquiry into the domain of the *real* that mechanisms can be uncovered which can explain the *empirical* and the *actual*. Critical teacher educators should thus be prepared to question social, philosophical, economical and historical aspects of the contributions made, whilst switching between the *empirical*, the *actual* and the *real* (Sayer 2000), and have an awareness of the tensions and complexities (Apple 2013, 62) involved in this work. As in any other form of pedagogy, subject knowledge and expertise in the facilitation of dialogue is thus crucial.

Finally, I have suggested that the teaching of social justice should play a greater role in ITE, but also that higher education providers must continue to provide dialogue and *real* domain depth and criticality in ITE to help student-teachers make sense of the inequalities they will experience within their practice. In a wider theoretical sense, this study has shown that critical realism provides an effective theoretical framework for understanding dialogic enquiry in the teaching of contentious and politically sensitive subjects.

Acknowledgement

I would like to thank Gail Edwards, Francis Jones and Heather Smith for their advice.

Disclosure statement

No potential conflict of interest was reported by the author.

Funding

This research was financially supported by the Newcastle University Institute for Social Renewal.

References

Alexander, R. 2006. *Towards Dialogic Teaching*. 3rd ed. Thirsk: Dialogos.
Apple, M. W. 2011. "Global Crises, Social Justice, and Teacher Education." *Journal of Teacher Education* 62 (2): 222–234.
Apple, M. W. 2013. *Can Education Change Society?* New York: Routledge.
Bakhtin, M. 1986. *Speech Genres and Other Late Essays*. Austin: University of Texas Press.
Baumfield, V., and M. Mroz. 2002. "Investigating Pupils' Questions in the Primary Classroom." *Educational Research* 44 (2): 129–140.
Brewer, M., J. Browne, and R. Joyce. 2011. *Child and Working-Age Poverty from 2010 to 2020*. Institute for Fiscal Studies. Accessed September 14, 2015. www.ifs.org.uk/comms/comm121.pdf
Browne, J., A. Hood, and R. Joyce. 2014. *Child and Working-Age Poverty in Northern Ireland over the Next Decade: An Update*. Institute for Fiscal Studies. Accessed September 14, 2015. www.ifs.org.uk/bns/bn144.pdf
Burbules, N. C. 1993. *Dialogue in Teaching – Theory and Practice*. New York: Teachers College Press.
Burbules, N. C. 2000. "The Limits of Dialogue as a Critical Pedagogy." In *Revolutionary Pedagogies*, edited by Peter Trifonas, 251–273. New York: Routledge Falmer.
Burbules, N. C. 2001. "Theory and Research on Teaching as Dialogue." In *Handbook of Research on Teaching*. 4th ed., edited by Virginia Richardson, 1102–1121. Washington, DC: American Educational Research Association.
Chandley, N., and R. Sutcliffe, eds. 2010. *SAPERE Handbook to Accompay the Level 1 Course*. 3rd ed. Oxford: SAPERE.
Chetty, D. 2008. *Philosophy for Children and Antiracist Education – To What Extent Does P4C Complement Antiracism?'* MA diss. London: Goldsmiths College, University of London.
Cochran-Smith, M. 2003. "Learning and Unlearning: The Education of Teacher Educators." *Teaching and Teacher Education* 19 (200): 5–28.
Cochran-Smith, M., and S. L. Lytle. 2009. *Inquiry as a Stance: Practitioner Research for the Next Generation*. New York: Teachers College Press.
Cooper, K., and K. Stewart. 2013. *Does Money Affect Children's Outcomes?* Joseph Rowntree Foundation. Accessed September 14, 2015. https://www.jrf.org.uk/sites/default/.../money-children-outcomes-full.pdf
Department for Education. 2011. *Teachers' Standards*. Accessed September 14, 2015. https://www.gov.uk/government/uploads/.../Teachers__Standards.pdf
DfE (Department for Education). 2015. *Pupil Premium: Funding and Accountability for Schools*. Accessed September 14, 2015. https://www.gov.uk/guidance/pupil-premium-information-for-schools-and-alternative-provision-settings
Department for Work and Pensions. 2015. *Households below Average Income: An Analysis of the Income Distribution 1994/95 to 2013/14*. Accessed September 14, 2015. https://www.gov.uk/government/statistics/households-below-average-income-19941995-to-20132014
Dewey, J. (1916) 1966. *Democracy and Education*. Toronto: Collier-Macmillan.
Dorling, D. 2011. *Injustice – Why Social Inequality Exists*. Bristol: Policy Press.
Easton, G. 2010. "Critical Realism in Case Study Research." *Industrial Marketing Management* 39: 118–128.
Edwards, G. 2014. "Standpoint Theory, Realism and the Search for Objectivity in the Sociology of Education." *British Journal of Sociology of Education* 35 (2): 167–184.
Freire, P. (1970) 2000. *Pedagogy of the Oppressed*. London: Continuum.
Gorski, P. C. 2012. "Perceiving the Problem of Poverty and Schooling: Deconstructing the Class Stereotypes That Mis-Shape Education Practice and Policy." *Equity and Excellence in Education* 45 (2): 302–319.
Grainger, K. 2013. *"The Daily Grunt": Middle Class Bias and Vested Interests in the 'Getting in Early' and 'Why Can't They Read?'*. Sheffield: Sheffield Hallam University.
Gregory, M. 2014. "The Procedurally Directive Approach to Teaching Controversial Issues." *Educational Theory* 64 (6): 627–648.

Hatcher, R. 2012. "Social Class and Schooling – Differentiation or Democracy?" In *Education, Equality and Human Rights – Issues of Gender, 'Race', Sexuality, Disability and Social Class*, edited by Mike Cole, 239–267. London: Routledge.

Haynes, J. 2002. *Children as Philosophers*. London: Routledge Falmer.

Hess, D. E. 2004. "Controversies about Controversial Issues in Democratic Education." *PS: Political Science & Politics* 257–261.

Hughes, J. A. 2012. "What Teacher Preparation Programs Can Do to Better Prepare Teachers to Meet the Challenges of Educating Students Living in Poverty." *Action in Teacher Education* 32 (1): 54–64.

Jones, O. 2012. *Chavs – The Demonization of the Working Class*. London: Verso.

Jones-Teuben, H. 2013. "'I Disagree with Myself!': Creative Thinking in a Key Stage 1 Community of Enquiry." PhD diss., Newcastle-upon-Tyne: Newcastle University.

Kershner, R., and S. Northen. 2010. "Children, Diversity and Equity." In *Children, their World, their Education*, edited by Robin Alexander, 110–126. London: Routledge.

Lefstein, A. 2006. *Dialogue in Schools: Towards a Pragmatic Approach*. Working Papers in Urban Language & Literacies. London: King's College London.

Lipman, M. 2003. *Thinking in Education*. Cambridge: Cambridge University Press.

Lofthouse, R., E. Hall, and K. Wall. 2012. "Practitioner Research." In *Research Methods in Educational Leadership and Management*, edited by A. Briggs, M. Morrison, and M. Coleman, 170–187. London: Sage.

Neumann, J. 2011. *Poor Kids*. True Vision for BBC. Accessed September 14, 2015. http://www.bbc.co.uk/programmes/b011vnls

O'Mahoney, J., and S. Vincent. 2014. "Critical Realsim as an Empirical Project – A Beginner's Guide." In *Studying Organizations Using Critical Realism: A Practical Guide*, edited by P. K. Edwards, Joe O'Mahoney, and Steve Vincent, 1–20. Oxford: Oxford University Press.

Reay, D. 2006. "The Zombie Stalking English Schools: Social Class and Educational Inequality." *British Journal of Educational Studies* 54 (3): 288–307.

Rogalsky, J. 2009. "'Mythbusters': Dispelling the Culture of Poverty Myth in the Urban Classroom." *Journal of Geography* 108 (4–5): 198–209.

Sayer, A. 2000. *Realism and Social Science*. London: Sage.

Smith, E. 2012. "An Introduction to Education and Social Justice." In *Key Issues in Education and Social Justice*, edited by Emma Smith, 1–17. London: Sage.

Smith, H. J. 2013. "Emotional Responses to Documentary Viewing and the Potential for Transformative Teaching." *Teaching Education* 25 (2): 217–238.

Smyth, J., and T. Wrigley. 2013. "Understanding Poverty in the Twenty-First Century." In *Living on the Edge: Rethinking Poverty, Class and Schooling*. edited by John Smyth and Terry Wrigley, 39–57. New York: Peter Lang.

Stenhouse, L. 1981. "What Counts as Research?" *British Journal of Educational Studies* 29 (2): 103–114.

The General Teaching Council for Scotland. 2013. *Standards for Registration*. Accessed September 14, 2015. www.gtcs.org.uk/standards/standards-for-registration.aspx

Thomas, G. 2007. *Education and Theory: Strangers in Paradigms*. Maidenhead: Open University Press.

Thomas, G. 2011. *How to Do Your Case Study*. London: Sage.

Warnick, B. R., and D. S. Smith. 2014. "The Controversy over Controversies: A Plea for Flexibility and for 'Soft-Directive' Teaching." *Educational Theory* 64 (6): 627–648.

Wegerif, R. 2010. *Mind Expanding – Teaching for Thinking and Creativity in Primary Education*. Maidenhead: Open University Press.

Wells, G. 1999. "*Dialogic Inquiry – Toward a Sociocultural Practice and Theory of Education*." Edited by Hawkins Brown Pea. Cambridge: Cambridge University Press.

Wilkinson, R., and K. Pickett. 2010. *The Spirit Level: Why Equality is Better for Everyone*. London: Penguin Books Ltd.

Wrigley, T. 2012. "Rethinking Poverty and Social Class: The Teacher's Response." In *Social Justice Re-Examined*, edited by R. Arshad, T. Wrigley, and L. Pratt, 145–165. Stoke on Trent: Trentham Books.

Student teachers' perceptions of the effects of poverty on learners' educational attainment and well-being: perspectives from England and Scotland

Sue Ellis, Ian Thompson, Jane McNicholl and Jane Thomson

ABSTRACT
This article reports on two UK initial teacher education studies from two contrasting contexts: a secondary school course in Oxford, England and a primary school course in Strathclyde, Scotland. The questions of how student teachers understand the effect of poverty on pupils' educational achievement, and what they as prospective teachers can do to effect change, are common concerns of the research studies reported here. The Oxford study illustrates the problematic issue of student teachers' perceptions of poverty, whilst the Strathclyde data suggest the potential power of a focused intervention to change views on poverty and education. A teacher identity framework is used to consider the interactions between external factors (schools, systems, communities of practice) and internal factors (knowledge, activities, thoughts, reflections), to understand how participation, alignment, agency and reification can support or undermine teachers' understanding and enactment of teaching for social justice.

Introduction

The strong correlation between child poverty and poor educational outcomes is well documented (e.g. Economic and Social Research Council 2011; Raffo et al. 2009). In the UK, arguably one of the most unequal societies in the developed world, research shows that educational inequalities surface in the preschool years (Sylva et al. 2004), but continue to grow in primary (elementary) and secondary (high) school years (Connelly, Sullivan, and Jerrim 2014). Yet not all pupils from impoverished backgrounds fail and there is research evidence to suggest both that good teachers make a difference and that negative stereotypes about impoverished children based on deficit assumptions can perpetuate inequality (e.g. Cummings et al. 2012; Gorski 2012).

Recent government discourse from the central UK government in Westminster, as well as from the regionally devolved governments in Scotland, Wales and Northern Ireland, has voiced significant concerns about this educational inequality. This focus has had some effect on policy and practice in initial teacher education (ITE). For example, ITE programmes in all four nations are expected to prepare beginning teachers to meet the needs of all learners, including those living in poverty. However, despite this focus of attention, there has been surprisingly little research in the UK on the perceptions held by student teachers on the effects of poverty on pupils' learning and well-being. The research that has been conducted in this area (e.g. Thompson, McNicholl, and Menter 2016) indicates that many student teachers hold unsophisticated attitudes towards the effects of poverty on pupils based on deficit models that attribute educational lack of success to problems located within pupils, parents and communities. Although the educational landscapes in England and Scotland are significantly different, ITE courses in both countries are subject to policy changes caused by the pressures of globalisation and standardisation of teacher training (Menter, Brisard, and Smith 2006).

This article is presented as an exploratory study on student teachers' perceptions of the effects of poverty on learners, an area without much directly relevant literature. The article reports on two UK ITE research studies from two contrasting contexts: a secondary school course in Oxford, England and a primary school course in Strathclyde, Scotland. The questions of how student teachers understand the effect of poverty on pupils' educational achievement, and what they as prospective teachers can do to effect change, are common concerns of the research studies reported here. As Jensen (2009) and others argue, it is essential that trainee teachers develop an understanding of the effects of poverty for the young people in their classrooms. The Oxford study illustrates the problematic issue of student teachers' perceptions of poverty, whilst the Strathclyde data suggest the potential power of a focused intervention.

The Oxford study, conducted in the academic year 2012–13, investigated how secondary student teachers' views on poverty were subjected to challenge and change during an ITE course in England. This mixed methods study highlighted some of the difficulties faced by teacher educators in challenging entrenched views on poverty and educational attainment. The Strathclyde study reports findings from a study of the impact of a literacy clinic project intervention aimed at changing primary school student teachers' understandings of, and attitudes towards, poverty and their own role in relation to challenging inequality. The project, based in one of the poorest parts of Glasgow, is designed to build primary level student teachers' fluency in real-time teaching responses in ways that provide a strong emotional and social dimension to their learning and impact on their professional identity. The project has been running for four years and involves a short-term intervention in which student teachers use their literacy-teaching knowledge to support children with reading problems. The literacy clinic project gives insight into the sorts of experiences that can change student teachers' attitudes and beliefs about poverty by enhancing their understanding and agency in terms of what they can do as teachers.

This article has two main aims: to disseminate the key findings from these very different studies about student teachers' perceptions of poverty in both England and Scotland, and to stimulate further discussion about how teacher education (whether school or university based) can ensure that the new generation of teachers meets the needs of pupils living in poverty. The authors conclude that there is much to learn from these studies about the effects of both school experience and University-led interventions on student teachers' understanding and professional response to teaching children from economically disadvantaged backgrounds.

Theoretical position

Theoretically, we draw on the concept of *identity* in relation to the transition from student teacher to teacher professional. Holland and Lachicotte define identity as 'a self-understanding to which one is emotionally attached and that informs one's behaviour and interpretations' (Holland and Lachicotte 2007, 104). Holland et al. (1998) develop the concept of positionality to denote that an individual's participation in activities in practice takes place from a particular stance or perspective. Identities in action develop as a 'heuristic means to guide, authorise, legitimate, and encourage their own and others' behaviour' (Holland et al. 1998, 18). This heuristic development of identity requires two distinctive forms of agency: improvisation (the openings whereby change comes about) and appropriation (the adoption and reshaping of professional knowledge).

However, the identities that individuals develop are 'social and cultural products' (Holland and Lachicotte 2007, 134) mediated through social and professional experience and through interactions with others (Edwards 2010). Identity formation is therefore both relational and situated. Professional identity formation reflects the social and cultural demands and motives involved in becoming a professional. These demands are multiple and often contradictory. Identity is premised as one's objectified self-image in relation to 'the ways of inhabiting roles, positions, and cultural imaginaries that matter to them' (Holland and Lachicotte 2007, 103). Norton-Meier and Drake, drawing on Holland et al. (1998), argue that one of the challenges for ITE programmes is 'to understand how to help university students integrate their histories of personal *figured worlds* of schooling and past *relational identities*' (Norton-Meier and Drake 2010; 204). Holland and Lachicotte's concept of the figured world refers to the way that individuals position themselves in relation to the 'socially and culturally constructed realms of interpretation and performance' (Holland and Lachicotte 2007, 115). The danger is that when faced with conflicting identities and multiple challenges, the pull of student teachers' long-held beliefs and experiences is invariably the strongest.

Whilst Holland and Lachicotte's conceptions are used in this article to talk about identity construction in a broad sense, a more specific teacher identity framework allows us to consider identity construction in terms of the interactions between external factors (schools, systems, communities of practice) and internal factors (knowledge, activities, thoughts, reflections). In this way, we aim to understand how professional identities, forged through participation, alignment, agency and reification (Wenger-Trayner et al. 2015), can be shaped in ways that support or undermine teachers' understanding and enactment of teaching for social justice.

ITE/poverty context in England and Scotland

Reducing the attainment gap associated with poverty is a high-profile policy issue in both England and Scotland (Department for Education (DfE) 2010; McNab 2015). In England, the policy solution is to devolve the resources, decisions and accountability to individual school administrations through a pupil premium (additional government funding targeted at children eligible for free school meals at any point in the past six years) (see Burn et al. forthcoming). It is unclear how effectively the pupil premium is being used by schools (Carpenter et al. 2013), or how success will be measured given the Government's abandonment of the 'contextual added value' attainment measures introduced by the previous Labour administration (Stewart 2011). 'Contextual added value' was a statistical comparison of a child's performance with children with similar prior performance and circumstances. In Scotland, the policy response has been to amend the *Children and Young People (Scotland) Act* to place a legal duty on local authorities to monitor and take steps to reduce inequalities of outcome linked to social disadvantage (Scottish Parliament 2015). A National Improvement Framework, which will include standardised tests, will support this (Scottish Government 2016).

Scotland and England have different mechanisms for measuring and monitoring attainment, but there is strong evidence that educational achievement is linked to economic disadvantage, with similar patterns in both countries. In England, nationally available data show that the gap is present when children enter schooling and widens as they move through the school system (Strand 2014). The data allow fine-grained analysis and shows that the gap exists in almost all schools, even those rated 'outstanding' by England's inspection body, Ofsted (Strand 2014). Such studies, and others indicating that most variation in school attainment is associated with qualities of school intake rather than aspects of schooling (e.g. Rasbash et al. 2010), have been interpreted by some theorists as evidence of schools' relative powerlessness to effect change given external home, community or peer-group factors (e.g. BERA 2014). The attainment pattern for schooling in Scotland is less well-evidenced, but appears to follow a similar pattern (Sosu and Ellis 2014). Analysis of the *Growing Up in Scotland* survey data indicates significant vocabulary differences in children from low and high-income households at age three, and that high-income children have an advantage of 13-months in vocabulary and 10 months in problem-solving abilities by age five (Bradshaw 2011). The gap widens as children move through school: aged 8 years, 72% of children from deprived backgrounds and 84% from the least deprived backgrounds perform well or very well in literacy. By 14 years, only 68% from deprived backgrounds perform well or very well compared with 90% from the least deprived backgrounds (Sosu and Ellis 2014).

There are undeniable tensions in national and international academic discourses around how far schools, teachers and schooling can influence attainment as central, peripheral or marginal agents of social change. Whilst some argue that 'gap talk' underplays the underlying social causes of disadvantage and represents a political desire to shift an impossible responsibility for educational success or failure to schools (e.g. Ball 2010; Gillborn 2008), others focus on identifying features of outlier schools, school systems, pedagogies or design interventions that demonstrate a narrowed gap (e.g. Darling-Hammond 2010; Holzman 2010; Kirp 2013; MacInnes 2009; OECD 2012; Stein and Coburn 2008).

The English data indicate, somewhat counter-intuitively, that the attainment of disadvantaged children tends to be lower where such children constitute a minority of the school population (Strand 2014). One explanation is that they become 'invisible' within the larger, economically advantaged, population. This implies that teachers and schools do impact on the poverty gap, and that addressing poverty-related attainment is an issue for all England's educators. In Scotland, the National Survey sample sizes are inappropriate for such fine-grained analysis but geographical distributions indicate that around two-thirds of children in poverty go to school in areas not categorised as deprived (SIMD 2009, 2012). In Scotland too, therefore, all teachers will teach some children in poverty and should be expected to take steps to close the gap.

In both countries, therefore, the challenge for ITE is to influence student teachers' professional understandings of, and commitment towards, delivering social justice and high academic attainment for children from economically disadvantaged homes. Yet studies suggest that many teachers hold deficit models of children in poverty (e.g. Cox, Watts, and Horton 2012; Gazeley and Dunne 2005; Lupton and Thrupp 2013) and that student teachers' pre-existing beliefs are difficult to change during ITE courses (e.g. Richardson 1996; Wideen, Mayer-Smith, and Moon 1998). Professional beliefs matter because they filter teachers' understandings, their aims, their observations and their responses to classroom events (Jacobs, Lamb, and Philipp 2010). Belief change is closely aligned to teacher identity (the sense of self, and who one wants to be) and to teacher agency (the capacity to act and, through this, develop new professional understandings).

The 'poverty' issue for ITE courses and education researchers becomes how to create the conditions for student teachers' understanding, identity and agency to flourish in ways that prompt their professional commitment to equity and an ability to deliver it for children in poverty. Whilst most ITE courses in the UK have an explicit commitment to social justice and children's rights, we could find no research studies of how ITE programmes realise this in terms of the poverty agenda, and what works to leverage effective change. English research does indicate that idealistic motivations do not reliably prompt effective improvisations (the openings whereby change comes about) or appropriations (the adoption and reshaping of professional knowledge) in early career teachers. Importantly, idealism accompanied by a failure to impact successfully on children's learning may lead to disappointment and disaffection (Day and Gu 2010).

Moore (2008) found that student science teachers' agency in delivering social justice was linked to broader constructs of their professional agency and identity as science teachers, as well as to their stance towards social justice. Research needs to deepen understanding of student teachers' views of poverty and of how ITE interventions work to gain traction and impact on their identity and knowledge.

Methods

Primary and secondary ITE contexts

There are some significant differences in the preparation of primary and secondary school teachers. The primary teacher needs to work across the curriculum and have significant skills in the teaching of literacy and numeracy in particular. The developmental needs of younger pupils means more attention must be paid to responsive teaching, instructional density (many outcomes from a single lesson) and to promoting home-school links. At secondary level, the vast majority of training concentrates on trainee teachers' specialisms. However, the trainee teachers in each sector are both involved in a social situation of development that requires them to empathise with, and understand the diverse learning needs of, learners as well as the contextual factors that can affect this learning. This article concentrates on the shared experience of developing an understanding of poverty and education from these contrasting ITE environments. Both the studies reported in this article are highly situated and the outcomes reported adopt an interpretive stance. The intention is to provoke a debate rather than deliver potential solutions. We would argue that this aim and the mixed-methods methodology across two different sites and teacher populations is justifiable given the lack of current research in this area. By triangulating the data, this article raises questions about the potential levers for change that may be available to ITE course designers and tutors.

Case one

The study *Student Teachers' Perceptions of Poverty and Educational Achievement* was carried out within the ITE programme at the University of Oxford in the academic year 2012–13. This research and the interventions that followed in subsequent years have been reported in detail elsewhere (Burn et al. forthcoming; Thompson, McNicholl, and Menter 2016). The study was concerned with the views held by ITE students on the effects of poverty on pupils' learning, well-being in school and educational achievement. The key research question guiding this study was: *in relation to learners living in poverty, in what ways and to what extent do beginning teachers' knowledge, skills and dispositions develop during their programme of study?* The study used a mixed methods approach (Mertens and Hesse-Biber 2013) involving the collection and analysis of both qualitative and quantitative data. Surveys and interviews were used as different but complementary lenses to investigate student teachers' perceptions and, ultimately, generate better understandings.

Qualitative and quantitative data were collected from two pre and post whole course survey questionnaires with the PGCE cohort. Comments from the surveys were coded and the results used to provide a statistical summary. At the end of the course, but before the second survey, semi-structured focus group interviews were also conducted. The pre and post course questionnaires were used to investigate student teachers' perceptions and their development over the course of the ITE programme. The first survey was delivered to 185 students and had an 85% response. The second was delivered to the 179 students remaining on the course with a 93% reply rate. A Professional Development Programme (PDP) 90 min session that dealt with issues of poverty and educational achievement was delivered to the whole cohort immediately after the first survey. This was designed as an intervention and provocation to challenge perceptions of poverty and educational attainment. The students were subsequently asked to reflect on the discussions in the light of their school experience in two placements on the course. In the second stage (the second survey and focus group interviews), the aim was both to gauge student teachers' perceptions of poverty and also to determine what influence various aspects of the course had had on their beliefs: placement schools, school mentors, university tutors, and university sessions.

Case two

The *Strathclyde Literacy Clinic* study reports evidence from a study designed to reshape student teachers' beliefs about children who live in poverty and their professional capacity to raise the literacy attainment of such children. The data were collected over two years from two separate student cohorts and the entire data-set consists of: the student teachers' written notes and reflections whilst working in the clinic; in-depth semi-structured interviews conducted towards the end of their clinic and participation; and written reflections made several weeks after clinic work had finished. This article reports the data from student teacher interviews and written reflections.

Thirty students who had indicated that they were willing to take part in the research were randomly selected for an in-depth interview. An experienced educational researcher who was not involved in the work of the literacy clinic and who did not know the students carried out the interviews. Each interview was transcribed as a detailed summary using students' own words and sent to the interviewee to confirm its accuracy and amend it if necessary.

These were anonymised and forwarded to the research team with details of the student teacher's gender, age, participating basis (credit/volunteer), and the year-group/cohort. Three researchers read and re-read the interviews and used an iterative process of thematic content analysis to create an analytic hierarchy, following the process described by Ritchie, Spencer, and O'Connor (2003). Participation in the research was voluntary, and student teachers were assured that the process was confidential and would not affect their grades on the course. Interviewees had the right to withdraw at any time.

The Strathclyde Literacy Clinics operate in schools serving high-poverty populations. About 80 ITE students participate annually, working in teaching teams of four. Each team works for 10 weeks with one child aged 7–10 years who has struggled to learn to read. The child has one 30-min withdrawal lesson from each team member (i.e. four lessons per week). Team members collect evidence about the child's learning assets and needs and use it to agree learning priorities that everyone works to deliver. Decisions are revised as new evidence emerges and are explored in tutorial discussions with academic tutors and other teams. The approach foregrounds 'the problem of enactment' (Darling-Hammond 2006) by focusing student teachers on responding fluently to knowledge as it emerges during teaching (Cazden 1983). Students write notes highlighting key actions/observations and reflections in a team file after the lesson rather than pre-lesson procedural guides or lesson plans. Continuity and coherence emerge through daily telephone updates between adjacent students in the teaching chain. These articulate the teaching on a day-by-day basis and promote a collaborative group dynamic based on shared knowledge, responsibility, pupil-focused preparation and reflection.

A Venn diagram (see Figure 1) acts as a 'boundary object' (adapted from Star and Griesemer 1989), allowing the group to share evidence that individuals may value and use in different ways. It prompts student teachers to incorporate into their teaching, evidence about the child's:

- *cultural capital*, knowledge, beliefs and experiences (of the world and literacy);

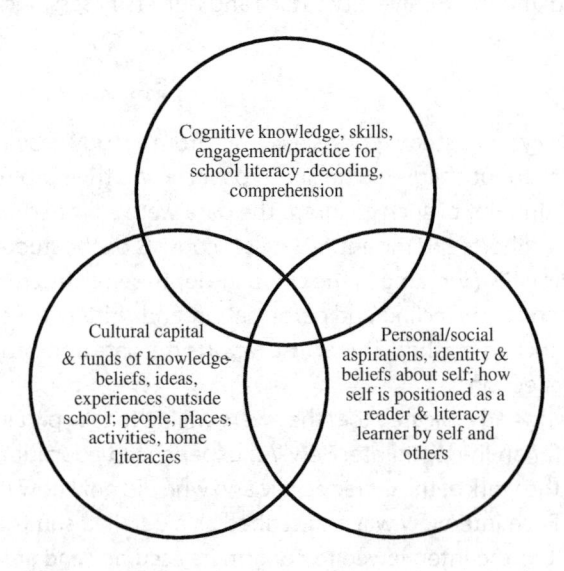

Figure 1. Venn diagram as a boundary object.

- *identity* as a reader and a literacy learner;
- *cognitive* knowledge and skills for literacy learning.

Although lightly specified, the boundary object has intuitive validity and serves two important functions in facilitating the work of individual student teachers and negotiation of meaning within student teams. First, it facilitates data collection and evidence use from multiple disciplines, specifically prompting teaching professionals to align their work to knowledge domains with different epistemological traditions and negotiate across them to work out what to teach, and how (Wenger-Trayner et al. 2015). Second, it promotes an 'assets based' discourse for teaching that positions young readers as agentic and instruction as bridging from the known to the unknown (González, Moll, and Amanti 2005). In much teacher discourse, the cognitive knowledge domain drives curriculum content and analyses of learning, but the boundary object evidence collected around cultural capital and identity invites consideration of how to use these aspects to drive cognitive development. Teachers consider how to use the funds of knowledge children bring to school (González, Moll, and Amanti 2005), how to adopt a situated, culturally determined view of literacy (Street 2000), how to attend to children's literate identities (Esteban-Guitart and Moll 2014), and to how they position themselves, and are positioned by others, as literacy learners (Dweck 1986). Highlighting the different epistemologies provides different lenses to examine practice, different definitions of what matters and student teachers learn to recognise, value and broker, different kinds of evidence. By understanding the insight each brings, they can locate their pupils, their teaching and ultimately themselves, within the wider 'landscape of practice' (Wenger-Trayner et al. 2015).

Findings

Case one/findings

In the Oxford study *Student Teachers' Perceptions of Poverty and Educational Achievement*, a pre-course survey asked the cohort of student teachers ($n = 185$) to respond to a series of questions about their attitudes to, and perceptions of, poverty and educational achievement. They were first asked to describe their own background income levels and 82% described themselves coming from middle to high income backgrounds. When the student teachers were asked what had the largest impact on pupils' educational outcomes, life choice and opportunities, the results were: Parents'/Carers' Attitudes to Education 81%; Social Class 8%; Income Levels 7%; gender 3%. These striking figures suggested that the vast majority of the cohort held deficit views about children in poverty by blaming attitudes rather than economic and social conditions.

The second survey ($n = 179$), conducted at the end of the course, began by asking the student teachers whether they agreed with the following assertion: *'There is a link between poverty and pupils' educational outcomes, life choices and opportunities'* ($n = 166$). The finding that 24% at the end of an ITE course disagreed that there was a link between poverty and educational achievement was a revealing finding for a course that had repeatedly made this link explicit through the sharing of research findings in University and school-based sessions. It can also be argued that the majority of the 76% of students who did believe there was a link between poverty and educational attainment fell back on deficit models for their interpretation of why this should be the case. One hundred and eighteen comments on the reasons for the given answers on this questions were coded for four different factors: parental deficit (41%); pupil deficit (19.5%); school factors (positive and negative) (7.5%); and socio-economic factors (32%). 18 comments were uncoded as they gave no reason or just restated the question.

Examples of statements suggesting that low expectations or aspirations held by parents was the main cause included:

> I think that students who come from less well off backgrounds are often (but not always) there because their parents have lower aspirations, therefore they are less likely to value their education leading to less opportunities in life. (Respondent 55)

> Pupils are highly affected by their family as a role model in terms of aspiration and attitudes to school. (Respondent 61)

Others attributed the main cause to the 'low aspirations' of pupils themselves.

The next question explored whether the student teachers believed that their views on poverty had changed during the course ($n = 166$). The fact that only 4% had completely modified their view and that 40% reported no difference backed up the research evidence that suggests that student teachers' views are hard to change.

An open question asked the students to give any reasons for a change of view. The qualitative data from the open question responses of the 61% of respondents whose views had changed were coded against the two themes of University (66 comments) and school influence (107 comments). 80% of comments identified the PDP programme as a shaping influence with smaller indications for curriculum session (9%), assignments, peers and university tutors (all 3%). Aspects of the school placements as a shaping influence included: working with pupils (57%); working with teachers (15%); own reflections and observations (17%), and communication with parents (6.5%).

The findings suggested overall that ITE programmes can challenge some entrenched views through: Professional Development Programmes; the choice of school environment; exposure to theory; and, reading of relevant literature. However, deficit models were widely accepted by some student teachers who viewed 'aspirations' (negative or positive) as more important than social class or poverty or any other structural inequalities.

From the university side of the course, the theoretical provocations from the PDP session were identified as an important factor for their change of view in 80% of 66 comments from those who did change their views. However, it is questionable whether a one off lecture session really was an important catalyst for their reflections on their subsequent school experience. From school experiences, 57% of comments indicated that working with pupils helped to shape prospective teachers' views. Other significant factors were teachers (15%) and their own reflections (17%).

Data from one of the focus group interviews revealed that the transformative effect of direct experience was very dependent on the social composition of placement schools. Some student teachers reported very little contact with pupils from impoverished backgrounds and felt that theoretical readings were therefore abstracted from their own social situation of development. This contrasted sharply with the experience of a minority of the student teachers in the focus group who described themselves as being placed in schools with significant levels of social deprivation:

> My [first placement] school had a high proportion of Free School Meal pupils and vulnerable children which gave me the opportunity to deepen my understanding of these issues through

working with the children in a pastoral setting and in the classroom. (Chloe, student teacher Oxford)

The conclusion drawn from this study was that identity is hard to change without direct involvement with pupils from impoverished backgrounds and with teachers experienced in working to alleviate the effects of poverty for these youngsters. The social justice agenda of the course, and direct input from both university and school educators, had some limited effect in changing student teachers' perceptions through discussion and explication. However, 40% of the cohort did not change their views. The prompts and provocations were ultimately relatively weak levers for change. The provocative PDP lecture had the most effect, but this did not break into the hard-to-reach perceptions of many of the student teachers. The majority of the student teachers held deficit models at the start and end of the course, and even those that accepted the correlation blamed the parents or a lack of imagination or ambition within the child. Simply being told that this was not true had little to no impact.

Case two/findings

Iterative thematic content analysis of the student teacher interviews and written reflections identified several mechanisms that supported the student teachers' agency and effectiveness in the literacy clinic. Three categories of response, related directly to the development of their professional identity, agency and knowledge of how to close the attainment gap, were identified as:

- understanding of poverty in the context of schooling;
- adaptive actions and applications to position learners more equitably;
- exercising professional agency and imagination to address the attainment gap.

The interrelatedness of these categories, and interwoven factors about the student teacher identities, the one-to-one context of practice and the group context of teaching, illuminate the complex ecology of teaching and of how professional engagement shapes the development of identity in relation to social justice.

Understanding poverty and schooling

The picture that emerged about student teacher understandings of poverty in the context of schooling indicated a step-change in their understandings of life in disadvantaged families and of how poverty impacts on educational attainment. This was so regardless of the student teachers' past placements in schools serving deprived areas or personal experiences of growing up in such areas. The evidence that emerged was that, after an initial stage of shock, the one-to-one discussions between the student teacher and child disrupted the student teachers' rather cosy institutional narratives and assumptions about schooling and presented an alternative pupil-narrative that commanded attention and action. They realised how organisational measures, such as within-class attainment groupings, negatively impacted on choice, enjoyment, self-esteem and friendships. Georgia's reaction to her pupil's view of schooling and literacy was typical of many interviewees:

> I was quite disturbed by it. A real eye-opener. I was shell-shocked by what he couldn't do and most of all his negative view of reading. I still worry about his future. I did find the experience

> enjoyable in a strange way though it was upsetting ... and I wanted to try really hard for him....
> (Georgia, student teacher Strathclyde)

The evidence collected during the teaching sessions led student teachers to question what the concept of home-school links really meant for children whose home lives did not fit the school's assumptions. These elements had been covered in previous university course content, reading and assignments, but acquired new, personalised meanings:

> Well you need to know your children. I've been aware of that before, but on placement you don't really think about the child's home life so much ... Their parents might be illiterate ... What's that say to school about 'sending the reading homework out'? (Helen, student teacher Strathclyde)

The mundane details of children's lived experiences of poverty, and of the school literacy curriculum, challenged stereotypes and gave new insights into poverty and schooling. It was clearly quite an emotional experience for many students. After the first six interviews, the researcher wrote a note to the research team saying:

> Each one I have done so far has shown visible emotional signs when discussing the levels of poor readers and the impact of poverty ... [it is in their] ... expressions, teary eyes, taking a moment or two to reflect on what to say next.

Adaptive teaching to link to pupil lives

Although emotions enhance student teacher learning by encouraging engagement, professional identity needs to be nurtured by more than emotion. Identity is about envisioning who you are and what you know as a professional and (re)presenting this narrative to yourself and to others. This process can sometimes get skewed in performative, whole-class placements where teaching is formally observed and assessed. However, the analysis related to specific adaptive behaviours revealed changes that were often small and seemingly un-dramatic but involved student teachers noticing different kinds of evidence and then using their knowledge differently which led them to re-frame their teaching. Evidence from the 'cultural capital' and 'identity' domains were particularly powerful levers to prompt changes that positioned the pupil as agentic. Analysis revealed three sub-categories of adaptive behaviours in the students' teaching. Each situated the child more powerfully in relation to the learning task. First, there were instances of student teachers re-framing tasks to position pupils' out-of-school knowledge as central to the work. They did this by building tasks around pupils' artistic talents, significant role models and personal aspirations. Second, they adapted their teaching to explain the reasons and purposes behind the tasks and instructional inputs. For example, one student teacher, Alice, told the interviewer:

> I said 'Why I am asking you these questions about this book, it isn't to test you or to catch you out, but I want to show you the sorts of things that readers think about when they read. That's what my questions are doing.' (Alice, student teacher Strathclyde)

Third, they demonstrated a deeper understanding of the wider context and cultural background that makes a task or text truly meaningful. Kathy captures this in describing how her understanding of what counts as 'important to know' shifted:

> Now I understand the importance of contextualising things. Developing activities that are based on the child's need – I already knew that mattered – but what I think now is you need more, because that's not enough. ... it's like teaching someone to swim without going in the water – without lots of context she can't get enough purchase to push her own way through. (Kathy, student teacher Strathclyde)

Analysis of student teachers' written reflections indicated that the boundary object facilitated adaptive teaching by focusing the student teachers on collecting and using different kinds of evidence. It dislocated their dominant (cognitive) knowledge frameworks for thinking about teaching and prompted them to improvise bridging-behaviours that linked teaching to pupils' lives and to how they felt.

The Professional Self: Agency, Imagination and the Poverty Gap

Learning to align a wider range of evidence in the context of use also prompted professional understanding and agency in relation to poverty. Working mainly within a single knowledge domain can lead professionals to linear thoughts and narrow interventions. By drawing explicitly on three knowledge domains, student teachers learned to re-frame problems and potential ways forward. This inevitably led to an expanded range of potential learning pathways and interventions with different underpinning theories of change. Professional judgement became more complex, less certain, and open to a wider range of challenges. For some, this underlined their own agency in relation to acting on professional knowledge and impacted on their professional identity in ways that made complete sense:

> It made me realize that when something doesn't work you need to find another way. As a professional you don't always follow the crowd – you have to see what else can be done. ... It has changed how I think about literacy and changed me as a teacher. (Lucie, student teacher Strathclyde)

The team discussions helped this process, assuaging the uncertainty of negotiating across different kinds of knowledge, working out how to weigh and use the evidence and how to proceed. Individual student teachers taught just once a week and had time to be curious, to wonder, to reflect and to research. Ideas had 'cooking-time' and were seasoned by other students' observations, questions and challenges. The one-to-one context supported professional agency and personalised insights whilst the team structure offered intrinsic motivation, safety, challenge and rapid success (because the child's progress reflected the work of four people). These aspects encouraged the student teachers to envisage their future professional selves as agentic and knowledgeable about how to address the attainment gap. This was even true for less confident student teachers, for whom professional knowledge, agency and identity were perhaps more fragile constructs. In her interview, Sharon described how the agency and knowledge that resided in the group helped her towards a more robust and positive personal professional identity. She characterised herself as someone who had 'failed a few things and had to work hard just to keep up'. Although she still indicated some vulnerability, she was clearly beginning to assume a stronger identity and agency for herself:

> I feel like we had, as a group, what we needed to be able to do it. We were told beforehand what to expect but it was a bit different out there and we had to change everything. It was very hard, because the child we were working with was really struggling, even compared with his peers who were also struggling. It was very rewarding, though, especially changing his perspective. He was at first very reluctant. It was a job of work to even get his energy up to try. He found it hard to remember the lessons ... so I had to learn to adapt to that. At the same time, seeing the difference in his ability and interest in learning gave me hope I can make that difference with my pupils in future. (Sharon, student teacher Strathclyde)

Discussion and conclusion

Empirical research from a range of epistemological traditions shows that children from poor backgrounds do better educationally and emotionally in some school contexts than others. Very few school populations contain no children in poverty and prospective teachers need to be attuned to noticing and addressing the needs of disadvantaged children. This is so whether they work in schools serving deprived communities with large population of such children or schools serving advantaged communities where children in poverty form a hidden minority. It is, quite simply, not ethical for ITE programmes and ITE researchers not to treat this as an urgent priority.

This article set out to discuss the perceptions of student teachers on poverty and educational attainment from two very different perspectives of a primary ITE course in Scotland and a secondary ITE course in England. The argument posed was that viewing the problem from contrasting perspectives could help to develop a new understanding of a common problem. What both studies make clear is that successfully challenging student teachers' understandings of social justice and equity in education is not just about direct experience. It needs input from literature, research provocations, and collaborative challenge, and is developed differently in different contexts of use. Poverty is complex. Not all young people who are impoverished will fail. Home, community, emotional, personal and school circumstances combine in different ways to impact on learning, and the process whereby student teachers come to understand the implications for their teaching are equally complex.

The Oxford intervention shows that whilst ITE courses can successfully challenge some preconceptions, there are limitations to simply telling student teachers what to think. If student teachers hold deficit models that essentially blame the learner, then a disruption or dislocation through direct or reported experience may be required to change these seemingly entrenched views. Hard to change does not mean impossible to change. As identity and perceptions are relational and situated, then it is important to consider both the choice of placements and also alternatives in provision around issues of poverty and learning. The Strathclyde Literacy Clinic intervention shows that professional knowledge and communities of practice can be levers for change, but professional identity is complex. It requires practical opportunities for student teachers to attend to the boundaries of knowledge and to align and realign themselves to a range of professional knowledge domains. These realignments offer tentative hope that, as student teachers learn to use different kinds of evidence and different ways of thinking, they can develop new understandings of their role in making schooling more equitable for children living in poverty. Traditional school placements may, however, not offer suitable spaces for this to happen.

The questions these studies raise for ITE educators concern the kinds of opportunities that we create for student teachers to explore their own attitudes and beliefs about poverty and educational attainment. Student teachers need opportunities to bring different kinds of research knowledge to bear on practice, and, through reification (the production of physical or conceptual artefacts), make it personal and meaningful. This may mean challenging their past histories, their *figured worlds* of schooling and past *relational identities*, through the creation of new supportive but challenging communities of practice. Agency, beliefs and identity matter, because if student teachers believe there is no link between poverty and achievement or that the attainment gap is inevitable, then they will not address pupils' needs. Simply relying on placement experiences, and strong, well-established courses with social justice as a core value may not in itself be enough to change long-established patterns of belief. There is an urgent need to understand the links between social justice and teacher identity.

The studies also raise questions about the sorts of learning spaces that support student teachers in bringing professional knowledge, agency and identity together in ways that prompt them to pay careful attention to the effects of one course of action rather than another, and what each brings into focus or omits. ITE courses need to develop the structure and circumstances whereby student teachers can understand and adapt from cultural difference and personal learning identity.

Hall et al. (2012) show that agency is frail amongst student teachers who have little power in school placements and are often struggling to create and maintain conflicting aspects of their own professional identity. The two studies reported here show that ITE programmes perhaps could focus more explicitly on exploring, and attending to, how identity is forged from daily encounters with pupils, with educational ideas and with data. If identity develops across different contexts and is central in creating or inhibiting professional knowledge and self direction, ITE programmes need to design many contexts in which student teachers can explore how to address the needs of children living in poverty, and monitor their impact. ITE courses cannot assume school placements will do this.

All professionals have to negotiate large-scale political dilemmas as active players in a policy framework. However, how they do this may not be in an overt way but through the situated formation of professional identities. Hilary Janks claims that what she calls the 'big P' of Politics, which addresses the large-scale political issues around inequality, is connected to the 'small p' of politics, the power of small political acts through the daily actions and interactions that make the professional political. These 'small p' acts are still political. They are:

> the minute-by-minute choices and decisions that make us who we are. …it is about how we treat other people day by day; it is about whether or not we learn someone else's language or recycle our own garbage. Little p politics is about taking seriously the feminist perspective that the personal is the political. (Janks 2012, 151)

In the context of equitable education, the development of the personal agency of student teachers, their choices and decisions as beginning teachers, means understanding and addressing the social reality for pupils living in poverty.

Disclosure statement

No potential conflict of interest was reported by the authors.

References

Ball, S. J. 2010. "New Class Inequalities in Education: Why Education Policy May be Looking in the Wrong Place! Education Policy, Civil Society and Social Class." *International Journal of Sociology and Social Policy* 30 (3/4): 155–166.

BERA. 2014. *Poverty Not Schools to Blame for Exam Results*. Accessed September 9th, 2015. https://www.bera.ac.uk/bera-in-the-news/poverty-not-schools-to-blame-for-exam-results-gap

Bradshaw, P. 2011. *Growing Up in Scotland: Changes in Child Cognitive Ability in the Pre-school Years*. Edinburgh: Scottish Government.

Burn, K., T. Mutton, I. Thompson, J. Ingram, and R. Firth. forthcoming. The Impact of Adopting a Research Orientation Towards Use of the Pupil Premium Grant in Preparing Beginning Teachers to Understand and Work Effectively with Young People Living in Poverty. *Journal of Education for Teaching*.

Carpenter, H., I. Papps, J. Bragg, A. Dyson, D. Harris, K. Kerr, L. Todd, and K. Laing. 2013. *Evaluation of Pupil Premium*. London: Department for Education.

Cazden, C. B. 1983. "Can Ethnographic Research Go Beyond the Status Quo?" *Anthropology and Education Quarterly* 14: 33–41.

Connelly, R., A. Sullivan, and J. Jerrim. 2014. *Primary and Secondary Education and Poverty Review*. London: Institute of Education.

Cox, B. J., C. Watts, and M. Horton. 2012. "Poverty Perceptions of Pre-Service Teachers and Social Work Candidates." *Journal of Studies in Education* 2 (1): 131–148.

Cummings, C., K. Laing, J. Law, J. McLaughlin, I. Papps, L. Todd, and P. Woolner. 2012. *Can Changing Aspirations and Attitudes Impact on Educational Attainment? A Review of Interventions*. York: Joseph Rowntree Foundation.

Darling-Hammond, L. 2006. "Constructing 21st-Century Teacher Education." *Journal of Teacher Education* 57 (3): 1–15.

Darling-Hammond, L. 2010. *The Flat World and Education: How America's Commitment to Equity Will Determine Our Future*. New York: Teachers College Press.

Day, C., and Q. Gu. 2010. *The New Lives of Teachers*. London: Routledge.

Department for Education (DfE). 2010. *The Importance of Teaching*. Accessed February 10th, 2016. https://www.gov.uk/government/uploads/system/uploads/attachment_data/file/175429/CM-7980.pdf

Dweck, C. S. 1986. "Motivational Processes Affecting Learning." *American Psychologist* 41 (10): 1040–1048.

Economic and Social Research Council. 2011. *Child Poverty Casts a Long Shadow Over Social Mobility. Evidence Briefing*. Swindon: ESRC.

Edwards, A. 2010. *Being an Expert Professional Practitioner: The Relational Turn in Expertise*. Dordrecht: Springer.

Esteban-Guitart, M., and L. C. Moll. 2014. "Funds of Identity: A New Concept Based on the Funds of Knowledge Approach." *Culture & Psychology* 20 (1): 31–48.

Gazeley, L., and M. Dunne. 2005. *Addressing Working Class Underachievement*. Brighton: University of Sussex.

Gillborn, D. 2008. *Racism and Education: Coincidence or Conspiracy?*. London: Routledge.

González, N., L. Moll, and C. Amanti. 2005. *Funds of Knowledge: Theorizing Practices in Households, Communities, and Classrooms*. New York: Routledge.

Gorski, P. C. 2012. "Perceiving the Problem of Poverty and Schooling: Deconstructing the Class Stereotypes that Mis-shape Education Practice and Policy." *Equity & Excellence in Education* 45 (2): 302–319.

Hall, K., P. Conway, R. Murphy, F. Long, K. Kitching, and D. O'Sullivan. 2012. "Authoring Oneself and Being Authored as a Competent Teacher." *Irish Educational Studies* 31 (2): 103–117.

Holland, D., and W. Lachicotte. 2007. "Vygotsky, Mead and the New Sociocultural Studies of Identity." In *The Cambridge Companion to Vygotsky*, edited by H. Daniels, M. Cole, and J. V. Wertsch, 101–135. New York: Cambridge University Press.

Holland, D., W. Lachicotte, D. Skinner, and C. Cain. 1998. *Identity and Agency in Cultural Worlds*. Cambridge, MA: Harvard University Press.

Holzman, M. 2010. *Yes We Can: The Schott 50 State Report on Public Education and Black Males*. Cambridge, MA: Schott Foundation for Public Education. Accessed February 10th, 2016. http://www.Blackboysreport.org/bbreport.pdf

Jacobs, V. R., L. L. C. Lamb, and R. A. Philipp. 2010. "Professional *Noticing* of Children's Mathematical Thinking." *Journal for Research in Mathematics Education* 41 (2): 169–202.

Janks, H. 2012. "The Importance of Critical Literacy." *English Teaching: Practice and Critique* 11 (1): 150–163.

Jensen, E. 2009. *Teaching with Poverty in Mind*. Alexandria, VA: ASCD.

Kirp, D. L. 2013. *Improbable Scholars: The Rebirth of A Great American School System a Strategy for America's Schools*. Oxford: Oxford University Press.

Lupton, R., and M. Thrupp. 2013. "Headteachers' Readings of and Responses to Disadvantaged Contexts: Evidence from English Primary Schools." *British Educational Research Journal* 39 (4): 769–788.

MacInnes, G. 2009. *In Plain Sight: Simple, Difficult Lessons from New Jersey's Expensive Effort to Close the Achievement Gap*. New York: Century Foundation.

McNab, S. 2015. Nicola Sturgeon: Judge Me on Education Record. *The Scotsman*, August Tuesday 18, 2015. Accessed September 9th, 2015. http://www.scotsman.com/news/education/nicola-sturgeon-judge-me-on-education-record-1-3861506

Menter, I., E. Brisard, and I. Smith. 2006. *Convergence or Divergence? Initial Teacher Education in Scotland and England*. Edinburgh: Dunedin Academic Press.

Mertens, D. M., and S. Hesse-Biber. 2013. "Mixed Methods and Credibility of Evidence in Evaluation." *New Directions for Evaluation* 138: 5–13.

Moore, F. M. 2008. "Agency, Identity, and Social Justice Education: Preservice Teachers' Thoughts on Becoming Agents of Change in Urban Elementary Science Classrooms." *Research in Science Education* 38: 589–610.

Norton-Meier, L. A., and C. Drake. 2010. "When Third Space is More Than the Library." In *Cultural-historical Perspectives on Teacher Education and Development*, edited by V. Ellis, A. Edwards, and P. Smagorinsky, 196–211. London: Routledge.

OECD. 2012. *Education at a Glance 2012: Highlights*. OECD Publishing. Accessed January 8th, 2016. http://dx.doi.org/10.1787/eag_highlights-2012-en

Raffo, C., A. Dyson, H. Gunter, D. Hall, L. Jones, and A. Kalambouka. 2009. *Education and Poverty: A Critical Review of Theory, Policy and Practice*. York: Joseph Rowntree Foundation.

Rasbash, J., G. Leckie, R. Pillinger, and J. Jenkins. 2010. "Children's Educational Progress: Partitioning Family, School and Area Effects." *Journal of the Royal Statistical Society: Series A* 173 (4): 1–26.

Richardson, V. 1996. "The Role of Attitudes and Beliefs in Learning to Teach." In *Handbook of Research on Teacher Education*, edited by J. Sikula, 102–119. New York: Macmillan.

Ritchie, J., L. Spencer, and W. O'Connor. 2003. "Carrying out Qualitative Analysis." In *Qualitative Research Practice: A Guide for Social Science Students and Researchers*, edited by J. Ritchie and J. Law, 219–262. London: SAGE Publications.

Scottish Government. 2016. *National Improvement Framework for Scottish Education - achieving excellence and equity*. Edinburgh: HMSO. Accessed January 8th, 2016. www.gov.scot/Publications/2016/01/8314

Scottish Index of Multiple Deprivation (SIMD). 2009. Accessed January 8th, 2016. http://www.gov.scot/Topics/Statistics/SIMD/Background-Data-2009

Scottish Index of Multiple Deprivation (SIMD). 2012. Accessed January 8th, 2016. http://www.simd.scotland.gov.uk/publication-2012/

Scottish Parliament. 2015. *Education (Scotland) Bill Stage 1 Parliamentary Business- Bills 87330 Holyrood*. Edinburgh: Scottish Government. Accessed January 8th, 2016. http://www.scottish.parliament.uk/parliamentarybusiness/Bills/87330.aspx

Sosu, E., and S. Ellis. 2014. *Closing the Attainment Gap in Scottish Education*. York: Joseph Rowntree Foundation.

Star, S., and J. Griesemer. 1989. "Institutional Ecology, 'Translations' and Boundary Objects: Amateurs and Professionals in Berkeley's Museum of Vertebrate Zoology, 1907–39." *Social Studies of Science* 19 (3): 387–420.

Stein, M. K., and C. E. Coburn. 2008. "Architectures for Learning: A Comparative Analysis of Two Urban School Districts." *American Journal of Education* 114 (4): 583–626.

Stewart, W. 2011. "League Tables to Ignore Race and Poverty." *Times Educational Supplement Newspaper*, June 3, 2011. Accessed January 8th, 2016. https://www.tes.com/article.aspx?storycode=6086535

Strand, S. 2014. "Ethnicity, Gender, Social Class and Achievement Gaps at Age 16: Intersectionality and 'Getting It' for the White Working Class." *Research Papers in Education* 29 (2): 131–171.

Street, B. 2000. "Literacy Events and Literacy Practices: Theories and Practice in the New Literacy Studies." In *Multilingual Literacies: Comparative Perspectives on Research and Practice*, edited by M. Martin-Jones and K. Jones, 17–29. Amsterdam: John Benjamin's.

Sylva, K., E. Melhuish, P. Sammons, I. Siraj-Blatchford, and B. Taggart. 2004. *The Effective Provision of Preschool Education (EPPE) Project: Findings from the Preschool to the End of Key Stage 1*. London: DfES.

Thompson, I., J. McNicholl, and I. Menter. 2016. Student Teachers' Perceptions of Poverty and Educational Achievement. *Oxford Review of Education* 42 (2): 214–229.

Wenger-Trayner, E., M. Fenton-O'Creevy, S. Hutchinson, C. Kubiak, and B. Wenger-Trayner, eds. 2015. *Learning in Landscapes of Practice: Boundaries, Identity, and Knowledgeability in Practice-based Learning*. London: Routledge.

Wideen, M., J. Mayer-Smith, and B. Moon. 1998. "A Critical Analysis of the Research on Learning to Teach: Making the Case for an Ecological Perspective on Inquiry." *Review of Educational Research* 68 (2): 130–178.

Seeing disadvantage in schools: exploring student teachers' perceptions of poverty and disadvantage using visual pedagogy

M. L. White and Jean Murray

ABSTRACT
This paper describes exploratory research into the development of innovative visual pedagogies for investigating how pre-service student-teachers articulate their views about the effects of poverty on educational attainment. Social class emerges as the strongest factor in poverty and educational disadvantage in the UK. The resulting issues are often awkward for students to discuss and conventional pedagogies may not have effective 'reach' here. Findings from this study showed that the visual methods deployed gave students pedagogically well-structured spaces for the expression and exchange of a diversity of views about poverty and social class, engaging them in both heated discussions and prolonged 'silences'. However, the pedagogies did not challenge the stereotypical deficit models of 'the poor' which some students expressed. Nevertheless, we argue that reconfigured versions of these visual pedagogies have considerable potential for innovative social justice work in teacher education.

Introduction

The UK is one of the most unequal societies in the 'developed world' (Wilkinson and Pickett 2009), with all the damage to the social, educational and moral fabric of society, which such extreme inequality can bring. Not surprisingly then, educational inequalities, often associated with social and economic disadvantage in general and with living in poverty in particular, persist (DfE 2010). Nearly half of the poorest children in England (those eligible for free school meals) fail to achieve nationally recognised qualifications at age 16 (DFE 2011). The UK is not alone in this depressing picture, of course: evidence quoted in an OECD report (OECD 2006) shows that the adverse impact of living in challenging socio-economic circumstances on children's academic attainment is statistically significant in 53 of the 54 OECD countries.

Despite this grave situation, the precise effects of poverty on children's achievements, beliefs and aspirations remain significantly under-researched, as are schools' and teachers' views on poverty and educational disadvantage and how these issues might be most effectively tackled. We also know very little about how student-teachers on pre-service courses in England conceptualise poverty and are prepared to work with children from deprived socio-economic circumstances in proactive and effective ways.

It seems essential to us, and to many other teacher educators, that pre-service programmes should develop student-teachers' awareness and understanding of such social justice issues and equip them to respond appropriately in their teaching. But given the lack of research, a major issue is how we, as teacher educators, can respond to these multiple challenges (Goodwin and Kosnik 2013). How do we establish relevant ways to work with pre-service students to prepare them to teach pupils living in poverty and coming from diverse backgrounds? In particular, what types of pedagogies might prepare student-teachers for the experiences they may have of working in schools in socio-economically deprived areas? And how do we develop students' awareness of schools where poverty, though less prevalent and perhaps less visible, still has a significant, detrimental effect on a minority of learners (Thompson et al. 2014)?

In this paper, we describe and analyse one initiative to develop pedagogical frameworks for discussing issues around poverty and its effects on educational attainment. This initiative is called 'Picturing Poverty'; it is designed to be a three-stage pedagogical research project, but the work presented here is the first and experimental stages of that larger project. The focus is on a research-informed enquiry with pre-service students training to be English teachers, exploring appropriate pedagogies to discuss some of the complex intersectionality in England between poverty, social class, disadvantage and educational attainment in East London schools.

This research is located at a time when the ubiquity of digital and web technologies means that visual materials and methods are increasingly accessible and affordable to educators. Although the use of photography in anthropology, sociology and cultural studies is well documented (Banks 2001; Pink 2007), in educational practice, ethical concerns of anonymity and censorship have limited its use (Pauwels 2010; Prosser 1998) and it is only now becoming more common place (Thomson 2008).

Our starting point for the design of this project was an emphasis on visual pedagogies to explore students' thinking about poverty and deprivation in education. This focus is partly designed to draw:

> attention to the process through which knowledge is produced. Pedagogy addressed the 'how' questions involved not only in transmission or reproduction of knowledge but also in its production. Indeed, it enables us to question the validity of separating these activities so easily by asking under what conditions and through what means we 'come to know'. How one teaches ... becomes inseparable from what is being taught and, crucially, how one learns. (Lusted 1986, 2–3)

The specific aim of the workshop is to develop visual pedagogies as a means of exploring how student-teachers articulate their views on, and experiences of, the effects of poverty and deprivation in education. As we indicate below, these issues are often seen as challenging and conflicted discussion topics for which more conventional pedagogical strategies may not have effective 'reach'. But we should stress that the pedagogies in use here are exploratory and experimental, and that, in this pedagogical research enquiry, we are not engaged in a quest to 'prove' their effectiveness. The workshop also had a secondary focus on using images in the classroom and offered suggestions for visual learning as pedagogy. This was relevant for these students as some may teach Media Studies in future.

Visual pedagogies are developed as 'a model of collaboration' (Harper, 1998, 35), between teacher educator/researcher and student-teachers/participants. Here, the importance of photography is not just as a pedagogical tool to be used in place of or in addition to other methods, rather we see it also as a research practice and a methodology that demands collaboration and the consideration of questions of agency – 'the starting place of doing' (Oakeshott 1975, 32) asking who has the authority to speak for whom? (Behar 1996). The structure of the pedagogical enquiry also owes much to Freire's (1970) problem-posing pedagogy, the process of working together to explore community issues. This is a pedagogy which recognises that people bring their knowledge and experience into the classroom and is bound to engaging with issues of social justice to frame the practices of teaching and learning.

Poverty and class in schooling and teacher education

Poverty, injustice and disadvantage in education, long important themes in educational discourses in the UK, have become renewed areas of concern in this century as the levels of social inequality in British society have increased (Dorling 2011). Analysis of educational outcomes for the UK in international surveys such as PISA reveals a growing achievement gap in which children from marginalised groups have poorer educational outcomes and consequently often poorer employment and life chances in comparison to their more economically or socially privileged peers. The economic crisis of 2008, the recession, the slow recovery from it between 2008 and 2014 and draconian cuts in welfare benefits by the previous Coalition government (2010–2015), and the 'promise' of yet more cuts to come from the current Conservative government, have only exacerbated these trends and the resulting concerns for those concerned with equity issues. Some have argued that the market-led education and social policies introduced by successive governments have led to greater social and economic polarisation in schooling (Smyth and Wrigley 2013).

Further issues are around the intersectionality of socio-economic marginalisation in England; living in poverty is clearly 'co-related' with class, ethnicity and gender. The effects of population distribution over time in both urban and rural settings are also important to consider (Dorling 2011). Definitions of poverty have long been contested (Townsend 1979), but for a number of writers, social class emerges as the strongest factor in poverty and educational disadvantage (Reay 2006; Smyth and Wrigley 2013). As Jones (2011, 5) notes, there are multiple ways in which historically rooted ideas of 'class' continue to operate as powerful social underpinning structures in British society. In his view, contemporary policy and media statements attempt to gloss over these 'class' issues, presenting stands above 'class and sectional interests' and divisions. Smyth and Wrigley (2013) similarly note that in educational terms, 'the official policy discourse, while acknowledging poverty (or at least disadvantage) is virtually silent about class' (2). These authors make 'a conscious decision to break that silence', stating that in their views 'poverty derives from class, in the senses of differences of power and position' (ibid). For Reay (2006), social class remains 'the troublesome un-dead of the English education system' (289), this is not least because 'social class injustices have never been adequately tackled within education' (291).

These analyses of 'silences' around social class and education at policy levels mirror the discomfort which many English people feel in discussing class issues. This discomfort can be compounded by an all-too-familiar national trait of not wishing to cause offence by inadvertently using the 'wrong' or 'politically incorrect' terms (Fox 2004). But talking about class in England is complex, since, paradoxically, as Jones (2011) identifies, this polite, ignoring, seemingly politically correct, silence can also exist alongside the derogative use of terms such as 'chav' to denote members of the working class. Jones sees this term as now encompassing 'any negative traits associated with working-class people – violence, laziness, teenage pregnancies, racism, drunkenness' and being 'a term of pure class contempt' when 'used by a middle-class person' (8). In this kind of discourse, prejudices around the working class, their 'respectability', work ethics (or lack of them) and the causes of any resulting socio-economic marginalisation continue to create derogatory, judgemental and homogeneous stereotypes of many of those living in poverty as 'the poor'. For this project, the implications of these multiple paradoxes of 'silence', political correctness and 'derogation' are that in asking student-teachers to talk about poverty and education, we are also asking them to discuss issues of class which many will find difficult and uncomfortable. This is then certainly an area in which more conventional pedagogies may not have effective 'reach' (Thompson et al. 2014), hence our experimentation with the affordances offered by visual pedagogies.

A further issue is that aspects of the current context for pre-service teacher education in England do not support innovations in teaching for social justice. The system, which has been under almost continuous reform since 1984, has high levels of regulation, accountability and compliance characterising the increasingly fragmented and school-led provision (Gilroy 2014). There are now multiple routes into teaching, but regardless of the route followed, student-teachers spend at least two-thirds of their time learning in their placement (practicum) schools. This places particular importance on the learning occurring in those schools.

All routes aim to prepare students to teach diverse groups of learners, including pupils who are marginalised and disadvantaged. Student-teachers are assessed against a short list of 'baseline' standards for all teachers (DFE 2011); these have been described as 'regulatory rather than developmental in intent' (Beauchamp et al. 2013, 6). They do not, however, make direct reference to the promotion of social justice, and there are therefore, predictably, no specific references to social class. There are similarly no references to the 'achievement gap' which features so strongly in government discourse, nor to the need for teachers to engage with marginalised or disadvantaged pupils, living in poverty, who may be under-achieving in terms of education. The Standards do stress the more generic areas of inspiring, motivating and challenging pupils (Standard [S]1), promoting 'good progress and outcomes' for all (S2) and adapting 'teaching to respond to the strengths and needs of all pupils' (S5). But the omission of explicit references to social justice agendas is not helpful to many teacher educators and student-teachers who see these agendas as being central to their avowed practices.

Pre-service cohorts in England, despite the previous New Labour government's initiatives to diversify the teaching force, still tend to be dominated by students from more socio-economically advantaged ('middle class' in conventional British terms) households and geographical areas and from the 'white British'/Caucasian ethnic majority. This demographic suggests that few student-teachers will have sustained personal experience of living in poverty, or other types of disadvantage. But we should note that a commitment to diversity does not have to be embodied in 'difference' or membership of a minority and/or disadvantaged group (Goodwin and Kosnik 2013). Many student-teachers, for example, bring rich life, work and academic experience into pre-service programmes that influence the ways in which they understand the material, sociocultural and educational effects of poverty; many have strong commitments to 'making a difference' in society; and many will go on to work as teachers in schools in under-privileged areas, attended by pupils from multi-cultural, -ethnic and -linguistic backgrounds who live in poverty and consequently face significant social, economic and educational disadvantages.

As indicated above, in England, we know very little about student-teachers and their preparation for working with children living in poverty. Cox et al.'s (2012) research in the USA, however, shows that students' attitudes to poverty often follow stereotypical patterns, rely primarily on middle class norms and are deeply engrained. Gorski (2012), also in the USA, discusses how such 'poverty-based stereotyping' feeds an ideology of deficit and 'mis-directs' practices and policies for schools. In this and similar research, student-teachers and other educators are positioned as largely 'resistant' to challenges around teaching for social justice and change. Other US studies, in contrast, show student-teachers strongly committed to social justice agendas on entry into teacher education, to challenging social and educational stereotypes and to critiquing schooling (Beyer 2001; Sleeter et al. 2004). This does not, however, mean that these aspirations can be channelled into positive and effective teaching to combat disadvantage.

Thompson et al.'s research is one of the few large-scale studies of student-teachers' attitudes set in England (2014, 7). Their findings suggest that 'deficit models were widely accepted by many of the student-teachers' in their sample group who 'saw "aspirations" as more important and influential on children's achievements than social class or poverty'. As the authors comment, following Gorski, such deficit views from student-teachers can lead to low expectations in the classroom, and this in turn may impact negatively on the effectiveness of students' teaching during the practicum. But Thompson et al. also acknowledge that many students enter teacher education wanting to 'make a difference' in the lives of children as learners. The issue here, again, is how such aspirations might become the principles that underpin effective pedagogies to combat social and economic disadvantage in schools.

A further issue around creating pedagogies for social justice in teacher education is the demographic of teacher educators. Goodwin and Kosnik (2013, 341) describe teacher educators in the USA as a group predominantly 'mono-cultural, mono-racial in make-up'. The same categorisations would apply to many teacher educators in the UK, with the additional comment that most, like their student-teachers, would come from relatively privileged socio-economic backgrounds. From these demographics, it might seem that as a group teacher educators, like their students, will have little sustained experience of living in poverty and disadvantage. Many teacher educators, however, have worked in schools in socio-economically disadvantaged and/or ethnically and linguistically diverse areas and therefore have experience of working with pupils from diverse backgrounds living in poverty (Goodwin and Kosnik 2013; Murray and Maguire 2007). Indeed, commitments to working in this area of social justice have often been forged in that teaching experience, in the sustained experiences of preparing student-teachers or in researching educational disadvantage.

Picturing poverty: a pedagogical research initiative

The setting for this pedagogical research enquiry is a teaching-intensive university in a densely urban context in East London, which has long been the area of the city where new immigrants to England first settle. The London Borough of Newham is at the heart of the university's catchment area and hence many of the students have placements within schools in this community. Historically, this has been one of the most disadvantaged boroughs in London (Aldridge et al. 2013; Newham Case Report 83, 2014). Newham was host to the Olympic games in 2012 and although the area has benefited from £9 billion of private investment (Centre for Economic and Business Research 2013) and is now seeing some significant re-development and 'gentrification', the borough still has the second highest level of child poverty in London. In 2014, the Newham Household Panel Survey noted that more than half (55%) of the borough's children live in households in poverty, compared to 17% nationally (London Borough of Newham 2013). Since September 2009, all Newham's primary school children have received free school meals in recognition of this.

A large number of pupils in Newham schools receive a 'pupil premium' because they live in socio-economic disadvantage; this 'premium' is additional government funding awarded to 'publicly funded schools in England to raise the attainment of disadvantaged pupils and close the gap between them and their peers', with each of these 'disadvantaged pupils' over the age of 11 currently attracting a payment of at least £935 (DfE 2015, 1). The pupil premium is now commonly used as a measure of the levels of disadvantage in schools or regions. Nationally, the average percentage of pupils in each school receiving the pupil premium is 27%; in East London that figure rises to over 70% in some schools. An Ofsted inspection report on the university partnership noted that these 'challenging urban schools' provide 'ethnically, socially, economically and culturally diverse contexts' (Ofsted 2012, 14). The report continues that these schools are learning environments which demand 'perseverance and commitment' (12) from the student-teachers working within them.

The Post Graduate Certificate of Education (PGCE) students within the teacher education programme at this university are amongst the most ethnically diverse cohorts in the country (approximately 22% of all students belong to Black or Ethnic Minority groups in an average intake, compared to a national average of approximately 14%). Socially, the majority of students come from relatively privileged socio-economic groups, although some will have been the first in their families to go to university. Many of them start their teaching careers in the multi-ethnic, -cultural and -lingual schools of East London.

In this research, all students on the PGCE English course (total cohort $n = 16$) were invited to participate in a workshop with a clear focus on visual pedagogies and engaging in 'the process of critically analysing and learning to create one's own messages – in print, audio, video, and multimedia, with emphasis on the learning and teaching of these skills through using mass media texts' (Hobbs 1998, 16). The workshop was part of the planned programme for the whole cohort, but was not assessed. The project was conducted following strict ethical guidelines, approved by the university, with all students given full choices about participation. In consideration of the potentially sensitive nature of the data, participants were given additional assurances of confidentiality and anonymity. For this reason, pseudonyms have been used here.

The research design used visual and qualitative data collection methods, including documentary analysis of written materials generated during the workshop and the session notes from the teacher educator, content analysis of questionnaires completed by students, interviews with a relevant teacher educator and photo analysis of the visual materials produced during the workshop. Records of the placement schools for each student were also made available. All of this data were used to form and inform the findings presented here.

Using visual pedagogical strategies

The workshop included various activities briefly described in non-sequential order below. It began with the sharing of stories about motivations to enter teaching and experiences of school placements. This sharing was intended to locate the workshop firmly within the context of the pre-service course, highlighting the importance of experience and reflection (Schön 1983), and exploring how these narratives might affect the student-teachers' current educational beliefs and pedagogical choices (Knowles and Holt-Reynolds, 1991). The students told stories about their experiences as pupils in school and while beginning to train as a teacher. Without exception, personal narratives here were positioned as informing the choices that they made ('I'm doing a PGCE because I want to get a good job – I'm poor now but that will change I hope!') and their attitudes to social class and poverty ('I was the first person in my family to go to university but I knew others in school who went ... I will be able to help my students (*pupils*)').

What you think you see – and what you don't

The teacher educator also provided an analysis of a photograph by Betsy Schneider after posing a series of questions using the SHOWED interview schedule (Wang et al. 2004, 912) to frame discussions of the visual images used:

(1) What do you See here?
(2) What is really Happening here?
(3) How does this relate to Our lives?
(4) Why does this concern, situation or strength exist?
(5) How can we become Empowered through our new understanding?
(6) What can we Do?

In discussions of the Schneider (2003) photograph, students were concerned to address the ethical issues raised by the image and they approached the subject matter (a young child who is in what appears to be a plastic bucket) with reluctance. One student-teacher suggested 'this is about being poor' adding 'the boy is dirty' while another suggested that 'he looks uncomfortable ... he is looking right at me and I feel bad, like something is wrong'. Within this type of visual pedagogical approach, the act of seeing and the gaze (Mulvey 1989; Sontag 1979) are central to theorising and making meaning from visual representations. The discomfort felt by the audience (in this instance the student-teachers) reflects the shift of focus from the subject of the image to the social identity and experience of the viewers. Students were 'relieved' to find out that the photographs were of the photographer's child and that the image was 'rooted in the snapshot, originating from the experiences I have with the children, watching them grow and discover the world' (Schneider 2003).

One of the central tasks of the researcher or educator is to contextualise images (Davies 1999; Pink 2001, 2007), to provide detail on the context in which the image was made, as well as on the photographers' history and the context (and purpose). Throughout any visual research project the history and context of production and recording must be made clear because our interpretative practices have a material effect on the world; there is a materiality. The task allowed consideration of the complexities of a photograph and thinking about how ethical issues can shift as the site of the image changes. The analysis of the image addressed the ethics of photographic practice at the site of production, at the site of the image itself and in the social spaces of the audience viewing the work. In providing her analysis of the image, the teacher educator aimed to support students both in their future teaching and their effects to ensure a dialogical relationship between theory and practice.

Teacher power?

In an activity designed to make explicit the constructed nature of images, students were asked to represent the different roles they inhabit in the classroom. In pairs they used their camera phones to take a series of images which were then deconstructed. In this situated performance (Rose and Finders 1998), the students produced images that were structurally similar; in each photograph, hierarchical power relationships were represented through physical presence, spatiality and action. Those embodying the teacher role were positioned in the centre of the frame and physically pointed towards the interactive whiteboard, a pupil's work (represented in all images as in a static paper form) or standing over a pupil, who in each image appeared submissive or static. In these photographs, 'relations of power and discipline are inscribed into the apparent innocent spatiality of social life' (Soja 1989, 6). Just as ethnographers often photograph rituals and cultural activities during fieldwork (Pink 2001) it is perhaps to be expected that the classroom is a significant space for teachers where the semiotic resources of identity are embodied. Theorising the practice and analysis of photography, Bourdieu (1990 [1965], 6) considers that 'the most trivial photograph expresses, apart from the explicit intentions of the photographer, the system of perception, thought and appreciation common to a whole group' and, as Wright (1999, 9) notes, 'anyone who uses a camera or views a photograph will almost probably be subscribing, albeit unwittingly, to some or other theory of representation'. The process of image production, analysis, and reflection encourages reflexivity and the exploration of personal pedagogies, and we contend that 'how teachers and students use gaze, body posture, and the distribution of space and resources produces silent discourses in the classroom' (Jewitt 2008, 262).

Reading poverty

In another group activity, students were asked to offer *readings* of found visual texts from the eighteenth, nineteenth and twenty-first centuries, William Hogarth's *Gin Lane* (1751), an etching depicting a poverty-stricken area to the north of Covent Garden, a film still of Oliver Twist famously asking for more food and a promotional image from Channel Four's Skint (2013). Hogarth, made famous by his portraits of London life, depicts a dystopian life, with gin addicts fallen in the street, a half dressed mother dropping her child and in the background a corpse being thrown into a coffin. The image of Oliver Twist is a still from David Lean's 1948 film of the Dickens classic. Set in the slums of Victorian London the director presents the orphan's quest as a darkly gothic moral tale. The final image is another still, this time from a Channel 4 observational documentary series telling 'intimate stories of how people live with the devastating effects of long term unemployment' (Channel 4, 2013). Although set in the north of England, this series mirrors the struggles with poverty found in many socio-economically deprived areas of London.

The texts were chosen as they variously represent and depict poverty: they gave students the opportunity to interpret them through the lens of their own experience and using their own value systems. Media theorists have long argued that media (and visual) engagement is not a passive act and viewers/readers actively shape cultural meanings (Buckingham 2000). In popular culture generally, and in these images specifically, poverty is *othered* through the language used to describe the experience of those living in poverty, and in the imagery used, to define and ultimately stereotype people. Here, it is not the poor who represent themselves.

Images were used as a stimulus to generate discussion (Harper 2002) and to enable students to talk about poverty in the abstract. In these ways they were able to explore the lived experiences of others, engaging in the kind of processes which Vygotsky (1978) describes in young children as 'play without action'. Here, the 'playing' comes through students drawing from their personal and cultural resources of visual experiences, referencing familiar visual forms, styles and discourses. From a pedagogical point of view the activities also provided the students with an opportunity to critically analyse visual texts and focus on the three sites of meaning making (production of an image, image itself and the audience) outlined by Rose (2001), knowledge that will be vital when they later work with pupils in schools.

Talking about poverty: beliefs and silences

Following these various activities using visual pedagogical approaches, the students were asked to discuss and agree on a definition of poverty. As indicated earlier, such definitions have long been contested (Townsend 1979) and terms relating to class, social or economic disadvantage and inequality are often used interchangeably in talking about poverty in England. Here, and throughout the workshop, the students also tended to conflate poverty with other social issues such as unemployment, alcohol or drug dependency and those who require financial support (benefits) from the state. While one group defined poverty as 'inequality – a lack of access to food, shelter and education', another group focussed on 'deprivation' and noted that those in poverty would have 'limited experience of culture and opportunities', that they were likely to have 'poor health and hygiene', and might feel 'a sense of isolation'.

When prompted to provide individual definitions of poverty, the most significant and prolonged silences in the workshop occurred. Here, Louise, eventually responding when everyone else was silent, said 'It's a touchy subject. Everyone's experience is different'. Charlotte then agreed, adding, 'This is outside my frame of reference so it's all new to me and you don't really know what to say. It feels bleak …'. Pooja added, 'This is hard – I don't know the right words …'. Most expressed some consensus with Louise's view that class is strongly related to poverty and it 'still plays a huge role … social class and what pupils have access to has a huge impact on development and opportunity'. Sophie said, 'I didn't really think about it (*poverty*) before starting the course'.

Discussion of poverty and children's lives in school proved to be a slightly easier topic, although here too there were silences and senses of hesitation in speaking out. Students identified factors such as the roles of parents, schools and pupils themselves in overcoming educational under-achievement. Pooja stated:

> Households play, in my opinion, a huge role in a child's attitude, as with their right kind of support and encouragement they would go on to pursue their dreams and goals …. People who may struggle with poverty may not see their education as a priority as they may have bigger issues to consider.

Louise saw differentiations in parental attitudes, saying 'Sometimes education is not an immediate concern/interest and therefore isn't always pushed whereas with other parents it is the main priority'. Some students stressed the power of pupils' individual agency in overcoming disadvantage. Rania stated:

> I do not consider income levels as determinous (sic) in people's aspirations. I believe that children coming from very poor families have aspirations and are hardworking and really (emphasis in the original) want to do something with their lives.

Similarly in Sophie's view, pupil agency could overcome parental attitudes, 'sometimes parents can have an impact but pupils are their own people so they will not always follow what their parents do'. Jessica added, 'It is totally dependent on an individual's aspirations and goals as to whether they want to do well and succeed and it is not necessary predetermined by social class' (sic). Other students showed understanding and empathy for the living conditions of pupils and the limitations these might impose, even on the most motivated. Typical statements included: 'some pupils have a large amount of responsibility at home. Sometimes working for extra money and they might be exhausted'; 'When students live in poverty there is a lack of working space or quiet space at home'; and 'Pupils who might be from a low income household might not have access to the latest technology or travel or theatre opportunities so this will affect them'.

When discussing their practicum, some students considered that they had been placed in schools where issues of poverty impacted on the lives of pupils, but it was not an issue they had considered or discussed. Placements had clearly been diverse, but all talked about their school experiences positively, describing their work in the school and their roles as part of a school community. Senses of belonging and commitment were demonstrated in the language they used describing '*our* students (*pupils*)', 'those students that were part of *our* school community', and 'the students in *my* school' identifying the centrality of their work, but experiences in school had differed markedly. Lucy, for example, described her placement in a school in a deprived area as being 'really diverse ... many students are new to the country and the pupil premium is used to pay for their breakfast and a study space so that kids can do their homework'. Charlotte said, 'At my school the school works closely with parents, welfare officers and Newham to ensure pupils and families have access to help'. Like Lucy, she had clearly seen these practices demonstrated in her school and had a clear sense of how the school supported disadvantaged pupils and their parents. In contrast, Jess had been in a school where 'parents pay for tutors but they [*the pupils*] don't care: they know that they will be ok and get good jobs'. Jess felt that she had had little experience of seeing how schools work with pupils living in poverty.

One student-teacher contrasted her experiences at her first placement school with those she anticipated at her second school, which she had already visited. She talked about her desire to work in a school with similar pupils to those in her first placement and the importance of an affinity with the school ethos:

> I know that it will be different at [*placement two school*] when I go there, you can just tell by what teachers say about students and their expectations really, I want to work in a more challenging school where students might be the first in their family to go to university or they have problems and we can help, that's what we should do. At [*placement two school*] they just expect, they know that they will do well without really trying. At [*placement one school*] everyone was really committed to making a difference ...

At some schools students reported a 'silence' about poverty and social class, which mirrored the silence on these issues in the university element of the programme. Pooja stated:

> We never talked about this (*in the university*) and in school we know it's true but you don't ask teachers about kids and poverty, like we know the ones who have a hard time but we don't talk about it or ask them.... I thought about when I was in school but I don't [*think*] we understood class or money like it wasn't there but it was.

Concerned about this absence, Pooja asked her mentor about her own experiences of pre-service education, 'I talked to my mentor in school about this and … they did not talk about class or poverty on her course (*either*)'.

While student-teachers drew on personal, often limited, experiences of poverty and disadvantage, they were alert to the expectations that they felt were appropriate for the profession: as Sophie stated,

> I was very lucky growing up but I do see poverty as a real issue and I know friends and family who have [*experienced a*] hard time … we don't think about it but in school we see it [*poverty*] everyday'.

Considering the impact of poverty and disadvantage on education was 'much harder to think about' and one student noted 'teachers need to be supported by the school – a teacher on their own is powerless to deal with poverty' later adding 'you feel so helpless. It's frustrating but what can I do?'

Here, recognition of the challenges in defining poverty and its effects on educational achievement reflects the need to explore the complex issues of teacher identity discourses and consideration of 'how language that challenges traditional educational paradigms is obligated to create new categories in order to reclaim new spaces of resistance, to establish new identities, or to construct new knowledge/power relations' (Giroux 2005, 17).

Conclusions

The first findings of this pedagogical research initiative indicate that many of the student-teachers had little personal experience of disadvantage. In the workshop, they were sometimes reluctant to define poverty and its relationship to class, fearing that they might 'get it wrong'. As one student stated, 'I think you know but you don't want to upset people by pointing it out'. Our findings suggest that many of the group saw issues of poverty and disadvantage as alien, unfamiliar, uncomfortable and 'other', viewing the issues through the lenses of their own often middle class and norm-referenced perspectives. Some, like Charlotte quoted above, pushed the discussion away altogether by stating that the issues were 'outside my frame of reference', or like Sophie, confessed that they had never considered them before starting the pre-service course.

Our findings also indicate that some of the students identified limited aspirations of parents, schools and pupils as important factors in educational under-achievement. Stereotypical views of lack of parental aspirations, in particular, were often explicitly or implicitly positioned as more influential on children's learning than material or cultural factors around poverty. In this use of deficit models, based on stereotypical and homogenised ways of understanding poverty, our findings mirror those of other studies of student-teachers (Cox et al. 2012). Other students, such as Rania and Sophie, saw pupils themselves as sometimes having positive aspirations and being able to use personal 'agency' to overcome disadvantage. These views seem more positive at first sight but here, again as in previous research (Smyth and Wrigley 2013), the responsibility for educational achievement is devolved to the individual and their ability (or inability) to overcome the effects of poverty. Again, aspirations and personal efforts are seen as more influential than the material and cultural effects of poverty. However, a few students' views, like those of Louise, were more nuanced and show more consistent indications of awareness of the intersectionality of poverty, class and other forms of deprivation than in the earlier study of ITE students in England by Thompson et al. (2014) and in the work of Cox et al. (2012) in the USA.

As we have indicated above, there were significant silences and pauses during the workshop, together with senses that the questions under discussion were 'hard' or 'new' or 'bleak' as topics. We argue that the narratives constructed and shared in this research cannot be disarticulated from those silences. Understanding silence depends on the context in which it occurs, how it is interpreted and by whom, but it has long been accepted that silence does not just represent an *absence* in conversation (Tannen 1985) and that '(L)istening to silences can be just as instructive as listening to voices' (Losey 1997, 191). The words the students speak (and the deficit views of 'the poor' which they sometimes express) therefore need to be read alongside their awkward silences as indicative of a pre-service education version of the familiar English trait of not causing offence by inadvertently using the 'wrong' language in an area of discussion seen as 'other'. Here, these silences effectively close down or close off the topics under discussion, often rendering both student-teachers and teacher educator unable to speak freely or, indeed, sometimes, to speak at all.

These group silences in the workshop are reinforced by other silences or absences in teacher education. We also found silences on poverty and social class at the meso or institutional levels of the research: the university programme, for example, included a strong commitment to teaching about the broad principles of social justice, but there was no direct focus on the educational factors associated with socio-economic disadvantage or preparation for working in schools of high poverty. The silence at the university was in some cases compounded by the variable provision for student-teacher learning within the placement schools. In some schools, the student experience was of yet more silence on poverty and social class issues, and, again, atmospheres in which 'you don't ask teachers about kids and poverty', sometimes again because of fear of 'getting it wrong', causing 'offence' or not knowing the 'right words'. In other schools, it was clear that student-teachers were able to work in supportive, insightful and seemingly effective ways with children living in poverty. In a pre-service system which is now largely school led, the variability in this provision matters greatly for individual and communal student learning. In these silences, university and schools alike are open to Reay's (2006) critique that social class injustices are inadequately addressed in both pre-service teacher education and schooling. Finally, we also recognise silence at the macro level of pre-service education; the Teaching Standards in England, as indicated above, do not directly reference broad issues of social justice or have any specific focus on combating educational inequalities caused by poverty.

As stated above, our intention in designing this workshop was to explore and experiment with ways in which visual pedagogies might challenge and facilitate student discussions. There was never any intent to 'prove' the effectiveness of these pedagogies and we did not set out to measure any changes in students' attitudes. Nevertheless, our findings enable us to reflect on the strengths and weaknesses of these pedagogies. The strengths, as we see them, are that the visual methods used engaged the students in sometimes heated discussions of images of poverty and class; they focused their attention on some of the issues around poverty and educational attainment and gave them pedagogically well-structured 'spaces' in which they could express their views and experiences, as they wished to do so. 'Listening' to the views of others, through both silences and interchanges of opinions, made them aware of the diversity of views and of how difficult and contested issues around poverty and class are. We would also hope that, in the longer term, the workshop might make the student-teachers think more deeply about pupils living in poverty that they teach in their placement schools.

Some readers might see it as a 'weakness' of the workshop that a number of the students expressed stereotypical deficit models of the poor, yet our aim was only to *explore how* they articulated their views on and experiences of the effects of poverty and deprivation in education and not necessarily to challenge thinking. This exploration was intended to provide a starting point for later stages of the project. We would argue that, as the baseline for social justice work, all teacher educators need to know and understand their students' views. Nevertheless, following Gorski (2012), we acknowledge that such poverty stereotyping and ideologies of deficit are certainly not 'neutral', not least because they can impact adversely on children's educational outcomes. In retrospect then, we could, and perhaps should, have challenged the deficit models expressed, for example, by citing research which contradicts such thinking (see Jones forthcoming; in this issue). Such challenges could not, however, be processes of judgement by which students' views were labelled as simply inadequate or wrong. Rather the workshop could perhaps have included more work on exploring personal and professional identities and past experiences for the students. Such work can, of course, be 'uncomfortable and challenging', not least because 'identity is rooted in personal histories and … some of the underlying fixed positions are deeply held ethical positions' (Boylan and Woolsey 2015). As these authors recommend, compassionate pedagogies are needed here, with orientations to kindness and empathy rather than judgement (ibid, 66). For us, further work on visual pedagogies offers the ideal vehicle for such identity work, since as Pink (2007, 17) states 'images are 'everywhere' …. They are inextricably interwoven into our personal identities, narratives, lifestyles, cultures and societies, as well as with definitions of history, space and truth'.

With every indication that English society will continue to be characterised by inequality (Wilkinson and Pickett 2009), it is vital that student-teachers are aware of the patterns of educational under-achievement often associated with social and economic disadvantage in general and with living in poverty in particular. To achieve this undoubtedly, teacher educators in universities *and* schools need more sophisticated ways of teaching about issues of poverty, class and educational under-achievement; and these need to be pedagogies that might guide students beyond stereotypical deficit views. We therefore consider it vital that in both the university element of the programme and while on school placements, student-teachers have the opportunity to talk about their own views and experiences in relation to the complex relationships between social and economic deprivation and the effects of poverty on educational achievement. In taught sessions at the university using visual materials as stimulus to generate talk and discussion should, in our view, be considered as viable pedagogical strategies, allowing for both abstract and sometimes metaphorical discussions before moving on to the more challenging talk of lived experience. Whilst we are not suggesting that images should replace words as the dominant mode of pedagogical practice (or representation), like others (Emmison and Smith 2000; White 2009), we are asking for more consideration to be given to visual knowledge production. Over the past decade the growth of new digital technologies has changed the way we interact with visual culture, how we access, read, produce and share visual materials. We no longer need a camera when we engage in photographic practices and often a mobile phone is used in place of specialised photographic equipment. Pictures can be easily uploaded to the Internet and shared creating new forms 'for self-narration and representation' (Richter and Schadler 2009, 171). Yet, these new social emphases on the visual are not always well represented in the pedagogies of teacher education.

In developing this research project, we now aim to run a revised version of the workshop working from the evaluation of the initiative described here. In the further interlinked stages of the project, we will investigate how spaces and places of poverty affects the possibilities for the (re)construction of knowledge and identities, challenging deep cultural and ethical beliefs as students work with learners in schools in deprived communities. We also want to develop a bespoke theoretical framework for analysing the results of later stages of the project. For this, we intend to combine perspectives on teaching for social justice, research on learning to teach and studies of place/space and spatiality. We will aim to explore how the places and spaces of poverty in local schools (and the often under-developed and impoverished geographical landscapes in which they exist) both structure, and are structured by, the social practices of schooling and teacher education. In designing this framework, we are then interested in how distinctive spaces and places affect teacher educators' pedagogies and student-teacher learning. Following Hargreaves (1995, 32), we argue that 'what it means to *be* in teacher education … can only properly be understood by firmly locating our studies of teacher education in space as well as in time'.

Finally, to emphasise how important it is that we find new pedagogies for social justice which overcome the silences about class and educational disadvantage and start to challenge compassionately pre-service teachers' understanding of these relationships, we conclude with the words of Reay (2006, 304),

> Social class remains the one educational problem that comes back to haunt English education again and again and again; the area of educational inequality on which educational policy has had virtually no impact.

Disclosure statement

No potential conflict of interest was reported by the authors.

References

Aldridge, H., S. Bushe, P. Kenway, T. MacInnes, and A. Tinson. 2013. *London's Poverty Profile*. New Policy Institute. http://www.londonspovertyprofile.org.uk/LPP_2013_Report_Web.pdf.
Banks, M. 2001. *Visual Methods in Social Research*. London: Sage.
Beauchamp, G., L. Clarke, M. Hulme, and J. Murray. 2013. *Policy and Practice within the United Kingdom* (Research and Teacher Education: The BERA-RSA Inquiry). London: BERA. https://www.bera.ac.uk/wp-content/uploads/2013/12/BERA-Paper-1-UK-Policy-and-Practice.pdf.
Behar, R. 1996. *The Vulnerable Observer: Anthropology that Breaks your Heart*. Boston, MA: Beacon Press.
Beyer, L. 2001. "The Value of Critical Perspectives in Teacher Education." *Journal of Teacher Education* 52 (2): 151–163.
Bourdieu, P. 1990 (1965). *Photography: A Middle-Brow Art*. Oxford: Polity Press.
Boylan, M., and Ian Woolsey. 2015. "Teacher Education for Social Justice: Mapping Identity Spaces." *Teaching and Teacher Education* 46: 62–71.

Buckingham, D. 2000. *After the Death of Childhood: Growing up in the Age of Electronic Media*. London: Polity.
Centre for Economic and Business Research. 2013. https://www.newham.gov.uk/Pages/News/Nine-billion-pounds-of-private-investment-in-Stratford,-Newham,-since-the-2012-gaames-were-announced.aspx
Cox, B., C. Watts, and M. Horton. 2012. "Poverty Perceptions of Pre-service Teachers and Social Work Candidates." *Journal of Studies in Education* 2 (1): 131–148.
Davies, C. A. 1999. *Reflexive Ethnography: A Guide to Researching Selves and Others*. London: Routledge.
Department for Education (DfE). 2010. *The Importance of Teaching: The Schools White Paper*. London: Department for Education.
Department for Education (DfE). 2011. *Training Our Next Generation of Outstanding Teachers: Implementation Plan*. London: Department for Education.
Department for Education (DfE). 2015. *Carter Review of Initial Teacher Training (ITT)*. London: Department for Education.
Dorling, D. 2011. *So You Think You Know About Britain?* London: Constable.
Emmison, M., and P. Smith. 2000. *Researching the Visual*. London: Sage.
Fox, K. 2004. *Watching the English*. London: Hodder & Stoughton.
Freire, P. 1970. *Pedagogy of the Oppressed*. London: The Continuum Publishing Company.
Gilroy, P. 2014. "Policy Intervention in Teacher Education: Sharing the English Experience." *Journal of Education for Teaching* 40 (5): 622–632.
Giroux, H. 2005. *Border Crossings: Cultural Workers and the Politics of Education*. 2nd ed. New York: Routledge.
Goodwin, L. A., and C. Kosnik. 2013. "Quality Teacher Educators = Quality Teachers?: Conceptualizing Essential Domains of Knowledge for those who Teach Teachers." *Teacher Development: An International Journal of Teachers' Professional Development* 17 (3): 334–346.
Gorski, P. 2012. "Perceiving the Problem of Poverty and Schooling: Deconstructing the Class Stereotypes that Mis-shape Education Practice and Policy." *Equity and Excellence in Education* 45 (2): 302–319.
Hargreaves, A. 1995. "Towards a Social Geography of Teacher Education." In *Teacher Education in Industrialised Nations: Issues in Changing Social Context*, edited by N. Shimahara and I. Holowinsky, 87–124. New York: Garland.
Harper, D. 1998. "On the Authority of the Image: Visual Methods at the Crossroads." In *Collecting and Interpreting Qualitative Materials*, edited by N. Denzin and Y. Lincoln, 130–149. London: Sage.
Harper, D. 2002. "Talking about Pictures: A Case for Photo Elicitation." *Visual Studies* 17: 13–26.
Hobbs, R. 1998. "The Seven Great Debates in the Media Literacy Movement." *Journal of Communication* 48 (1): 16–32.
Jewitt, C. 2008. "Multimodality and Literacy in School Classrooms." *Review of Research in Education* 32: 241–267.
Jones, H. Forthcoming. "Discussing Poverty with Student Teachers: The Realities of Dialogue." *Journal of Education for Teaching*.
Jones, O. 2011. *Chavs: The Demonization of the Working Class*. London: Verso.
Knowles, J. G., and D. Holt-Reynolds. 1991. "Shaping Pedagogies through Personal Histories in Pre-service Teacher Education." *Teachers College Record* 93: 87–113.
London Borough of Newham. 2013. *Newham Household Panel Survey – Wave 7*. London: Newham.
Losey, M. K. 1997. *Listen to the Silences: Mexican American Interaction in Classroom and the Community*. Norwood, NJ: Ablex.
Lusted, D. 1986. "Why Pedagogy?" *Screen* 27: 2–14.
Mulvey, L. 1989. *Visual and Other Pleasures*. London: Macmillan.
Murray, J., and M. Maguire. 2007. "Changes and Continuities in Teacher Education: International Perspectives on a Gendered Field." *Gender and Education, Special Edition* 19 (3): 125–132.
Newham Case Report 83. 2014. *CASE Report 83 114*. London: LSE.
Oakeshott, M. 1975. *On Human Conduct*. Oxford: Oxford University Press.
OECD. 2006. *Education at a Glance 2006*. Paris: OECD.
Office for Standards in Education. 2012. *Initial Teacher Education Inspection Report HMI 0700771*. London: OfSTED publications.

Pauwels, L. 2010. "Visual Sociology Reframed: An Analytical Synthesis and Discussion of Visual Methods in Social and Cultural Research." *Sociological Methods and Research* 38 (4): 545–581.
Pink, S. 2001. *Doing Visual Ethnography: Images*. Media and Representation in Research. London: Sage.
Pink, S. 2007. *Doing Visual Ethnography*. 2nd ed. London: Sage.
Prosser, J. 1998. *Image-Based Research: A Sourcebook for Qualitative Researchers*. London: Falmer.
Reay, D. 2006. "The Zombie stalking English Schools: Social Class and Educational Inequality." *British Journal of Educational Studies Special Issue on Social Justice* 54 (3): 288–307.
Richter, R., and C. Schadler. 2009. "See My Virtual Self: Dissemination as a Characteristic of Digital Photography – The Example of Flickr.com." *Visual Studies* 24 (2): 169–177.
Rose, G. 2001. *Visual Methodologies: An Introduction to the Interpretation of Visual Materials*. London: Sage.
Rose, S. K., and M. J. Finders. 1998. "Learning from Experience: Using Situated Performances in Writing Teacher Development." *Writing Program Administration* 22 (1): 33–51.
Schneider. 2003. The Tub [ONLINE]. Accessed 5 February 2015. http://ves.fas.harvard.edu/people/betsy-schneider
Skint: Episode 1, Channel 4, 13 May 2013.
Schön, D. 1983. *The Reflective Practitioner. How Professionals Think in Action*. London: Temple Smith.
Sleeter, C., M. Torres, and P. Laughlin. 2004. "Scaffolding Conscientization Through Inquiry in Teacher Education." *Teacher Education Quarterly* 34 (1): 81–96.
Smyth, J., and T. Wrigley. 2013. *Living on the Edge: Re-thinking Poverty, Class and Schooling*. New York: Peter Lang.
Soja, E. 1989. *Postmodern Geographies*. London: Verso.
Sontag, S. 1979. *On Photography*. Harmondsworth: Penguin.
Tannen, D. 1985. "Silence: Anything But." In *Perspectives on Silence*, edited by D. Tannen and M. Saville-Troike, 93–111. Norwood, NJ: Ablex.
Thompson, I., J. McNicholl, and I. Menter. 2014. "Student Teachers' Perceptions of Poverty and Educational Achievement". Paper presented to the BERA Conference, London, September.
Thomson, P. 2008. "Children and Young People: Voices in Visual Research." In *Doing Visual Research with Children and Young People*, edited by P. Thomson, 1–19. Abingdon: Routledge.
Townsend, P. 1979. *Poverty in the United Kingdom*. London: Allen Lane and Penguin Books.
Vygotsky, L. 1978. "The Role of Play in Development." In *Mind in Society*, translated by M. Cole, 92–104. Cambridge, MA: Harvard University Press.
Wang, C., S. Morrel-Samuels, P. M. Hutchison, L. Bell, and R. M. Pestronk. 2004. "Flint Photovoice: Community Building among Youths, Adults, and Policymakers." *American Journal of Public Health* 94 (6): 911–913.
White, M. L. 2009. "Ethnography 2.0: Writing with Digital Video." *Ethnography and Education* 4 (3): 389–414.
Wilkinson, R., and K. Pickett. 2009. *The Spirit Level: Why More Equal Societies Almost Always Do Better*. London: Allen Lane.
Wright, T. 1999. *The Photography Handbook*. London: Routledge.

Index

1.0 programmes 45; assessing teacher quality 47–48; challenges 45–46; learning-centred and learner-centred 47; teachers as saviours 47
2.0 programmes 48–54; college goal 54; discrete classroom management techniques 50–52; financial aid for students 49–50; focus on compliance 52; funding independent programmes 48–49; GREAT 49; measurable student growth 52–53; teacher-as-technician approach 50–52; teacher--community interactions 53–54
3.0 programmes 54–57; community teachers 56–57; foundation 54–55; place-based learning 55–56; value community expertise 55

academic research: research-literate teachers 23–24
accountability: university-based programmes 46
achievement gap: adaptive teaching linking to pupil lives 120–121; breaking the connection with parental income 19; closing 119; England and Scotland links to economic disadvantages 113; England and Scotland policies 112–114; link to economic disadvantage 113; low expectations/aspirations by parents 118; New Zealand 80; parent in-school involvement 6–7; problem of teacher quality 80; professional agency and knowledge to address gap 121; understanding poverty in context of schooling 119–120; *see also* education outcomes
adaptive teaching: linking to pupil lives 120–121
agency: professional agency and knowledge to address attainment gap 121; pupils overcoming disadvantages 136–138
analysing visual texts 134–135
assessing teacher quality: measurable student growth 52–53; preparation 1.0 programmmes 47–48
assumptions: challenging 87
attitudes towards poverty *see* perceptions of poverty

Bank Street model 47
barriers to learning: cultural deprivation 70; hidden 71; individual circumstances 68; parent relationships 69; parental attitudes 69
Beacon Schools 17
behaviour tracking systems 52
BES (Best Evidence Syntheses) 81
big P of politics 123
BME (black and minority ethnic backgrounds) 71
building relationships and reciprocity 86–87

Centre for the Use of Research and Evidence in Education (CUREE) 24
challenges and pressures on teachers: economic and social crisis 40
challenging assumptions and stereotypes 87
charter management organisations (CMOs) 48–49
children: academic achievement and parental attitudes 69; agency in overcoming disadvantages 136–138; effects of poverty on well-being 36–38; emotional outcomes 83; poverty in Portugal 32–33; poverty of relationships 69; social outcomes 83
Children and Young People Act 113
Church Green academy 67–69
classroom management: behaviour tracking systems 52; discrete techniques 50–52
Closing the Gap (CTG) 24
CMOs (charter management organisations) 48–49
Coalition government education/teacher education policies 19–25; compensatory initiatives 20–21; diversification of provisions and increased parental choice 26; diversification of schooling 20; diversification of teachers 21–22; reducing the role of universities 22–24; similarities with Labour government policies 26; social inequality and outcome gaps elimination 24–25; teacher quality 26–27; *see also* PPG
Community of Enquiry 98; critical realism 98–99; empirical issues bringing out actual

INDEX

views 106–107; ethics 101; facilitator neutrality 102–103; procedurally directive dialogue disadvantages 105; purposeful dialogue 104–105; reciprocity 103–104; stigmatisation of disadvantaged families 102; study context 99–100; study methods 100–101
community teachers: 3.0 programmes 56–57; valuing expertise of community 55
compensatory initiatives: Coalition government education policies 20–21
contextualising images 133–134
converter Academies 20
critical realism 98–99; empirical issues bringing out actual views 106–107; facilitator neutrality 102–103; reciprocity 103–104; stigmatisation of disadvantaged families 102
CTG (Closing the Gap) 24
cultural deprivation: barrier to learning 70
cultural dimensions of teaching/teacher education 42
CUREE (Centre for the Use of Research and Evidence in Education) 24

defenders (1.0 programmes) 45; assessing teacher quality 47–48; learning-centred and learner-centred 47; teachers a saviours 47; university-based programme challenges 45–46
deficient mindset of people experiencing poverty 8
deficit ideology 7; language 11; people experiencing poverty deficient mindset 8; resultant deficit model 61–62
demographics of teachers 131
demonstrable competences of teachers 22
dialogic enquiries 97–98; critical realism 98–99; empirical issues bringing out actual views 106–107; ethics 101; facilitator neutrality 102–103; procedurally directive dialogue disadvantages 105; purposeful 104–105; reciprocity 103–104; stigmatisation of disadvantaged families 102; study context 99–100; study methods 100–101
direct experience with children 75
discrete classroom management techniques 50–52
diversification 71; Coalition government education policies 20–22; education provisions 26; ITE programme organisational structure/recruitment processes 21–22; teacher quality 26–27; teachers 130–131

EAL (English as an additional language) 71
early intervention: ECM (Every Child Matters) 16
EAZ (Education Action Zones) 15–16
ECM (Every Child Matters) 16–18

economic disadvantages: challenges and pressures on teachers 40; effects on children's well-being 36–38; link to educational achievement 113; Portugal crisis 32; strategies for handling at school 38–41; teachers' role in promoting equity 38–39
edTPA 47–48
Education Action Zones (EAZ) 15–16
education outcomes: addressing gaps 26; eliminating gaps through educational interventions alone 24–25; New Zealand 80; parental attitudes 69; socio-economic influences on underachievement 91; transforming by raising young people's aspirations/attitudes 19; *see also* achievement gaps
education policies 2; Coalition government 19–21; diversification of provisions and increased parental choice 26; education outcome gaps 26; Labour government 15–17; New Zealand 79–80; reducing achievement gap associated with poverty 112–113
education sector crisis in Portugal 33–34
Educational Endowment Foundation (EEF) 24
educational underachievement: socio-economic impact 96–97, 107
EEF (Educational Endowment Foundation) 24
EEF/Sutton Trust Toolkit 24–25
effects of poverty on children's well-being 36–38
EiC (Excellence in Cities) 16
emotional outcomes: MTchg programme 83
empirical issues bringing out actual views 106–107
engagement with school students: building relationships and reciprocity 86–87; challenging assumptions and stereotypes 87; knowing learners as individuals 86; setting high expectations for students across broad learning domains 87
England: educational achievement link to economic disadvantage 113; ITE poverty agenda 114; London Borough of Newham 131–132; reducing attainment gap associated with poverty 112–114; social class 129–130; socio-economic marginalisation 129; *Student Teachers' Perceptions of Poverty and Educational Achievement* study 115; teacher diversity 130–131; *see also* Picturing Poverty initiative; PPG
England government education/teacher education policies; Coalition government 19–25; diversification of provisions and increased parental choice 26; Labour government 15–19; similarities in addressing education outcome gaps 26; teacher quality 26–27

INDEX

English as an additional language (EAL) 71
equity literacy 6; commitment to equity 10–11; socio-economic family involvement disparity 6–7
equity-centred ITE programmes 81–84
ethics: dialogic enquiry study 101; reinforcing in teaching/teacher education 42
Every Child Matters (ECM) 16
Excellence in Cities (EiC) 16

facets of practice for equity 81–82; MTchg programme 83–84
facilitator neutrality 102–103
family involvement: socio-economic disparity 6–7
family-community relationships: teacher-centric approach 53–54
federal funding: non-university teacher preparation programmes 48–49
federal regulations for teacher education programmes 46
financial aid for student teachers: preparation 2.0 programmes 49–50
Finland: teachers as researchers 23
food emergency programme in Portugal 32
A Framework for Understanding Poverty 8
free schools 20
funding: financial aid for student teachers 49–50; non-university teacher education programmes 48–49; *see also* PPG

generational injustice 11
generational poverty 11
gestures for redirection 52
government education/teacher education policies: Coalition government 19–25; diversification of provisions and increased parental choice 26; education outcome gaps 26; Labour government 15–19; teacher quality 26–27
GREAT (Growing Achievement Training Academies for Teachers and Principals Act) 49
grit ideology 9–10

hidden barriers to learning 71
hierarchical power relationships through images 133
high expectations for students across broad learning domains 87
Hilltop academy 69–70

identity formation 112; adaptive teaching linking to pupil lives 120–121; changing views 118–119; professional agency and knowledge to address attainment gap 121; social justice links to 122–123; understanding poverty in context of schooling 119–120

ideologies: deficit 7–8, 11; grit 9–10; shifts to cultivate equity literacy 11–12; structural 7, 10–11
The Importance of Teaching 22
inclusion: Labour government education policies 15
independent teacher preparation programmes funding 48–49
individual circumstances as barriers to learning 68
initial teacher education programmes *see* ITE programmes
innovative social justice *see* visual pedagogies for social justice
inquiry stance 84; ITE programmes 87–88; MTchg 91
institutional and personal histories interplay 73
interplay of personal and institutional histories 73
inter-professional collaboration: ECM (Every Child Matters) 16
ITE (initial teacher education) programmes 2–3; changing views on poverty 118–119; demonstrable competences of teachers 22; equity-centred 81–84; facets of practice as philosophical and practice frame 88; inquiry stance 87–88; lack of inclusion of poverty issues in curriculum 39–41; modified perceptions of low SES schools and students 90; national curriculum by Labour government 17; omission of social justice agendas 130; organisational structure diversification 21–22; perceptions on preparation to work in low SES schools 89–90; Portugal restructuring 34–35; poverty agenda 114; primary *versus* secondary teachers 114; professional learning conceptions 63–64; recognising not challenging inequities 91; recruitment processes diversification 21–22; reducing the role of universities 22–24; research orientation towards PPG funding *see* PPG research project; silences on poverty and social class 138; socio-economic influences on underachievement 91; teacher inquiry 91; visual materials to stimulate discussions 139–140; *see also* social justice ITE

knowing learners as individuals 86

Labour government education/teacher education policies 15–19; Excellence in Cities 16; diversification of provisions and increased parental choice 26; EAZ (Education Action Zones) 15–16; ECM (Every Child Matters) 16; inclusion 15; similarities with Coalition government policies 26; specialist

INDEX

schools/sponsored academies 16–17; Sure Start initiative 16; teacher education policies 17–19; teacher quality 26–27
language: deficit ideology framings 11
learner-centred teachers 47
learning-centred teachers 47
Lemov, Doug: *Teach Like a Champion: 49 Techniques that Put Your Students on the Path to College* 50–51
limited powers of education to compensate for poverty 97, 107
local programmes: Sure Start initiative 16
London Borough of Newham 131–132
low expectations/aspirations by parents and attainment 118
low SES (socio-economic communities) schools: building relationships and reciprocity 86–87; challenging assumptions and stereotypes 87; education outcome inequalities 80; facets of practice as philosophical and practice frame 88; knowing learners as individuals 86; modified perceptions of 90; MTchg inquiry stance 87–88; MTchg student teacher preparation perceptions 89–90; recognising not challenging inequities 91; setting high expectations for students across broad learning domains 87; socio-economic influences on underachievement 91

Māori 80; Te Ao Māori course 83
MATCH teacher residency 49
measurable student growth 52–53
meritocracy: success 5
MET (Measures of Effective Teaching) Project 81
Midway City School 70–72
MTchg programme 82–84; building relationships and reciprocity 86–87; challenging assumptions and stereotypes 87; facets of practice as philosophical and practice frame 88; facets of practice for equity 83–84; inquiry stance 84, 87–88; knowing learners as individuals 86; methods 84–85; modified perceptions of low SES schools and students 90; perceptions on preparation to work in low SES schools 89–90; recognising not challenging inequities 91; setting high expectations for students across broad learning domains 87; socio-economic influences on underachievement 91; teacher inquiry 91

national curriculum: ITE programmes 17
national educational policies on poverty 2
national standards: Qualified Teacher Status 17–18
neoliberal market-based teacher education policies: Labour government 17–19

New Opportunities programme 33
New Zealand: achievement gap 80; education policies 79–80; facets of practice for equity 81–82; indigenous population 80, 83; Registered Teacher Criteria 79; RITE 79; *see also* MTchg
non-university teacher preparation programmes funding 48–49

occupational socialization: teacher education 19

Pacific Island students in New Zealand 80
Pākeha 80
parent involvement: attitudes towards academic achievement 69; income and educational achievement connection 19; poverty of relationships 69; socio-economic disparity 6–7
parental choices: increasing 26
Pasifika students 80
PaTE (Poverty and Teacher Education) 1
perceptions of poverty: changing views 118–119; during practicums 36–38; identity formation 112; professional learning 63–64; resultant deficit model 61–62; shaped by prior experiences 74; understanding poverty in context of schooling 119–120
personal and institutional histories interplay 73
philanthropic funding: non-university teacher education programmes 48
Philosophy for Children 98
Phoning Parents 53–54
Picturing Poverty initiative 128–129; analysing visual texts focusing on three sites of meaning 134–135; belonging and commitment 136; contextualising images 133–134; defining poverty with visual pedagogies 135–137; hierarchical power relationships 133; potential for innovative social justice 138–140; pupil agency in overcoming disadvantage 136–138; silence about poverty and social class 137–138; strengths of visual pedagogies 138–139; visual materials for student teacher education 139–140; weaknesses of visual pedagogies 139
place-based learning: 3.0 programmes 55–56
political dimensions of teaching/teacher education 42
Portugal: challenges and pressures on teachers 40; child poverty 32–33; economic crisis 32; education sector crisis 33–34; effects of poverty of children's well-being 36–38; handling poverty issues at school 38–41; ITE restructuring 34–35; lack of inclusion of poverty issues in ITE programme 39–41; New Opportunities programme 33;

INDEX

student-teachers' perceptions of poverty 36–38; teachers promoting equity and social justice 38–39
poverty: context of schooling 119–120; defining with visual pedagogies 135–137; derives from social class 129–130; effects on children's well-being 36–38; individual circumstances 68; relationships 69; silence 137–138; strategies for handling at school 38–41; teacher attitudes 2–3
Poverty and Teacher Education (PaTE) 1
power relationships through images 133
PPG (Pupil Premium Grant) research project 62–64; adopting research orientation 72–73; Church Green academy 67–69; direct experience with children 75; Hilltop academy 69–70; interest in research literature 75; interplay of personal and institutional histories 73; Midway City School 70–72; participant object motives 73–74; project design 64–65; questionnaire data 65–67; revelations 74; student teachers' attitudes shaped by prior experiences 74
primary ITE course *see Strathcylde Literacy Clinic* study
primary school teacher preparation *versus* secondary school teachers 114
prior experiences shaping student teacher attitudes 74
procedurally directive dialogue 97–98; disadvantages for teaching social justice 105
professional agency and knowledge to address attainment gap 121
professional learning system 63–64
Project RITE (Rethinking Initial Teacher Education for Equity) 79
promoting equity and social justice 38–39
Pupil Premium Grant *see* PPG
purposeful dialogue 104–105

Qualified Teacher Status: national standards 17–18
quality of teachers 26–27; educational underachievement 80; measurable student growth 52–53; New Zealand Registered Teacher Criteria 79; preparation 1.0 programmes 47–48

reactive moves to misbehaviour 52
reciprocity: building relationships 86–87; dialogic enquiry 103–104
recognising not challenging inequities 91
recruiting untrained teachers 22–23
redirection gestures 52
reformers (2.0 programmes) 48–54; college goal 54; discrete classroom management techniques 50–52; federal funding 48–49; financial aid for students 49–50; focus on compliance 52; GREAT 49; measurable student growth 52–53; philanthropic funding 48; teacher-as-technician approach 50–52; teacher-community interactions 53–54
reinforcing ethical, cultural, social, political dimensions of teaching/teacher education 42
relationships: building 86–87; poverty 69
Relay Graduate School of Education 49
Relay Instruction Delivery Methods Reader 51
research literature: interest towards 75
research orientation towards PPG 62–63; adopting 72–73; Church Green academy 67–69; direct experience with children 75; Hilltop academy 69–70; interest in research literature 75; interplay of personal and institutional histories 73; Midway City School 70–72; participant object motives 73–74; PPG overview 64; project design 64–65; questionnaire data 65–67; revelations 74; student teachers' attitudes shaped by prior experiences 74
research-literate teachers: developing 23–24
resources: university-based programme losses 45–46
resultant deficit model 61–62
revelations by student teachers 74
RITE (Rethinking Initial Teacher Education for Equity) 79

Schools of Education 49
Scotland: educational achievement link to economic disadvantage 113; reducing attainment gap associated with poverty 112–114; Strathclyde Literacy Clinic 115–117
secondary ITE course in England *see Student Teachers' Perceptions of Poverty and Educational Achievement* study
secondary school teacher preparation *versus* primary school teachers 114
sense of belonging and commitment 136
setting high expectations for students across broad learning domains 87
silence about poverty and social class 137–138
Sit Up, Listen, Ask and Answer Questions, Nod Your Head, Track the Speaker (SLANT) 52
small p of politics 123
social class: poverty connection 129–130; silence 137–138; teacher attitudes 2
social dimensions of teaching/teacher education 42
social justice: challenges and pressures on teachers 40; effects on children's well-being 36–38; eliminating through educational interventions alone 24–25; links with teacher identity 122–123; strategies for handling at

INDEX

school 38–41; teachers' role in promoting 38–39; *see also* dialogic enquiries

social justice ITE: empirical and actual 107; increase understanding of difficulties faced by pupils living in poverty 96, 107; socio-economic impact on educational underachievement 96–97, 107; structural nature of poverty and limited powers to compensate for it 97, 107

social outcomes: MTchg programme 83

socio-economic disparities 6; deficit ideology 7–8; grit ideology 9–10; impact on educational underachievement 96–97, 107; influences on underachievement 91; in-school parent involvement 6–7; marginalisation in England 129; pupils overcoming 136–138; resultant deficit model 61–62; shifting towards structural ideology 11–12; structural ideology 10–11

specialist schools 16–17

The Spirit Level 71

sponsored academies 16–17

standardised assessment data: teacher quality 52–53

standards: emphasizing teachers' demonstrable competences 22

Standards for Qualified Teacher Status 18

stereotypes: challenging 87

stigmatisation of disadvantaged families 102

Strathclyde Literacy Clinic study 115–117; adaptive teaching linking to pupil lives 120–121; boundary object 116–117; closing the attainment gap 119; poverty in the context of schooling 119–120; professional agency and knowledge to address attainment gap 121

structural ideology 7; commitment to equity 10–11; shifts to cultivate 11–12

structural nature of poverty: student teacher understanding of 97, 107

student teachers: attitudes shaped by prior experiences 74; changing 118–119; demographics 131; diversity 130–131; handling poverty issues at school 38–41; identity formation 112; increase understanding of difficulties faced by pupils living in poverty 96, 107; lacking training on poverty issues in ITE programmes 39–41; modified perceptions of low SES schools and students 90; omission of social justice agendas 130; perceptions of poverty during practicums 36–38; perceptions on preparation to work in low SES schools 89–90; primary *versus* secondary preparations 114; professional agency and knowledge to address attainment gap 121; professional learning system 63–64; reinforcing ethical, cultural, social, political dimensions of teaching/teacher education 42; revelations 74; role in promoting equity and social justice 38–39; sense of belonging and commitment 136; silence about poverty and social class 138; socio-economic impact on educational underachievement 96–97, 107; *Strathclyde Literacy Clinic* 115–117; structural nature of poverty and limited powers to compensate for it 97, 107; *Student Teachers' Perceptions of Poverty and Educational Achievement* study 115, 118–119; understanding poverty in context of schooling 119–120; visual materials to stimulate discussions on poverty 139–140; *see also* dialogic enquiries

Student Teachers' Perceptions of Poverty and Educational Achievement study 115; changing views on poverty 118–119; low expectations/aspirations held by parents 118

success: meritocracy 5

Sure Start Initiative 16

symptoms of unequal society 71

Te Ao Māori course 83

Teach First programme 18–19

Teach for America (TFA) 48

Teach Like a Champion: 49 Techniques that Put Your Students on the Path to College 50–51

Teach Now programme 21

Teacher Education Forum of Aotearoa New Zealand (TEFANZ) 85

teacher education policies: Coalition government 21–25; Labour government 17–19; occupational socialisation 19; quality teachers 26–27

teacher identity framework 112; adaptive teaching linking to pupil lives 120–121; changing views 118–119; professional agency and knowledge to address attainment gap 121; social justice links to 122–123; understanding poverty in context of schooling 119–120

teacher preparation programmes in USA 45; defenders 45–48; federal regulations 46; reformers 48–54; transformers 54–57

teacher-as-technician approach 50–52

teacher-centric approach: family-community relationships 53–54

teacher-community interactions 53–54

teachers: attitudes on social class and poverty 2; challenges and pressures from economic/social crisis 40; demographics 131; inquiry 91; reinforcing ethical, cultural, social, political dimensions of teaching/teacher education 42; as researchers 23–24; role in promoting equity and social justice 38–39; as saviours 47

INDEX

Teaching and Learning Research Programme (TLRP) 81
teaching practices for positive education outcomes *see* facets of practice for equity 81–84
TEFANZ (Teacher Education Forum of Aotearoa New Zealand) 85
TFA (Teach for America) 48
TLRP (Teaching and Learning Research Programme) 81
transformers 54–57; community teachers 56–57; foundation 54–55; place-based learning 55–56; value community expertise 55
Troops to Teachers programmes 21

underachievement: socio-economic impact 96–97, 107
understanding difficulties faced by pupils living in poverty 96, 107
unequal society symptoms 71
universal prevention: ECM (Every Child Matters) 16
university-based programmes; challenges 45–46; reducing the role 22–24
untrained teachers: recruiting 22–23
USA: federal regulations for teacher education programmes 46; 1.0 programmes 45–48; 2.0 programmes 48–54; 3.0 programmes 54–57; teacher preparation programmes 45

visual pedagogies for social justice 128–129; analysing visual texts focusing on three sites of meaning 134–135; belonging and commitment 136; contextualising images 133–134; defining poverty 135–137; hierarchical power relationships 133; potential for innovative social justice 138–140; pupil agency in overcoming disadvantage 136–138; silence about poverty and social class 137–138; strengths 138–139; student teacher education 139–140; teacher demographics 131; weaknesses 139

well-being of children: poverty effects on 36–38